The Boardinghouse in
Nineteenth-Century America

CONTENTS

Illustrations follow page 76

Acknowledgments

Those who helped me with this project would more than fill what the nineteenth-century humorist Thomas Butler Gunn called a "boarding house on a large scale." But they would by no means inhabit a cheap establishment, for their time and assistance have been precious indeed.

If I kept a boardinghouse, Angel Kwolek-Folland, Michael McGerr, and Shirley Wajda would be my star boarders. Each read the entire manuscript in record time and provided invaluable suggestions for sharpening and broadening its argument. Morton Keller made his way through a sizeable chunk of a very rough draft. I continue to be grateful for his careful reading, cheerful encouragement, and unparalleled knowledge of the nineteenth century. The late Susan Porter Benson read numerous proposals and draft chapters, responding with her characteristic mix of unstinting support, witty commentary, and common sense advice—all of which I will greatly miss. I am indebted to Leigh Ann Wheeler for her perceptive critiques of several chapters. I also thank the many people who commented on conference papers, talks, proposals, and individual chapters for their thoughtful and always useful advice: Judith Allen, George Alter, Susan Armeny, Peter Baskerville, Elizabeth Blackmar, Mansel Blackford, Mary Blewett, Stephanie Bower, Bettina Bradbury, Ruth Hutchinson Crocker, Hasia Diner, Laura Driemeyer, Ellen Dwyer, Carolyn Goldstein, Michael Grossberg, Peter Laipson, John Lauritz Larson, Susan Lewis, the late Roland Marchand, Phyllis Martin, Scott Martin, Laura Plummer, Susan Porter, Elyce Rotella, Mary Ryan, Steven Stowe, Andrew Sandoval-Strausz, and Christiane Diehl Taylor. I am grateful, too, to audiences at Brandeis University, the Lowell National Historic Park, Eastern Kentucky University, and Indiana University and to those who attended presentations at meetings of the Berkshire Conference on Women's History, the Canadian Business History Conference, the Centre for Business History in Scotland, the Social Science History Association, the Society of Historians of the Early

American Republic, the Organization of American Historians, and the Urban History Conference. My notes and bibliographic essay reflect my intellectual debts to numerous scholars, but I owe particular gratitude to those whose work provided the essential building blocks for this study: Elizabeth Blackmar, Jeanne Boydston, Paul Groth, and Susan Strasser.

If, as the foregoing suggests, writing is rarely a solitary endeavor, neither is research. I could not have conceived of this book, let alone written it, without the help of colleagues who alerted me to sources I otherwise never would have discovered. If not for Shirley Wajda, I would have remained ignorant of the diaries of Susan Parsons Brown Forbes and Jacob Deterly. I learned from Chris Bobel that *It's a Wonderful Life* includes a boardinghouse scene. Angel Kwolek-Folland introduced me to "boardinghouse betties." James and Roberta Diehl suggested that I consult *Our Boardinghouse;* Margaret Puskar-Pasewicz recommended *Ten Dollars Enough.* Peter Molin made note of every boardinghouse reference he encountered as he researched his own dissertation on "genteel gothic." Judith Allen, Shane Blackman, Claude Clegg, Daniel A. Cohen, Ruth Crocker, Laura Driemeyer, Candace Falk, Benjamin Feldman, Susan Ferentinos, Kathryn Fuller, Nancy Godleski, Daniel Gregory, E. Haven Hawley, Helen Horowitz, Thomas McGraw, Richard P. Morgan, Susan Porter, Don Rittner, Thomas St. John, Eric Sandweiss, David Schmid, Helen Sheumaker, Philip Scranton, Andrea Tone, and Richard Wilke suggested possible leads, often generously sharing the results of their own research. Stephanie Bower told me about the correspondence of Richard and Antoinette Barker and introduced me to their custodian, the late Virginia Barker Bickel Putney Dalton. I am grateful beyond words to Mrs. Dalton and to her son Moseley Putney for allowing me access to these marvelous letters. I've had the good fortune to work with four superb research assistants. Patricia Cunningham diligently explored the collections of various and sundry archives, uncovering numerous references to boardinghouses. Kathie Miller Danner's discoveries helped me to contextualize key sources. Lynda Yankaskas searched the R. G. Dun credit ledgers and transcribed barely legible entries. Jamie Warren cheerfully and efficiently searched newspapers, city directories, and sundry other sources and checked footnotes.

I owe enormous debts to many wonderful archivists and librarians: Anne Engelhart, Diane Hamer, Jane Knowles, and Sarah Hutcheon at the Arthur and Elizabeth Schlesinger Library; Laura Linard, Timothy Mahoney, and Laura Cochrane at the Historical Collections Department of Baker Library; Michael Nash, Marjorie McNinch, and Lynn Catanese (without whom I never would have discovered the correspondence of Julia du Pont Shubrick and Alice Flagg Simons) at the Hagley Museum and Library; Peter Drummey and Kimberly Nusco at the Massachusetts Historical Society; Jeanne Solensky at Winterthur Library; and the staffs of the American Antiquarian Society, the Newberry Library, and the Western Reserve Historical Society. Closer to home, at Indiana University's Herman B Wells Library, History Librarian Celestina Wroth and the very able staffs of the Interlibrary Loan and Government Documents and Microforms departments provided essential research support. My deepest gratitude as well to Richard Cradick and the staff of Indiana University's Photographic Services; Geoffrey Smith, Elva Griffiths, James Smith, and Jeffrey Rudzinski of the Rare Books and Manuscripts Collections of the Ohio State University Library; and Jaclyn Donovan of the American Antiquarian Society for expert and timely help in reproducing illustrations.

Fellowships from the Newberry Library and the Hagley Museum and Library underwrote my initial forays into boardinghouse history. Indiana University, my institutional home, has been exceedingly generous in its support. I am grateful for gifts of time and money in the forms of a Summer Faculty Fellowship, a research grant and course release from the College of Arts and Sciences Humanities Institute, and a sabbatical leave. John Bodnar, former chair of the History Department, and Kumble Subbaswamy, former dean of the College of Arts and Sciences, deserve special thanks for securing me additional release time and research funds.

Working with the Johns Hopkins University Press has been a rare pleasure. I thank Robert J. Brugger for his patience, encouragement, and astute reading of early chapters and Amanda Slaybaugh for keeping the *i*'s dotted and the *t*'s crossed and for going above and beyond the call of duty to secure illustrations in the correct digital format. Julia Ridley Smith's superb copyediting saved me from numerous errors. Once again I am incredibly lucky to have secured the services of James O'Brien, indexer extraordinaire. Linda Forlifer kept the production process on track.

I am grateful to friends, colleagues, and students, including Judith Allen, Susan Armeny, Stephanie Bower, Maria Bucur, Ann Carmichael, the late William B. Cohen, Ellen Dwyer, David Edmunds, Susan Ferentinos, Jo Ellen Fitzgerald, Sarah Knott, Angel Kwolek-Folland, Pamela Laird, James Madison, Phyllis Martin, Dot McCullough, Tamara Miller, June Namias, David Nord, Thomas Pegram, Margaret Puskar-Pasewicz, Jeanne Peterson, Susanna Robbins, Jane Rogan, Bonnie Laughlin Schultz, Jennifer Stinson, Susan Lewis,

Leah Shopkow, Susan Tananbaum, David Thelen, Shirley Wajda, Margaret Walsh, and Leigh Ann Wheeler, for their insights—historical and otherwise—camaraderie, and good cheer.

I thank my family—Michael Gamber, Claudia August, and Margaret and Gordon Byers—for their love and encouragement. As someone who frequently presided over crowded multigenerational households, Elinor David would have sympathized with the trials and tribulations of boardinghouse keepers. For that and many other reasons, I regret that she did not live to see the completion of this book. Last, but most certainly not least, I thank Tim Byers and Ian Byers-Gamber for making our house a home.

Portions of this book appeared in slightly different form in "Away from Home: Middle-Class Boarders in the Nineteenth-Century City," *Journal of Urban History* 31 (March 2005): 289–305, and "Tarnished Labor: The Home, the Market, and the Boardinghouse in Antebellum America," *Journal of the Early Republic* 22 (Summer 2002): 177–204. I thank D & B (formerly Dun & Bradstreet) for granting me permission to cite the records of R. G. Dun & Co.

*The Boardinghouse in
Nineteenth-Century America*

Houses and Homes

Writing in the late 1990s about the increasing prevalence of grown children living with their parents, the etiquette expert Judith Martin ("Miss Manners") deplored the tendency of both parties to view their circumstances as "some sort of landlord-boarder arrangement." While she acknowledged that grown-ups residing in multigenerational households deserved greater autonomy and privacy than did minors, she insisted nevertheless that "a family household is not a boarding house, where people are supposed to pretend they have no interest in one another's private lives."[1]

Miss Manners is known for her fondness for quaint anachronisms, and her boardinghouse analogy, which probably only dimly resonated with her readers, is no exception. Indeed, the idea that the home, or, as Miss Manners put it, the "family household," is not a boardinghouse has a long history. It was a staple of nineteenth-century popular discourse, a moral certainty to which commentators as diverse as Sarah Josepha Hale, a prolific author of domestic fiction and "editress" of the genteel *Godey's Lady's Book*, and the iconoclastic poet Walt Whitman subscribed. Hundreds of self-appointed cultural authorities—journalists, humorists, writers of "fact" and fiction—joined Hale and Whitman in chronicling the disappointments, annoyances, and even dangers of boardinghouse life. They wrote for different purposes, with varying degrees of sophistication and satire, and they spoke to different, albeit often overlapping, audiences. But all agreed that boardinghouses were not homes.

Home, in their eyes, represented far more than a place of residence. Ideally the private abode of the nuclear family, it furnished a refuge from a market-driven world, governed proper relations between the sexes, provided moral guidance and emotional support to its inhabitants, and upheld republican government and social order. Its antithesis—in theory if not in fact—was the boardinghouse, a public establishment where strangers of both sexes mingled freely, fueling crime, vice, and social anarchy. Worst of all, in boardinghouses the moral contagions of the market invaded social relationships that ideally remained untainted by base economic concerns. For in boardinghouses women washed, cleaned, and cooked for money, services that elsewhere they presumably provided out of love. In an era dominated by powerful—if often illusory—dichotomies between home and market, public and private, love and money, boardinghouses emerged as unsavory counterparts to idealized homes. Or, to put it another way, they offered nineteenth-century Americans a means of defining home by representing everything that home was not.

"Be it ever so humble . . ."

Without a doubt the nineteenth century was the golden age of the home.[2] Ministers, journalists, authors of prose and poetry, lyricists, and editors of ladies' and general interest magazines, along with ordinary Americans, celebrated the virtues of home. They sang songs like "Home, Sweet Home" (perhaps the century's most popular ballad), recited poems like "My Own Fireside," and read novels that depicted heaven as a home.[3] Historians have most often identified these sentiments with the white, native-born bourgeoisie. Certainly, middle-class writers dominated popular discourse; certainly, members of the middle class were best positioned to turn domestic longings into material realities. Nevertheless, celebration of home transcended class, ethnic, and racial lines. "Wouldst thou listen to its gentle teaching, All thy restless yearning [home] . . . would still!" exclaimed the African American *Christian Recorder*. "Home! Sweet home! . . . Home is the flowery pathway of life, where the nobler passions of humanity blossom, in unspotted purity; the sacred shrine where all our longing, vagrant, pilgrim fancies love to worship," the *Boston Pilot* rhapsodized for the benefit of its largely Irish Catholic readers.[4]

It had not always been this way. As late as the 1830s and 1840s, home in the sentimental sense represented a novel and, in many senses, alien concept. Before that time, *home*, generally interchangeable with *household*, had no special meaning. And boarding, which would become the bête noire of midcentury moralists, was a familiar practice. Taverns and boardinghouses accommodated travelers and served as more or less permanent residences for some people. Members of eighteenth- and early nineteenth-century households, rural and urban, commonly included nonrelatives, often apprentices, who received room and board in exchange for their labor, or "helpers," who participated in less formal agreements.[5] Such arrangements neither precluded exploitation nor ensured domestic harmony. But only with the rise of home as a cultural icon did numerous Americans begin to perceive boarding as a social problem.

Yet, if the nineteenth century was the golden age of the bourgeois home, it was also the age of the boardinghouse. In cities and many towns, people of all classes were at least as likely to live in boardinghouses as in homes. What historians call the market revolution, a series of related developments that included the expansion of commercial agriculture, the beginnings of industrialization, the emergence of a working class dependent on wages, the rise of a salaried white-collar middle class, and massive urban growth, could never have been accomplished without boardinghouses and the labor of those who kept them. As rural populations outstripped local land supplies, as overfarming exhausted the soil, as farm machinery and manufactured goods reduced demand for agricultural and household labor, as bad harvests and unpredictable commodity prices spawned foreclosures, and as urban adventure beckoned, increasing numbers of men and women abandoned the American countryside to become merchants, clerks, salesmen, mechanics, and seamstresses in New York, Boston, Philadelphia, and countless smaller cities. At the same time, thousands of immigrants, propelled by famine, political upheaval, and economic dislocation, left Ireland, Germany, Britain, and France (and later Eastern Europe) for the United States. Some journeyed west to take up farming, but most had little choice but to pursue urban employments—as day laborers, domestic servants, and factory hands. As city populations expanded dramatically (by some estimates as much as 800% during the first half of the nineteenth century), so too did the number of establishments that offered room and board to rural migrants, European newcomers, and assorted people who could not or would not live in "homes."[6]

Social historians have estimated that somewhere between a third and a half of nineteenth-century urban residents either took in boarders or were boarders themselves.[7] A more precise reckoning is not possible, in part because few who kept boarders openly advertised that fact, in part because landladies—stung by accusations that allied them with a heartless marketplace—often adopted vague and confusing terminology. Contemporaries nevertheless recognized boarding's ubiquity. "Like death, no class is exempt from it," humorist Thomas Butler Gunn quipped in 1857; a year earlier Whitman had claimed, "it is probable that nearer three quarters than two thirds of all the adult inhabitants of New York city . . . live in boarding-houses." Gunn and Whitman's hyperbole aside, the boardinghouse was so common that even its detractors

described it, albeit not entirely accurately, as an "American institution," a symbol of the uniquely transient nature of American life.[8]

The same developments that increased the demand for "American institutions"—the expansion of urban manufactures and commerce, the dramatic
increase in the numbers of city residents in need of shelter, and the emergence
of economies based less on custom than on cash—helped give rise to the
domestic ideal that nineteenth-century Americans came to call the home. As
employers—no longer bound by craft traditions—increasingly declined to
house their employees, homes became the private abodes of loving families. As
artisan workshops gave way to factories and retail stores, "home" became distinct from "work." Merchants, clerks, laborers, and mechanics left their residences each morning for countinghouses, dry goods stores, workrooms, and
docks, returning home in the evening and perhaps for their midday meals. As
the exigencies of the marketplace seemingly enveloped all interactions, the
private home became a sanctuary. It was a place where love, not money,
reigned supreme.

Powerful as they were, these beliefs rested on convenient fictions. Regardless of commentaries that distinguished "home" from "work," housewives
of all classes, save the very wealthy, worked hard indeed. They washed,
cooked, swept, scrubbed, and stitched, arduous tasks in an era that featured
few labor-saving devices. The authors of advice manuals and prescriptive
fiction resolved the apparent contradiction between domestic ideology and
everyday reality by defining unpaid household labor as something other than
work. "What do you think I am doing?" exclaims a character in Hale's *Keeping House and House Keeping* (1845). "I am learning to make puddings, pas-
try, and bread! What I once thought such a drudgery now makes every day
pass pleasantly." What one historian aptly terms "the pastoralization of
housework"—a perception that bedevils stay-at-home parents to this day—
found widespread support, even among housewives themselves. A woman
hastily scribbling a letter or diary entry by candlelight might describe a
twelve-hour marathon of washing, sewing, cooking, and cleaning and conclude that she had not "done anything."[9]

The prevalence of paid labor within homes provided potentially more trou-
blesome challenges to the notion that "home" and "work" were distinct categories of experience. Even solidly middle-class housewives frequently contributed to family coffers by taking in sewing, laundry—and boarders. They
rarely, however, recognized this remunerated labor as real work, typically
reporting their occupations to census takers as "keeping house." What is more,

considerable numbers invited wage laborers—domestic servants—into their homes. To be sure, bourgeois matrons did all they could to preserve the privacy of the family, an entity from which servants, as opposed to the "helps" of an earlier era, were decidedly excluded. They routinely banished servants—during those rare hours when they were not at "work"—to dreary basements or stifling attics and barred them from the family table—except as waitresses. Nevertheless, the presence of servants, like housewives' gainful employment, suggests that homes were neither truly private nor truly removed from the market.[10]

Those who penned syrupy tributes to domestic bliss confronted a related dilemma. Did the true value of home reside in its material manifestation, its emotional essence, or both? A veritable mountain of prescriptive literature warned against luxury and ostentation. But few writers expected their readers to live lives of material deprivation. Even as they emphasized sentiment over rampant materialism, most had particular physical structures in mind when they conjured up visions of home. Most often, they meant a single-family, detached, owner-occupied, increasingly suburban, dwelling situated somewhere between the opulent mansions of the idle rich and the squalid tenements of the urban poor.

"Blessings in Disguise" (1840), one of hundreds of sentimental short stories penned by the prolific T. S. Arthur, illustrates the tensions between the moral and material meanings of home. When Mr. Howard, a young Philadelphia merchant, learns that he has been "ruined," he and his wife forsake their "elegantly furnished mansion" on Chestnut Street for a two-story brick house in the decidedly déclassé borough of Southwark, dismissing their servants except for the cook and chambermaid. Once a shallow and selfish young woman, Emily Howard cheerfully renounces fashionable society, embracing instead the "seclusion of home." "Our world is now our own fireside. What need we care for all beyond it," she bravely declares. As their financial situation worsens, the Howards contemplate an even humbler standard of living. Opportune tidings, informing Mr. Howard that he has not failed after all, save them from the grim fates Arthur implies but does not name: residence in grimy tenements or dreary boardinghouses. Having learned to value "right objects" over ostentation, they decline to return to Chestnut Street. The Southwark residence, to be sure—somehow tastefully furnished despite the Howards' financial woes—conforms much more closely to the middle-class ideal than the elegant mansion they left behind. (Indeed, "Blessings in Disguise" can be read not so much as a diatribe against the market as an advertisement for a particular brand of refined middle-class taste.) Nevertheless, to contemporaries, it would have represented a dwelling beyond the reach of many middle-class urbanites, let alone those lower on the social scale. Arthur lets his characters off the hook by sparing them true poverty. Secure in their comfortable two-story house, attended by two servants, the Howards do not have to test their newfound rejection of things material.[11]

Arthur's audience would have perceived a certain logic to this ending which may elude modern readers, for nineteenth-century social commentators imbued material structures with moral meanings. They favorably compared model homes—with their careful apportioning of public and private space and rooms set aside for distinctive purposes—with crowded tenements and disreputable boardinghouses. They contrasted the "sunshine" of the suburbs and the countryside with the "shadow" of the city. In the process, they papered over class inequalities by turning economic categories into moral ones.[12] At other times the material and moral meanings of home diverged, though bourgeois writers quickly resolved potential contradictions. The protagonist of George Thompson's lurid city mystery *Venus in Boston* (1849) lives in "humble but decent poverty," sharing a tenement room with her grandfather and younger brother. "True, it was but a garret," Thompson notes, "yet that little family with hearts united by holy love, felt that to them it was a *home*." In keeping with the happy endings virtuous heroines deserve, the young woman does not remain in these squalid circumstances long. The editor of *Harper's Bazaar* and a popular essayist who specialized in moral advice to women and children, Margaret Sangster had more in common with Hale than Thompson, the equally productive author of semipornographic fiction. But she, too, embraced a seemingly expansive definition of home. Home could be almost anywhere—according to her *Home Life Made Beautiful*—a tent, a flat, or "simply a room or two in a boarding-house." Sangster wrote at the turn of the twentieth century, at a time when antiboardinghouse rhetoric was beginning to diminish. Implicitly acknowledging that even comfortably middle-class families could not always afford "homes," Sangster bestowed her approval on rented houses, apartments—even boardinghouses. Nevertheless, she quickly tempered her enthusiasm for alternative forms of housing, advising "young married people" to assume "at once the state and the responsibilities of householders" if at all possible. In the event it was not, she recommended "a modest apartment on an obscure street" over a boardinghouse because the former contained "more true homeliness." Those who chose boarding over housekeeping merely because "the exchequer is limited" were "cowardly." "Love, true love, must pulsate in the atmosphere of the new home," she insisted. Yet pressed to declare whether love was really *all* that mattered, Sangster, like most cultural commentators, would have had to answer *no*.

If idealized homes existed in isolation from the marketplace, real homes were very much immersed in complex and increasingly competitive rental and real-estate markets. Fewer than a third of the mid-nineteenth-century residents of cities like Buffalo, Kingston, and Poughkeepsie, New York, owned their own homes; in the metropolis the proportion was far smaller. Nor did fleeing the city guarantee home ownership. Three quarters of the inhabitants of late nineteenth-century Boston suburbs lived in rented dwellings.[13]

Nineteenth-century newspapers listed quantities and prices of pork, beef, cotton, and flour under the heading of "domestic markets," distinguishing commodities bought and sold within the boundaries of the United States from "importations." Few would have applied the phrase to the middle-class home. Yet, in more ways than one, homes were indeed domestic marketplaces. Nevertheless, the idea that home and market were distinct, even oppositional, entities stubbornly persisted.[14]

If the home furnished a refuge from the market; indeed, if its very existence justified the ruthless pursuit of self-interest in the marketplace, what then of the boardinghouse? It would be going too far to claim that boardinghouses alone resolved the tensions and contradictions so glaringly evident in the rhetoric that surrounded the home. But they certainly helped to do so. As nineteenth-century commentators struggled to understand the meaning of home, boardinghouses seemed to provide them with a ready contrast, encompassing all that homes were not. If homes were private, boardinghouses were public. If homes nurtured virtue, boardinghouses bred vice. Above all, boardinghouses were creatures of the marketplace. Paying cash for housekeeping services (and accepting cash for providing them) defied the social logic of the domestic ideal. In the period that enshrined the home as the foundation of moral life and simultaneously embraced the market as the overarching model for economic relations, distinguishing between home and boardinghouse provided Americans with one means of determining what could and what could not be sold.

Women's labor stood at the heart of this social equation, for boardinghouse keeping was women's work. Even when husbands and fathers styled themselves proprietors, wives and daughters, sometimes assisted by female servants, performed the labor that keeping boarders entailed. That boardinghouse keeping should have provoked hostility is at first surprising. It offered no dramatic challenge to existing sexual divisions of labor; little distinguished keeping a boardinghouse from keeping house. Relocated to the marketplace, housewifery underwent a kind of magical, albeit malevolent, transformation. If women's unpaid labors of love made houses into homes, women's market labor converted boardinghouses into hovels, even brothels. Yet as landladies and boarders would discover, maintaining the always permeable boundaries between love and money, home and market, boardinghouse and home proved difficult indeed.

American Institutions

Ubiquitous in the nineteenth century, the "American institution" largely has disappeared from the national landscape. Thus a word of explanation may be in order. Perhaps bed-and-breakfasts provide the closest present-day analogy, for boardinghouses, unlike lodging houses, provided meals, usually served at a common table, and housekeeping services in addition to shelter. Hotels, on the other hand, served food and drink to passersby as well as guests. Hotels were usually purpose built; thus they tended to be more luxurious, expensive, and architecturally elaborate than were boardinghouses. (Hence they were almost always run by men.) Boardinghouses, apart from the imposing structures erected by corporate employers, most often were converted dwellings— or simply "homes" with extra rooms to let. "Public" boardinghouses mimicked their more illustrious counterparts by offering meals ("board") to nonresidents; "private" establishments accommodated only the needs of the people who lived in them. To be sure, there was considerable overlap between these various sorts of institutions. The same building might be described as a small hotel by one observer, as a large boardinghouse by another. Some landladies accommodated both boarders and lodgers. Conversely, the proprietors of otherwise private boardinghouses welcomed "day boarders" who slept elsewhere. And, as we shall see, boarders and boardinghouse keepers drew infinitely flexible distinctions between public and private establishments, between taking in boarders and running a boardinghouse, between living in a boardinghouse and boarding with a private family.[15]

These distinctions represented only the tip of the proverbial iceberg, for there were many different kinds of boardinghouses. Contemporaries usually contented themselves with distinguishing between "genteel" and "mechanic" establishments or with assigning labels such as first, second, and third class (categories that had no fixed or official meaning). Beneath these surfaces lurked a bewildering heterogeneity. Thomas Butler Gunn, the author of *The Physiology of New York Boarding-Houses* (1857), was one of the few observers who grasped the enormous complexity of this varied social universe. Possibly a relation of the renowned physician John C. Gunn, possibly a man who had medical training himself, he rejected dichotomous and tripartite taxonomies in favor of "physiology," classifying his subject into no fewer than thirty categories. These included the usual class and ethnic suspects ("the cheap boarding-house," "the Irish immigrant boarding-house," "the Chinese boarding-house," and "the German 'gasthaus'") but also occupational, philosophical, regional, and moral affinities ("the actor's boardinghouse," "the medical students' boarding-house," "the boarding-house wherein spiritualism becomes predominant," "the vegetarian boarding-house," "the boarding-house frequented by Bostonians"). Clearly writing tongue-in-cheek, Gunn nevertheless captured something of the variety of available boarding experiences. An enthusiastic reviewer for *Frank Leslie's Illustrated Newspaper* certainly thought so: "He has taken the roof off every class of boarding-house in the city, and revealed to the world their inmates in all their wide variety of character and occupation, their style of living, and exposed the whole system in every degree of social status." Newspaper advertisements confirm that there was indeed a boarding-house for everyone: Swedenborgians, tailors, amateur musicians, "respectable colored people," Southerners, teetotalers, and disciples of the food reformer Sylvester Graham.[16] Even smaller cities and towns offered potential boarders a semblance of the variety they would find in places like New York, Philadelphia, Boston, Chicago, and San Francisco.

Like the houses they inhabited, boarders' experiences varied, often in direct proportion to the accommodations they could afford. They generally had little good to say—in part because many boardinghouses deserved their disagreeable reputations. Gunn, Whitman, Arthur, Hale, and countless other writers, both famous and unremarkable, usually based their observations not on imagination but on experience, rendering easy distinctions between "prescription" and "reality," "fact" and "fiction" problematic. Most probably knew a good deal more about boardinghouses than about homes (even Hale, that doyenne of domesticity, lived much of her life in boardinghouses). Not coincidentally, they typically invoked homes as abstract ideals—ideals they literally helped to construct—but reserved their thickest description for boardinghouses, depicting eccentric housemates, filthy bed linens, "grave-like bedrooms," and intolerable "cuisine" in vivid, if not loving, detail. However realistic their portrayals, the notion that boardinghouses could never be more than "substitutes for home," as Gunn put it, influenced their perceptions. Homes, however vague and romanticized, provided them with yardsticks by which to measure boarding life—and boarding almost always came up short.[17]

Popular literature both reflected nineteenth-century boarders' experiences and shaped their expectations. But never completely. Boarders understood their circumstances in varied and sometimes surprising ways. This book explores some of the many means by which landladies and boarders negotiated the imaginary but nevertheless palpable tensions between home and marketplace, boardinghouse and home. Some longed for the comforts of home. Others preferred boardinghouses to homes. Still others turned boardinghouses into homes.

CHAPTER ONE

Away from Home

In 1820, eighteen-year-old John Locke, the son of a congressman by the same name, left his home in Ashby, a rural community in northwestern Massachusetts, for Boston. Accompanied by his father, Locke made the journey so many young men and women would make—from countryside to city, from "home" to boardinghouse. The senior Locke probably secured him his first job—as a shop boy in a dry goods store—and settled him into his first boardinghouse, run by a "Mr. Thomas Stearns in Brattle St." Over the next few years, young Locke changed jobs and boardinghouses often, working his way up from shop boy to bookkeeper to "Head of the Clerks," moving in order to be closer to successive workplaces. The reminiscences Locke penned a decade later were brief and unremarkable. If he found boardinghouse life disreputable or barely tolerable, if he longed for home, he did not say so. He did, however "recollect" the names of many of his fellow boarders:

> George S. Galvin Mr. Bernard an Englishman—Mr. Caleb Stimpson, Hall Kelly, Mr. Hogans—William Page Esq. C H. Locke Mrs Dunnage & her daughters Anna & Hannah & Miss Baker Stephen Hooper Esq a Lawyer at Mr. Stearns— in Brattle Street. George S. Galvin Benjamin Poor James A. G. Otis—James Vila at Mrs. Stannifords. Abraham N. Hewes Hall—Blake Callender—Two Miss Nuttings Miss Sarah Swain—Ladd—at Mr. Wescotts . . . Mr. Bains an Englishman—at Mr. Grays

Perhaps because he wrote before the canon of domesticity—always fragile—had fully crystallized, Locke referenced none of the themes that moralists, humorists, novelists, advice writers, and boarders themselves (categories that were far from mutually exclusive) would eventually fashion into folklore. And in 1850, Locke, forty-eight years old and a clerk in the Boston Customs House, was still a boarder, living with his wife, four children, and elderly father in a fashionable boardinghouse on Federal Street.[1]

Locke's residential history raises intriguing questions, for it unfolded amid increasingly insistent cultural dichotomies—house versus home, home versus market, virtue versus vice, public versus private. How did boarders understand their experiences? Did they see themselves as bohemian rebels against middle-class propriety? Social outcasts condemned to dens of iniquity? Lonely hearts who pined for "real" homes? Locke's terse prose provides few answers— although, as we shall see, that he remembered the names of his fellow boarders is worth noting.[2]

Fortunately, other boarders had more to say. This chapter tells the stories of four: a youngish single woman, an elderly widow, a middle-aged husband, and a young man in his early twenties. Two were securely anchored in the respectable middle classes (one clearly a member of the local elite); two inhabited the murky margins between the working classes and the middling sorts. As befits this relatively diverse group, the experiences they recorded shared much but also diverged. Each endured—albeit to differing degrees—the discomforts that accompanied boarding life: the absence of privacy that supposedly characterized homes and dependence on landladies and servants to provide what one satirist derisively termed the "comforts of home."[3] Each encountered moral danger in varying—if mostly harmless—guises. Each, in short, confronted at least implicitly what it meant to be a boarder in an era that celebrated "homes." The daily lives of people like Susan Brown Forbes, Catherine Thorn, Richard Barker, and Timothy O'Donovan furnished the raw material from which humorists, journalists, novelists, and short story writers produced their often-scathing critiques; conversely, popular social commentary provided a lens through which lodgers might view their circumstances. Yet, in the end, these four boarders—even the most stereotypical among them— navigated the nebulous territory between home and market, public and private, and house and home with more subtlety and grace than most boardinghouse critics were willing to admit.

"Our Family at 34.": Susan Parsons Brown (1856–1861)

Susan Parsons Brown left her hometown of Epsom, New Hampshire, for Boston at the tail end of March 1856. Snow still lay on the ground, so her father took her by horse sled to the house of a family friend. From there another friend of the family drove her by wagon to Concord. At Concord, Brown boarded a train that took her to Boston.[4]

This was not the first time that Brown had been away from home or even the first time she had visited Boston. At thirty-two, the former Lowell mill girl and peripatetic teacher was a veteran of such journeys. Still, her move to Boston represented the most dramatic contrast with her previous rural and small-town life. There she quickly found work. After a brief and disappointing stint in a wholesale millinery workroom, where "all days pass very much alike," she accepted the position of English teacher for the city's Jewish school.[5]

Unlike characters in Victorian melodramas, Brown was hardly alone in the city, even if she was away from home. Boston and nearby Cambridge teemed with relatives and friends with Epsom connections. Nor did moving to the city mean permanent exile. Brown returned to Epsom during school vacations, and her parents, sometimes separately, sometimes together, frequently visited her in Boston. Brown's story is not one of urban anomie but of urban community—a community linked by intricate ties between city and country. Through church, school, and respectable entertainments, she strengthened old acquaintances and forged new ones. But Brown's primary attachments were to what she called "our family at 34," the inhabitants of her boardinghouse at 34 Oxford Street. Her story offers a compelling example of how one lodger fashioned her boardinghouse into a home.

Very likely, Brown chose "34" because its keeper, Mrs. R. H. Haskell, was no stranger but rather the daughter of a family friend and a recent migrant to the city herself. (Possibly, the forty-four-year-old Haskell was even a relation.) Brown joined a household fairly bursting at the seams. In addition to Brown and her landlady, the "family" included two married couples, at least seven young clerks and salesmen who worked downtown in dry goods stores, a Miss Richardson, who seems to have been an invalid, and a servant. City directories suggest that Haskell's husband was still alive during Brown's first two years in Boston, but Brown never mentioned him; nor did she note his death. This was not unusual; it was common for keepers' husbands to disappear from boarders' view. Boardinghouse keeping was women's work; landladies, not their spouses, typically met potential boarders, collected rents, and presided over dining tables.

Although the composition of Brown's boardinghouse family would change frequently, the general pattern would remain the same: a married couple or two, a few single women, and a majority of young salesmen and male clerks who worked downtown on Summer, Winter, and Washington Streets in the city's commercial district.[6]

Although she always referred to her as Mrs. Haskell or Mrs. H, Brown acted more or less as a sister or daughter to her landlady. For a time, she and Haskell slept in the same room (a situation that perhaps spoke less of intimacy than of a shortage of available space). She accompanied Haskell on "bonnet hunting" expeditions, on social calls, and to Fourth of July fireworks. She ran errands for her. When Haskell left for a two-week visit to her mother in Pittsfield, Brown took over the management of the household, baking pies and cakes on Saturdays and interviewing prospective lodgers.[7] When Haskell faced financial difficulties, Brown lent her money. (She did not, however, hesitate to charge interest.)[8]

Brown forged relationships not just with her landlady but with the whole of the "family" at 34. She carefully recorded the arrival of new boarders and the departure of old ones. Each New Year's Day she took an inventory of the household's inhabitants, noting that "the family at 34 consists of . . ." or "our family at 34 consists of . . ." Brown's nomenclature was more than merely semantic; the inhabitants of 34 did indeed act something like a family. When Brown was sick, "Dr. Downs" (Mr. Downs, a fellow boarder and singing master) gave her medicine.[9] Sometimes the entire household joined together for May Day excursions, New Year's games of blind man's bluff, or an occasional "popped corn party."[10] On one New Year's Day, the boarders gathered in the parlor for a "presentation" in Mrs. Haskell's honor.[11]

More often, the family split into smaller, usually mixed-sex groups. All told, Brown spent surprisingly little time in the company of the other women, married and single, who lived at 34. She sallied forth into the world—on walks around the Common, to church, to lectures, to meetings—usually accompanied by one or more male boarders, even venturing to attend Catholic services with one Mr. Staple. She saw no moral danger in these excursions; after all, she was with members of her "family." Indeed, Brown played a central role in maintaining 34's respectability by organizing an "English grammar class" for the household's young male clerks. (In this she was not unique; Elizabeth Dorr, a teacher who boarded in nearby Dorchester, volunteered to give a German housemate lessons in English pronunciation.) Their dutiful attendance suggests the depth of their own commitment to self-improvement.[12]

Some of Brown's relationships with male boarders were mere friendships. Brown took a sisterly, even motherly, interest in Charles Dodge, a clerk some ten years her junior. She mended his coats and took pride in his accomplishments. "Dodge cast his *first* vote," she noted on Election Day in 1856.[13] Her interest in other boarders was more than sisterly. Although she was in her early thirties, Brown did not lack for suitors. She seems to have been choosy rather than desperate. A previous acquaintance from Epsom, John Cate French, courted her in Boston; in June 1856, however, they had "much conversation" in Mrs. Haskell's parlor "and parted 'friends.'"[14] For a brief period later that summer, a courtship with Alexander Lyle, one of the dry goods salesmen, blossomed. He and Brown sat in the parlor "chatting until the wee hours" on several occasions. The romance soon fizzled, and *"Mr. Lyle left boarding here"* [Brown's emphasis] the following February.[15] By June, Brown had identified another prospect, a new boarder named Alexander Forbes. Brown welcomed Forbes and his roommate, both recently arrived from Scotland, with a bouquet of flowers, because they were "new-comers & strangers."[16] The twenty-one-year-old Forbes, a clerk at Turnbull and Churchill's downtown dry goods store, quickly joined Brown's social circle. Soon he was accompanying her to church, Young Men's Christian Association (YMCA) meetings, and public lectures.

If Brown's initial interest limited itself to friendly sympathy, the tide quickly shifted toward romance. Soon Brown and Forbes were "chatting" in the parlor until the "wee hours."[17] Forbes, for his part, scrawled a hasty note to Brown on a scrap of newspaper torn from the *Boston Herald*. Perhaps he furtively passed it to her at breakfast or dinner, or slipped it into her hand as they passed on the stairs: "Miss Brown I love you." Finally, in December 1857, Brown obliquely noted that she and Forbes had "decided on a question that has been in agitation."[18] In other words, they were engaged. They did not marry until August 1859, a year and a half later. After a ceremony and brief honeymoon in Epsom, they returned to Mrs. Haskell's boardinghouse to begin married life. ("The first night of our married life in 34," the new Mrs. Forbes noted in her diary on August 13, 1859.) In this they were typical of newlyweds, who often chose boardinghouses over homes. Their marriage changed the allocation of boardinghouse space and sociability. They moved together into a new room, and as a married couple they could invite fellow boarders of either sex into their "private" domicile within the larger household.[19]

With its mixed assemblage of men and women, married and single, 34 was typical of middle-class boarding establishments. At first glance, its composition and ever-changing cast of characters suggests the fulfillment of moralists' dire warnings. In nineteenth-century parlance, 34 was a "promiscuous" or mixed-sex establishment. Haskell and her boarders lived in close proximity, even on terms of physical intimacy—evident when Brown noted in a diary entry that Dodge's "colic" (probably manifested by vomiting) had awakened the household.[20] Yet, all evidence suggests that 34 Oxford Street was an eminently respectable residence; very likely it was on the YMCA's list of respectable boarding places for young men new to the city.[21]

Brown was not an especially expressive diarist. Nevertheless, it is clear that she considered 34 Oxford Street home and its inhabitants her family. How did she negotiate the dichotomy between house and home, between "den" and respectable domicile? Brown must have encountered conventional definitions of *home* when she attended Edwin Hubbell Chapin's lecture, "Woman and her Work" which she pronounced "very excellent."[22] Still, home—as glorified in novels, household manuals, and ladies' magazines—may have been a less than familiar concept to her. Her reading tended toward the classics rather than the domestic, toward Shakespeare rather than *Godey's Lady's Book*. And Brown was no stranger to boarding. She had lived in a boardinghouse during her eight-month stint in 1843 as a weaver in Lowell; as a teacher in various New Hampshire towns she had always boarded with local families.[23] Her own family in Epsom sometimes took in boarders.[24] For Brown, as for many other Americans of her time, the isolated nuclear family and the idealized home were far more alien than living in the midst of the assorted and mostly transient individuals who made up the family at 34.

Nor can Brown's expansive (and in the view of bourgeois moralists, misguided) definition of family be attributed solely to rural innocence. She was no naïf; she was thoroughly familiar with the moral dangers of the city. Numerous YMCA speakers, whose lectures she attended, must have made the theoretical case. Yet Brown had more immediate knowledge. Vice even crossed the threshold of 34 in the person of James Haining, a fellow boarder whom Brown feared was "going the way to destruction." A young man might take one of many "ways to destruction" in antebellum America—drinking, gambling, sex, Sabbath-breaking, laziness, extravagance—Haining's particular vices are anyone's guess. In any case, he left 34, perhaps not voluntarily, before he could do much damage. Mrs. Haskell quite likely evicted him, for maintaining the respectability of one's establishment was an essential part of the work of boardinghouse keeping. Still hoping for Haining's reformation, Brown sent him a book titled *The Young Men of the Bible* before he left Boston for New York.[25] Whether this gesture had the desired effect is unclear. Possibly it did, for less than a year later "Jas. Haining returned from N. Y. to board here again," resuming his employment at Turnbull and Churchill's (the same dry goods store where Alexander Forbes worked).[26]

Perhaps Brown perceived no tension between boardinghouse and home because she didn't have to. Mrs. Haskell's domicile most likely was *not* a "boardinghouse"; rather—although twenty-five to thirty boarders crossed her threshold each year and although she housed seven to ten of them at any one time—in Brown's view she very likely offered accommodations in a "private family."[27] Middle-class establishments that housed boarders were *private fam-*

ilies; working-class ones were *boardinghouses.* This flexible definition of family assuaged anxieties about living arrangements and clearly distinguished respectable establishments from disreputable ones. "Privacy" was an elastic concept that conferred an aura of respectability on otherwise "promiscuous" households.

Within two years of the Forbes's marriage, Mrs. Haskell gave up boardinghouse keeping, and the couple, in keeping with social expectations, moved to "our own house." "Our own house" was not exactly what one might expect. Strictly speaking, it was not their own; they rented it for $550 a year.[28] Nor was it the private dwelling that "our own house" might imply. Instead, it was a boardinghouse of their own.

At Home and "Abroad": Catherine Thorn (1880–1890)

Boardinghouses tended to attract people at particular stages of life, most often young single men and women like Susan Brown and newly married couples. The reverse was true for Catherine Thorn, whose boardinghouse provided a refuge in old age.

Born in England, Thorn was the wife of a prominent local physician, state representative, and city mayor, and lived much of her life in Troy, New York. In 1880, five years after the death of her husband, she moved to the Clark House, a fashionable boardinghouse located just a few blocks from her former home. Thorn had other choices. She might have followed her friend Mrs. Griswold, who lived at the Protestant Episcopal Church Home for the Relief of the Aged, the Infirm, and the Destitute. Thorn was aged—she was seventy-eight when she moved to Clark House—though hardly infirm or destitute. Nor is it likely that a widow of means would choose any of the city's several "homes" that advertised their availability to the deserving poor. Thorn was not without a home, either literally or figuratively; she did not sell her house on Third Street but rented it out instead. Rather than inhabit an old age "home" or her own "private" home, Thorn, a lonely widow whose only son had died several years before, chose the sociability of a boardinghouse. Moving to Clark House, she joined a multigenerational household as its eldest resident. She would remain there—indeed, she outlived its landlady Helen Price—until her death in 1890 at the age of eighty-nine.[29]

Like the household Mrs. Haskell managed some thirty years earlier, Mrs. Price's boardinghouse included a mix of single men (most of them clerks and salesmen), single women (mostly teachers), married couples, and widows.[30]

Thorn had an active social life, even if we exclude her housemates. Only icy winter sidewalks and occasional illness prevented her from making daily social calls. Numerous visitors—among them friends and relatives, her attorney, and, occasional supplicants, including her husband's former patients and her former servant ("poor old Biddy")—called for her at Clark House as well.[31]

Much calling also went on inside Clark House. In the evenings, boarders often gathered in each other's private parlors. (By the late nineteenth century, genteel boarders typically rented suites of two rooms, one in which to receive visitors, the other for use as a bedroom.) They made music (Thorn played the piano while others sang), gossiped, and played fiercely competitive card games of cribbage, casino, whist, and bezique.[32] Perhaps because she had long experience in a "traditional" nuclear family, perhaps because the available cultural categories had expanded by the 1880s, perhaps because "home" had become a more familiar institution by the late nineteenth century, Thorn never described her boardinghouse community as a family. Although she called Clark House her home, she clearly considered herself a boarder. Unlike Susan Brown, Thorn never came up with words to describe her relationship to her landlady and fellow boarders. Yet, they *were* somehow special to her, a fact best captured in Thorn's description of what they were not. In Thorn's parlance, callers who came from outside the boardinghouse were "visitors from abroad."[33]

Degrees of intimacy varied. Thorn's closest relationship in the early 1880s was with Fanny Whittemore, a music teacher in her early forties. "Miss Whittemore" was Thorn's most constant companion, accompanying her to Sunday services at the Unitarian church, to church fairs and socials, and to numerous musical and theatrical entertainments. This was Thorn's most informal relationship, the least governed by social protocol. "The room next mine is rented to a young gentleman," Thorn wrote, "so Miss W & I are placed under some restraint—but such is the fate of boarders." "Restraint" likely meant that Thorn and Whittemore could no longer call on each other in their nightgowns and wrappers (and the remark demonstrates the importance of propriety). Yet Thorn's friendship with Whittemore was also her most difficult relationship. Disagreements, misunderstandings, and "slights" abounded. Whenever she and Whittemore were not on speaking terms, Thorn was "cut" out of whatever social gatherings Whittemore convened.[34] These spats were usually short lived. On one occasion Thorn noted that their "solemn silence to each other" "ended as my quarrels generally do, in a make up." That evening they once again played casino. "I suppose [we] would both miss the other," Thorn remarked, had their estrangement endured.[35]

Thorn's associations were not entirely with members of her sex. She had a similarly trying, though perhaps less intense, relationship with Mr. Briggs, a curmudgeonly bachelor. David Briggs, thirty-three years old in 1880, had boarded with Mrs. Price since 1871, relocating with her twice before she assumed the proprietorship of Clark House. During the seventeen years in which he was Price's boarder, Briggs rose from salesman to co-owner of Marshall and Briggs's collar manufactory.[36] His "queer ways" and general grouchiness inspired Thorn's irritation and affection. He brought her newspaper articles he thought she would find interesting and advised her on her own submissions to the *Troy Daily Times.* Thorn in turn advised Briggs on matters of the heart. "Mr. Briggs . . . appealed to me about sending his monogram to some lady," she wrote. "Advised him to beware."[37]

Was Clark House a family? Thorn did not use that term; indeed, she explicitly described herself as a "boarder." But, like the "family at 34," its inhabitants constituted a mixed assortment of middle-class types—salesmen, clerks, businessmen, teachers, widows, newlyweds—and elderly ladies. Like "34," it housed an ever-changing cast of characters, bolstered by a few long-term boarders, including Briggs and Thorn. And, like "34," despite the transience of its population, Clark House functioned something like a family home. When Sarah Buell, a (probably) consumptive invalid, died, her body was laid out in Clark House's parlor. (Conveniently, the household included an undertaker, William Madden, among its boarders.) All of the boarders save Thorn, who was ill at the time, attended the funeral. They offered comfort to Buell's husband and children, who continued to live at Clark House.[38] Mrs. Price nursed Thorn when she was unwell and brought her meals in bed. (She did not necessarily do so cheerfully; the obligation to nurse sick boarders was a common complaint of landladies). Miss Whittemore and Mr. Briggs, among others, went for the doctor and picked up medicines, including a bottle of port.[39] Before the advent of more specialized institutions, boardinghouses provided a variety of social services in exchange for rent; in that sense they were very much like "homes." Places like Clark House testified as well to the desire of "respectable" boarders to avoid old age "homes" and hospitals, ventures indelibly imprinted with the stamp of charity.

To be sure, Clark House was no paradise for Thorn. Her quarrels with Whittemore caused her much distress. Even though surrounded by fellow boarders, she was often lonely and melancholy, lost in thought about her departed husband and son or, as she called them, her "poor lost boys."[40] But, if in the end Clark House did not constitute Thorn's "family," perhaps it came close. David Briggs, her housemate for nearly a decade, was among her pall-bearers.[41]

"A Southern Man": Richard Barker (1888–1894)

Richard Barker was by no means a black sheep. But he seems to have been the least successful son of a prominent Kentucky family that included a cele-brated jurist and future president of the University of Kentucky. Barker learned the legal profession in New York, probably shortly after the Civil War. (It is not clear whether he attended law school or apprenticed with an experi-enced attorney; either would have been possible during this period). He com-pleted a "post-graduate course at the University of Virginia" at some point during his career. By 1875, he had returned to New York to practice law, although with only sporadic financial success.[42]

We know next to nothing about Barker's life as a New York bachelor, except that he lived for a time in a boardinghouse in Washington Place. His mar-riage in 1887 at the relatively late age of forty to twenty-year-old Antoinette Hutches (his "darling little girl" and "little wife") opens a window into Barker's residential and social experience.[43] His frequent separations from Nettie generated a voluminous correspondence that offers rich details of boardinghouse life. Spanning from 1888 to 1894, the Barker letters tell us much about the importance to men of domesticity, until recently assumed to be exclusively feminine terrain.[44] They also offer a nuanced dialogue on the varied meanings of *home.*

Like many urban newlyweds, the Barkers began married life as boarders. Like most city dwellers, they could not afford a home of their own. Residen-tial options proliferated in late-nineteenth-century New York; the Barkers might have chosen one of the newly erected apartment-hotels, which offered many of the same services as boardinghouses, albeit on a more luxurious scale, or a flat, which would have required Nettie, with the possible help of a servant, to keep house. Although advice writers who deplored married couples' pen-chant for boarding insisted that keeping house was always cheaper, both options were probably beyond the Barker's economic reach. Nor did Nettie nec-essarily wish to "go to housekeeping." Like many young middle-class wives, she seems to have preferred the sociability and the freedom—from the twin trials of housework and the servant problem—that boardinghouse life offered.

If the Barkers could not afford a house or a flat, they could not always afford a boardinghouse either. On the surface, Nettie's frequent visits to her parents in Galveston, her sister in Ohio, or Richard's mother in Louisville, were just that: visits. Yet Nettie tended to leave for visits when it became less than "convenient"—as she termed it—for her to live with Richard. In other words, Richard's earnings were not always sufficient to purchase genteel room and board for two (and eventually, three). When Nettie left the Manhattan boardinghouse kept by "Mrs. and Miss Brown" for an extended trip to Galveston, Richard stowed various possessions in other boarders' closets and moved into a smaller, single room.[45] "Visiting" was a necessary economic strategy and a necessity for keeping up appearances. Indeed, the financial burdens of first one, then two children and Richard's recently widowed mother's need for companionship conspired to keep the Barkers separated for much of the period between 1892 and 1894. After the autumn of 1891, Nettie, much to her disappointment, would never live in New York again.

A veteran boarder, Richard Barker took the inconveniences of boardinghouse life in stride. When a medium took up residence in an adjacent room, separated from his quarters only by a "thin partition," Barker gleefully recounted overheard séances, including one that summoned the ghost of an Indian chieftain named "Old Wild Cat." (He was happy to report, however, upon returning from a visit to Kentucky that a more substantial barrier had been installed in his absence.)[46] But his relationship to boarding—after his marriage, if not before—was complicated, for boarding often meant separation from Nettie. *Home* assumed a variety of meanings for him. *Home* was wherever Nettie was, *home* was his mother's house outside Louisville, and *home* was his current boardinghouse. (In the six-year period between 1888 and 1894, he lived in five different boarding establishments.)

Richard missed Nettie dearly, but boarding life offered compensations. He did not lack for society. Just as Susan Brown's Boston overflowed with people from Epsom, late nineteenth-century New York City was chock full of Kentuckians, and it is likely, moreover, that Barker chose boardinghouses that specifically catered to southerners. He found a home of sorts in the local Democratic Party, where he found support for his political views.[47] Still, many of Barker's New York friends and acquaintances were former landladies and housemates. The apparent transience of boardinghouse life was partly illusory; letters and diaries suggest that likeminded boarders tended to keep in touch with each other even after they no longer lived together. Indeed, it is difficult to underestimate the importance of boardinghouse ties. The Barkers met and befriended an elderly couple, Captain and Mrs. Phillips, at the Brooklyn boardinghouse in which they lived in 1889 and 1890. When Nettie was home, she nursed the elderly captain; when Nettie was away, Mrs. Phillips offered to do Richard's sewing for him. When the landlady's lease expired, Barker joined the Phillipses in their search for new lodgings. He continued to call on them after he had moved to other quarters.[48] Indeed, by the time he left New York for good in 1894, Richard had accumulated a circle of boardinghouse friends, who readily offered childrearing advice (which Richard passed on in letters to Nettie) or shopped for items that Nettie had requested from afar.[49]

Domesticity loomed large for Richard because he was so often separated from Nettie. Sympathetic servants at his final and favorite New York boardinghouse on West Eleventh Street redecorated his room to make it look more like "home." The African American cook, originally from Virginia, prepared him special dishes because, as she announced to the other boarders, "He is a southern man and I am a southern woman." The material artifacts of Richard and Nettie's shared domestic life assumed special importance. Returning alone to his Brooklyn lodgings in 1891, Richard waxed poetic over the things Nettie had left on the washstand—"many little bottles and little Dick's sponges." The Barker's oil stove (in an era before reliable central heating, boarders often furnished their own stoves) took on a symbolic importance far beyond its capacity to heat because it reminded Richard of their days together in the Brooklyn boardinghouse.[50]

No artifacts were as important to Richard Barker as photographs of his young son Richard. These photographs (which to reproduce, how many copies to order, which were the best) were a source of endless discussion between Richard and Nettie. They furnished Richard with a vital link to his absent family. They also enabled him to forge new relationships with other boarders. "There is a very handsome lady & her husband living here," Richard wrote Nettie in 1894. "They have no children . . . She saw my pictures on the bureau, passing the door, it being open, and came in & looked at them— so she told me at dinner tonight, begging pardon for the liberty. Says she never saw any thing more beautiful than little Richard with his fingers in his mouth & beseeches me to give her one. Other ladies heard her and said they must see that picture."[51] Indeed, Barker spent a good deal of his free time distributing Richard's photographs to current and former landladies and housemates. They continued to attract interest among the boarders, who felt free to go into Barker's room to show to "some friends who were visiting." One "borrowed our baby's picture this morning to show to her mother who is down on a visit from Albany. A lady in the house says it is the sweetest picture she ever saw."[52]

Little Richard's photographs introduced the senior Barker to the Hines family, who would become his most important companions in his final two years in New York. In many respects, Barker, the gentleman from Kentucky, and the German American Hines family were an unlikely match. Certainly, one-year-old Walter Hines's custom of drinking a daily glass of lager at the boardinghouse table gave Barker pause.[53] But in the end such cultural differences proved unimportant, for the Hineses offered Barker a surrogate family, and little Walter Hines, only a few months younger than Richard, a surrogate son. Richard was quick to assure Nettie that Walter paled in comparison to their own son. "He cannot speak nearly so plainly as Richard," he insisted. Subsequent letters offered similar developmental comparisons in which Richard always surpassed Walter. Nevertheless, Barker was extraordinarily frank about his relation to Walter: "he reminded me of . . . [Richard] as he quietly slept." "Sometimes I get remarkably lonely, thinking of you and little Dik. Sometimes I am depressed to such a degree that I jump up suddenly and run off to the Hines' room."[54] Richard gave Walter daily piggyback rides and frequently bought him presents. The two families exchanged letters and gifts. Mrs. Hines even "ghost wrote" a letter from Walter to young Richard.[55] The Barkers and the Hines families kept in touch for some time after Richard left New York, although they probably never met.

Boardinghouse life, coupled with separation from Nettie, did offer temptations, albeit of a fairly harmless sort. From what we can tell from the correspondence, Richard was a loving, faithful husband. Nevertheless, letters could reveal anxieties. "Good luck to you sweetheart and oceans of love and kisses from your Antoinette," Nettie wrote in September 1888, when the couple had not yet been married a year. In what might be termed a pre-Freudian slip, Richard responded, "In one of your letters you said 'good luck to your sweetheart.' I suppose you meant our friend Miss Southgate" (a boarder who had taken Nettie's place at the table during her absence). "No, indeed; I have no other sweetheart than my own dear little Nettie." Nettie's response was pointed and perceptive: "I *thought* I wrote 'good luck to *you* sweetheart,' and certainly meant to, for I had no thought of you having but one sweetheart— you see where your thoughts lie if you so readily selected Miss. S.—for that honored person—if there is more than one, your wife wishes to be counted out."[56] Some five years later, in 1892 (when Nettie was reluctantly but, as it turned out, permanently settled in her mother-in-law's residence outside Louisville), Richard assured her that he had resisted temptation. "They had a party at our house last night but I didn't go down to it. A rather handsome young woman who lives in the house asked me to come down & dance with her. I declined on various grounds, some expressed & some only thought— too tired, not dressed for party, can't dance, getting aged, a married man—wife & baby might not like it! Etc. etc."[57]

The boardinghouse at 145 West Eleventh Street, where "handsome young women" might ask gentlemen strangers to dance, was a far cry from the "family at 34," with its weekly grammar classes and careful moral supervision. Certainly, the several establishments that Barker inhabited sheltered more sophisticated, diverse, and cosmopolitan populations than did those who resided at the pious Mrs. Haskell's some forty years earlier or even at Clark House. This contrast tells us not only about the difference between New York and its more provincial counterparts but also something about the cultural distance—from earnest striving to casual self-confidence—the middle class had traveled over the course of the nineteenth century. Still, the sociological templates of Barker's boardinghouses would have been familiar to the inhabitants of Clark House or 34: respectable mixes of married and single men and women and respectable environments that offered both propriety and sociability. Just as 34's parlor offered Brown and her suitors a safe place for courtship, "handsome young women" who inhabited genteel boardinghouses could ask gentlemen boarders to dance without risking their reputations.

It would be many years before the Barkers had a home in the conventional sense of the word. They lived for a time in Arizona, where they rented a house, then returned to Louisville, where they resided with Richard's brother and sister-in-law. They did not move into their "own house" until 1912. As it turned out, Richard had little time to enjoy it. He died suddenly of a heart attack in 1916 at the age of sixty-eight.[58]

"A Good Deal of Contempt": Timothy O'Donovan (1883–1884)

Timothy O'Donovan was a victim of the industrial revolution. Sometime during the winter or spring of 1879, in one of the accidents that had become all too common in the late nineteenth century, the twenty-year-old line worker for the Pittsburgh, Cincinnati, and St. Louis Railroad (PC & SL) lost one of his legs. After several rounds of correspondence with George R. Fuller, an upstate New York manufacturer of "CELEBRATED ARTIFICIAL LEGS AND ARMS," he secured a prosthesis, which, despite Fuller's insistence that O'Donovan journey to Rochester for a fitting, he apparently purchased through the mail.

Whether O'Donovan's artificial limb lived up to Fuller's promises ("I will not hesitate to guarantee you a perfect fit and a leg that will be useful") is anyone's guess. In any case, losing a leg did not dampen his employment prospects. Misfortune instead propelled him into a white-collar job; after a period of training, he became a telegraph operator and ticket agent at the PC & SL's station at Walker's Mills, just west of Pittsburgh, eventually securing an additional post as the station's agent for the Adams Express Company.[59]

Then O'Donovan made what he came to consider a grave mistake: in January 1883 he joined the Brotherhood of Telegraphers. He disliked belonging to a secret society and found "the secrecy and ritual . . . all humbug . . . intended to deceive and impress the ignorant and timid." He acknowledged, too, the "risk of trouble in being a member" but believed that only "thorough organization" would improve telegraphers' wages and working conditions. In August the union authorized a strike, or so it seemed; O'Donovan soon learned that the strike order was a forgery—fabricated no doubt by a company agent provocateur. O'Donovan's participation, coupled with his "threatening letter" to a supervisor ("I did not intend it for that and think he has twisted what I wrote"), lost him both his jobs. He faulted not his employers but himself. He had been foolish to join a labor union. He would not repeat the error. "I leave it and will not again belong to any society for any purpose unless literary gatherings."[60]

O'Donovan may have erred in assuming the blame, but he had reason to be bitter. Losing his job with the PC & SL meant that he had to leave home to find another. After unsuccessful local interviews with Western Union and Jones and Laughlin, he secured a job as a telegraph operator (probably for Western Union) on the East Coast. Armed with a railroad pass issued by his new employer, he left for Connecticut.[61]

As far as the available evidence tells us, this was the first—and only—time O'Donovan left Allegheny County. Although he lived alone, probably in order to be close to the Walker's Mills station, his parents, brothers Michael and Peter, and sister Agnes lived nearby.[62] Finding another job meant leaving his family and his Irish Catholic community behind. Yet O'Donovan was hardly a provincial. The son of illiterate immigrant parents, he received at least a grammar school education and continued learning long after his formal schooling ended.[63] Apart from his antipathy toward collectivism, O'Donovan was the spitting image of the self-educated worker-intellectual described by labor historians. He subscribed to the *Irish World* and *Railroad Age* (splitting the cost of the latter with his brother Michael), but he also read Malthus,

Ricardo, Hume, Descartes, Montesquieu, De Tocqueville, John Stuart Mill, and Adam Smith. He supplemented his education in political economy with scientific and medical texts (*Darwin's Works, Physiology and Pathology of the Mind, Intellectual Development, Burton's Anatomy*) and books with a more practical bent (*Gould Brown's Grammar, Standard Practical Penmanship, Free Hand Drawing, Geometrical & Mechanical Drawing, Perspective*). Grammar and penmanship were necessary skills for a telegraph operator; O'Donovan's self-taught course in mechanical drawing supported his patent application for a new type of railroad-car coupler, perhaps intended to prevent the sort of accident that cost him his leg. (His efforts came to naught; although he secured the patent, the agent whom he engaged to market it proved "a swindling humbug.") As his wide-ranging reading suggests, O'Donovan was a man of many interests. Doctors allowed him to observe the autopsy of a "female infant" abandoned in the Walker's Mills cemetery. "Saw the heart, lungs, liver, stomach, bowels, bladder and womb in position, and experienced no difficulty in watching the operation, could have assisted if required."[64] Little wonder, then, that the intellectually curious telegrapher, now twenty-three years of age, saw his trip east as an adventure.

For O'Donovan this was an adventure worth preserving for future reminiscence, if not for posterity; hence, he recorded his journey in some detail. On the train he chatted with four students from Wheeling, West Virginia, on their respective ways to Exeter and the Rensselaer Polytechnic Institute (in Thorn's adopted city of Troy, New York) and more than held his own. The design of the Philadelphia to New York line impressed the observant railroad man— "almost perfect having scarcely any cuts or bridges those being short & low— nearly straight level line good road bed street rails etc. etc." Nothing, however, pleased him more than the newly completed Brooklyn Bridge. "It perfectly satisfied expectations I had of it or more than that giving real delight in appearance of stone work, also of Cables—guys etc.—seen them later in evening start the electric light on it this was pretty too seeing them all flash out brilliantly at one instant crowning the arch with light." The *City of Worcester*, the steamer that carried him from New York to New London, Connecticut, impressed him as well: "very fine compound engines first of kind I had seen this is of 2500 horse power 12 ft stroke of piston." O'Donovan's observations were sociological as well as mechanical. Wall Street made him feel "of very little account in this world's economy." Boston was different. "Here I feel as through you were in [a] great city and of full importance as an individual with known status and assured rights."[65]

After all of these amazing sights and mechanical marvels, everything else was bound to be a disappointment. Andover, Connecticut, his first posting, was "a dismal dreary place." Boarding in Andover was even drearier. His landlady was "a disagreeable unctuous looking person." At the table he found "repulsive looking bread unfit to eat other food still worse ugh!" Luckily, he was transferred to another station after only a few days. Life improved at East Thompson. There he stayed with a "nice family," who, in contrast to the "slovenly" cook at Andover, provided "right good board." He even briefly entertained thoughts of romance, for he found the two sisters with whom he boarded "right well educated good appearance and manners." One was already spoken for, but "Miss Jennie is most interesting."[66]

Such musings proved short-lived, for less than a week later O'Donovan was transferred to the western Massachusetts town of Bolton. He quickly discovered the disadvantages of his first boarding place. It was a half-mile from the railroad station (a fair distance for a one-legged man to walk), the rent (in his opinion) was excessively high, and there were too many other boarders. Neither did the tee-totaling O'Donovan appreciate that his landlady Mrs. Pomeroy sold "whisky on the sly, etc." After a week and a half with the Pomeroys, he moved to a more conveniently situated house that "seems much better"—though he was quick to note his landlady's girth: "enormously fat weighs 253."[67]

After a month and a half in Bolton, his employers reassigned him to the station at Willimantic, Connecticut—a mill town and railroad hub—where he spent the duration of his East Coast stay. At Willimantic it was much the same story. He boarded for a few weeks with a Mrs. Harris but quickly decided to move on, neatly summing up his reasons in the pages of his diary: "poor board and accommodations—high priced—undesirable acquaintances in people and boarders." He settled in at Mrs. Taft's, which "on first sight look[ed] much better." Predictably, the establishment failed to live up to his expectations. "Boarding and family do not wear so well as I find after a time. I have good deal of contempt for family and several of the boarders." Then he launched into a remarkable four-and-a-half pages of scathing social commentary. "Anderson is a stupid, bigoted chucklehead," he declared. Mr. Morrill, an agent for a sewing machine manufacturer, was "hollow chested, pigeon-toed, womanish, conceited, talkative, and a Methodist." Mr. Chadband, a photographer, "harmless enough, but very religious, very quiet and proper, has a horror of fun." (Here O'Donovan humorously alluded to the sanctimonious Reverend Mr. Chadband of Dickens's *Bleak House;* the real name of the photographer, who happened to be the Tafts' son-in-law, was Townsend.) The unmarred Crittenden sisters ("supposed teachers," he scoffed) were "supercilious and vain having really but meager education, and no ideas of manners but what they have gathered from etiquette books." One he considered "good looking," the other "ugly," mainly because she insisting on keeping her nose in the air. Dr. Hoagland, "a very small headed hang dog looking fellow" who "fondled"— evidently with her consent—the landlady's teenage granddaughter, fared no better; neither did W. T. Gardner, "a little monkey like fellow." The landlady's husband, a devotée of Spiritualism "in which he has stupid undoubting confidence," was "a senile decrepit old man but prides himself on his enlightenment and independence (though he is henpecked)."[68] And so on and so on. O'Donovan had very little good to say about almost anyone. All told, *he* was one with his nose in the air, and his fellow boarders probably disliked him as much as he disliked them. While there is delicious irony in contemplating a snobbish Irish Catholic looking down his nose at Yankees, Methodists, and Spiritualists, O'Donovan's rant suggests a good deal about his own social insecurities.

While O'Donovan was uncommonly vitriolic, he was not unique; much of the incessant transience of boardinghouse life reflected lodgers' search for congenial companions. Unfortunately for O'Donovan, Willimantic—a town with a rough reputation—offered few choices. While he favored colorful description over prosaic day-to-day accounts, O'Donovan did eventually forge relationships that bore at least surface resemblances to those at 34, Clark House, and West Eleventh Street during the sixth months he lived at Mrs. Taft's. Mrs. Page, "a very small plain old woman," frequently visited with him and gave him a stenography lesson; O'Donovan liked her even though she, too, believed in "spiritualist manifestation and kindred nonsense." For reasons he did not elaborate, he bestowed his approval on Bella Brown, a dressmaker—"about the best of them." S. C. Wheeler was "good hearted and honest," albeit "a good deal too fast for my idea." Yet here O'Donovan displayed uncharacteristic generosity. Wheeler was a good sort, after all, who "considers himself much more gay and reckless than he really is." Mr. Knox, the manager of the Willimantic station, was a "saucy good natured fellow" from whom O'Donovan parted "with some regret." The feeling was mutual; Knox gave O'Donovan a copy of *Lathrop's History of the American People* as a going-away present.[69]

These bright spots aside, O'Donovan *never* described his boardinghouses as "homes." He never described himself as living with "private families," never considered himself "a member of the family." There were good reasons, of course, for his alienation. O'Donovan was much farther from home, culturally if not geographically, than Susan Brown, Catherine Thorn, or even Richard Barker. An Irish Catholic, even an Irish Catholic inventor-intellectual, was bound to be an outsider in boardinghouses populated by the Yankee petty bourgeoisie. O'Donovan, indeed, was in something of a liminal state. Enough of snob to prefer these establishments, he bypassed "mechanic" boardinghouses—which housed the city's cotton- and silk-mill workers—where he would have found fellow Irishmen but also a good deal of whisky. Boardinghouse life itself was foreign to him; he had never, as far as we can tell, lived in one before. Even his parents seem never to have taken in boarders, though surely they could have used the extra income. Ironically, of all the people documented here, the Irish Catholic O'Donovan family most closely approximated what we tend to think of a middle-class Protestant domestic ideal. And Mr. Chadband's "horror of fun" aside, it was the Irish Catholic O'Donovan who condemned imbibing, flirtation, and fast behavior more harshly than did his Yankee compatriots. Most important of all in shaping his attitudes toward boarding and "home," O'Donovan never intended to stay in New England. That is precisely why his journal was not a diary in the conventional sense but a travelogue that documented his impressions of the places he visited and the people he met.

After six months in Willimantic and nine months away from home, O'Donovan had had enough of the Northeast—and enough of boarding. Armed with favorable reference letters from his East Coast employers, he left for Pittsburgh on May 19, 1884, even though no job awaited him. He took the same steamer from New London to New York, "not nearly as much dazzled by splendor of this boat as before." He spent some time sightseeing in Manhattan before boarding the train to Philadelphia, visiting Castle Garden ("a dismal, old barrick") and Battery Park (" a right handsome plot of ground"). He observed the trading at the Stock Exchange, and—still a working man at heart—decided that the brokers "would average well for intelligence, honesty and temperance and for health, physical development and personal beauty," but that they "lack[ed] earnestness and interest" in their "useless labors." In Philadelphia he found that the new Broad Street station was "scarcely the wonder one would be led to suppose from the mention in annual report of Penn R.R. Co." Indeed, nothing "dazzled" him on his return journey because home loomed large. By May 21 he was back in western Pennsylvania, stopping for a few days in Ebensburgh to visit relatives. On the twenty-seventh, his father met him at the Union Depot in Pittsburgh; together they rode home to Boston (Pennsylvania) where his mother awaited them. "Very glad to see them and find them so well," O'Donovan noted.[70]

On the fourth of June he was still pounding the pavement in Pittsburgh, looking for employment. Eventually, he found work, once again as a ticket agent. He hired a contractor to build a house in 1884 and married an Allegheny County girl (though evidently not an Irish one) four years later. By 1910, the O'Donovans—Timothy, Lucinda, and their four surviving children—had moved to the nearby Pittsburgh borough of Coraopolis, purchasing a house at 1030 State Avenue. Timothy finally abandoned the railroad business, opting instead to run a newsstand, assisted by his daughter Catherine and his son Edmond. By middle age he had achieved a modicum of lower-middle-class respectability. He was a homeowner, an independent entrepreneur, and a father of sons who worked as clerks and bookkeepers instead of risking life and limb on a railroad line. Successive census takers may have erred in describing Lucinda as having no occupation, but if she supplemented the family income, she evidently did not do so by taking in boarders. In more ways than one, Timothy O'Donovan never left home again.[71]

These four stories tell us much about nineteenth-century boardinghouse life—and by extension much about nineteenth-century society and culture. Perhaps most striking, the residences featured here were places where unrelated men and women lived together, ate together, socialized together, and occasionally mourned together. Experiences like Brown's, Thorn's, Barker's, and even O'Donovan's suggest that there was indeed a relationship between the mixed-sex composition of "respectable" boardinghouses and the maintenance of respectability. Far from countenancing "promiscuity" and vice, well-functioning boardinghouse communities sustained the good character of their inhabitants by showing that unrelated men and women could live together in propriety, if not always in harmony. Even though he frowned on flirting and "fondling," O'Donovan did not believe that he—or anyone else who lived at Mrs. Taft's—faced grave moral danger. Indeed—in an era when advertisements for "rooms to let, with board for the lady only," designated houses of assignation and boardinghouses that sheltered only women usually were brothels—carefully controlled heterosociability was one of the few ways boardinghouses could demonstrate respectability. That is precisely why employers who erected boardinghouses for female operatives and superintendents of "homes" for working girls took great pains to publicize their constant moral policing of their inhabitants. "Mechanic" boardinghouses might shelter only workingmen, but the identity of a residence that housed only women was immediately suspect.[72]

When Susan Brown, Catherine Thorn, Richard Barker, Timothy O'Donovan, and countless other Americans stepped across boardinghouse thresholds,
they immediately began negotiating constantly shifting boundaries between
acceptable and disreputable behavior, a task that in large part involved understanding which spaces they might inhabit—and with whom. Such distinctions
were lost on the *New York Tribune* editor who asked in 1878, "Who has ever
heard of a public boarding-house? The adjective would be completely super-
fluous, since any boarding-house . . . must be public."[73] To be sure, different
boardinghouse communities constituted themselves differently; the ten-person
"family" at 34 assembled with less formality, albeit greater propriety, than the
thirty-odd residents of Clark House or the inhabitants of a large hotel that
served food and drink to passersby as well as regular lodgers. Yet the *Tribune*
was only partly right, for even the most public of boardinghouses contained
private spaces. At the same time, privacy was an elastic concept. Consider
Brown's flexible definition of *private family* or Thorn's sense that she could
"call" with less formality on Miss Whittemore. Or consider that women
lodgers freely entered Barker's room to look at pictures of little Richard, staking their claims on potential or actual maternity. Or that Mrs. Page's visits to
Timothy O'Donovan's room were perfectly acceptable—Page's advanced age
ensured that social calls of this sort remained distinctly within the bounds of
propriety. (Interestingly, though, O'Donovan may have rewritten his history
with propriety in mind, for "Mrs. Page" might have been *Miss* Clara Page,
who at age thirty-two was not exactly "old.")[74] It was exactly these sorts of
transgressions that riled critics like the *Tribune* editor, who tarred them with
the taint of promiscuity and defined private families as encompassing far nar-
rower domestic circles than Brown imagined. Yet the thousands of Americans who lived not in "homes" but in boardinghouses suggest just how uncommon and, at times, just how unwelcome, domestic retirement really was. The
history of boarding reveals a middle class—and to some extent a working
class—for whom privacy remained important but that was far from private
in our sense of the word.

If boardinghouses were not exactly public, they violated bourgeois ideals in
other ways, for, to a limited extent, they played the role of social equalizers and
crucibles of diversity. To be sure, they excluded as much as they included; the
genteel establishments that housed Brown, Thorn, and Barker did not admit
manual workers and incorporated racial others, including Irish immigrants
and African Americans, only as servants. Whether O'Donovan could have
gained entry to any of them—even the relatively modest Mrs. Haskell's—is

doubtful. Yet he did gain entry to a succession of boardinghouses inhabited by New England Yankees, a measure of the degree to which "the Irish had become white" by the 1880s, but also a measure of boardinghouse diversity. And while O'Donovan grudgingly tolerated various white people he considered beneath him—Methodists and Spiritualists, for example—he was a racist who, in his quest for housing, never would have crossed the color line.[75] However, *within* limits, urban boarders mingled with people they might otherwise never have encountered. Raised in rural New Hampshire, Susan Brown met and married Alexander Forbes, a Scottish immigrant; what she would have perceived as his "difference" may have been what attracted her. Richard Barker, son of a plantation owner, became an honorary member of the German-American Hines family. Even the prickly O'Donovan made friends with "saucy good-natured" Protestants.

If nothing else, these accounts underscore boardinghouses' remarkable flexibility. They served as venues for courtship, schools for the upwardly mobile, old-age homes, and even hospitals. They testify to the myriad ways in which people created "surrogate families."[76] They challenge nostalgic narratives that evoke "traditional" families and households, for they reveal nineteenth-century living arrangements that were no less varied than our own. Ultimately, boardinghouses' attraction, even for the supposedly homeward-bound middle classes, shows us that communities of "strangers" *might* make houses into homes.

When novelists, journalists, and humorists wrote about boardinghouses, however, it was experiences like O'Donovan's—not Brown's, not Thorn's, not Barker's—that they typically imagined. Rotund landladies, flirtatious daughters, slovenly servants, boorish housemates, atrocious food—all played prominent roles in what had become a colorful folklore by midcentury. Certainly, O'Donovan's adventures had a material basis. Smallish and mid-sized New England towns offered none of the variety of boarding options one could find in cities like Boston, New York, or even Troy. Precariously balanced on the cusp between the working and middle classes, O'Donovan never could have afforded the amenities Catherine Thorn or Richard Barker's boardinghouses offered; nor would he have been welcome had he been able to pay. We might reasonably conclude that O'Donovan's story was more typical, more representative of run-of-the-mill boardinghouse experience. But there is also the distinct possibility that, for O'Donovan, life imitated art. We have no evidence that the seriously intellectual O'Donovan ever read lurid "city mysteries" or even humorists like Thomas Butler Gunn, although his ridicule of the "quiet and proper" Mr. "Chadband's" condemnation of dime novel westerns ("he seems to think they were intended to deceive") confirms his familiarity with at least some facets of nineteenth-century popular culture. Perhaps when he encountered his first boardinghouse, he saw exactly what he expected to see— or more accurately, ate exactly what he expected to eat and encountered exactly whom he expected to meet. In any case, popular culture by and large was on O'Donovan's side. That unhappy fact ensured that boardinghouse keeping—a task that required maintaining a constant (if often implicit) dialogue with numerous advocates of home, in addition to the daily trials of keeping house—was hard work indeed.

CHAPTER TWO

Keeping House

TO LET—A pleasant, furnished Lodging Room for gentlemen, in a private family at No. 6 Waverly place, within seven minutes walk of State st. References exchanged.

Boston Evening Transcript, June 13, 1863

Make no mistake. Susan Brown Forbes did not keep a boardinghouse. As the advertisement she placed in the *Transcript* made clear, she offered rooms in a "private family." Forbes defined *family* generously; she regularly entertained eight to ten lodgers at No. 6 Waverly Place, a house she and her husband had rented with the specific intention of taking in boarders. If her description seems less than accurate by the standards of the early twenty-first century, calling her abode a private family made sense to Forbes. "Private" residences required no licenses.[1] But the benefits of keeping a private family went beyond the practical. For one thing it distinguished the respectable household in Boston's largely Yankee eighth ward from what she would have considered the disreputable lodgings frequented by working-class and immigrant boarders. For another, it masked the economic relations that lay within, symbolically eclipsing No. 6's attachments to the commercial marketplace. Forbes was simply relying on common terminology when she composed the text of her ad; she probably gave these matters little conscious thought. After all, she was busy keeping house.

Hovering somewhere between the most genteel quarters and the mechanic and "emigrant" boardinghouses that sheltered Boston's expanding working class, No. 6 would have been termed a second-, possibly even a third-rate establishment in nineteenth-century parlance. Situated in a respectable but not quite fashionable neighborhood in the South End, No. 6 was within walking distance of the city's commercial downtown, a location that made it popular with clerks. No. 6 was convenient, then, but it boasted little of the cachet traded on by Miss Lavina Williams and her three unmarried sisters, proprietors of a genteel boardinghouse in Bowdoin Square to the northwest. Given that Forbes made do with one servant to the Williams's two, her "private family" would have offered comparatively few amenities, mirrored, perhaps, most clearly in the subtle distinctions between the two establishments' clientele. Both housed the white-collar middle classes. But No. 6 catered primarily to young salesmen and clerks, and the historic house in Bowdoin Square, which had once belonged to Harrison Gray Otis, to older, more established functionaries and merchants.[2]

Like Forbes, Louisa Morrill, a forty-year-old spinster in the year Forbes placed her ad, hailed from New Hampshire. But the successive boardinghouses she kept on Meridian Street, Leverett Street, and Crescent Place sheltered rougher crowds. Her boarders—a cosmopolitan mix of native New Englanders, Canadians, Europeans, and a sole African American—were mostly people who never would have crossed Forbes's or the Williams's thresholds: street vendors, printers, brush makers, seamen, liquor sellers, leather cutters, tailors, and tailoresses.[3] Even less likely to be found at Waverly Place or Bowdoin Square—except in the capacity of servants—were the laborers, teamsters, and washerwoman who resided at the widow Bridget Curtain's boardinghouse in the city's heavily Irish seventh ward.[4] To the north, on the lower slopes of Beacon Hill lived the majority of Boston's black community. There, Harriet Hayden, the wife of a prominent African American abolitionist, kept (with the help of an Irish domestic) eight boarders, all of them black and, except for a married couple, all of them men.[5]

Like boardinghouse keepers everywhere, Forbes, Williams, Morrill, Curtain, and Hayden inhabited different social worlds whose distinctions were reinforced by geography, though the actual physical distances between them were small. Nor did they necessarily have the same relation to the marketplace. Some took up boarding as a means of supplementing family incomes; others depended on it entirely. Some thought of themselves as boardinghouse keepers, others merely as "keeping house"—or like Forbes, as presiding over "private families." But all were in the business of boarding, providing food, lodging, and housekeeping services in exchange for cash. As a result, all trod treacherous cultural terrain. They kept houses in an era that glorified homes.

Getting Boarders

Most people who kept boarders never listed themselves in business directories or travelers' guides. They resorted to newspaper advertisements only

rarely; Forbes seems to have done so exactly once. They relied instead on circles of acquaintance—several veterans of 34 turned up at No. 6—and word
of mouth. On the face of it such strategies make perfect sense: why spend
money on directory listings or classified ads if you didn't have to? Yet refusing to advertise, paradoxically, *was* a form of advertising. In a culture that associated boardinghouses with crime, vice, and the machinations of a corrupt
marketplace, one of the surest means of attracting boarders was to deny that
you kept a boardinghouse. Hence, the proprietors of the most fashionable concerns claimed to host visiting friends, a ruse that shielded the reputations of
landladies and lodgers alike. Just as genteel landladies did not run boardinghouses, genteel boarders did not live in them. Market value lay in pretending
that there was no market.[6]

Landladies who stooped to advertising did not necessarily disagree. Influenced themselves by domestic ideology and shrewdly aware of domesticity's
market value, many antebellum boardinghouse keepers advertised their establishments as homes. One New York landlady described her house as a "quiet
and pleasant home"; another pledged to "secure" potential lodgers "a pleasant
home"; still another promised "the comfort and convenience of home."
Boarders entertained similar hopes, as did "three young gentlemen" who
"wish to obtain Board . . . where they can enjoy the substantial comforts of a
home."[7]

Forbes's 1863 ad made no such claim, and this was no anomaly. References
to home gradually declined, replaced in the last few decades of the nineteenth
century by inventories of specific amenities: first-class tables, handsome furnishings (claims that boarders quickly learned to take with several grains of
salt), hot and cold running water, private bathrooms, telephones, and, eventually, electricity. To be sure, earlier advertisers made sure to emphasize whatever
material advantages they had to offer. Like Forbes, however, they opted for
hazy descriptions: "pleasant rooms" had been a boardinghouse cliché at least
since the 1840s. Vague allusions gave way to appealing particulars as the century wore on. "LARGE FRONT room; hot and cold water; ample closets; bath on
same floor," read a typical ad from the 1880s; "attractive large rooms; private
bath; electricity; excellent table," read one from the teens.[8]

Advertisements like these—long on specifics, short on sentiment—
reflected certain matter-of-fact realities: the technological advancements that
revolutionized domestic life, the increasingly stiff competition for boarders
in an era when alternatives like apartments, flats, and suburban cottages were
ever more available, the rising cost of a line of type. Then, too, they suggest

that increasingly cosmopolitan urban boarders cared less for moral influences than for creature comforts. Yet home did not disappear entirely from land-ladies' lexicons; as late as 1915 a New York boardinghouse keeper could adver-tise her dwelling as "a satisfactory home for refined people." And if references to home declined over the course of the nineteenth century, the "private fam-ily" remained alive and well, both in the classifieds and in the popular imagi-nation. Or as "REFINEMENT" announced in 1888, "PRIVATE FAMILY WILL LET A FEW handsomely furnished rooms."[9]

The difference between a private family and a boardinghouse was partly a matter of entrepreneurial commitment and partly a matter of scale. But only partly. People who took in boarders in times of economic need did not neces-sarily consider themselves boardinghouse keepers; families who housed only one or two lodgers did not necessarily think of themselves as running board-inghouses. Landladies like Susan Forbes capitalized on precisely these impli-cations. Virtually every household in Forbes's immediate neighborhood included boarders. (Ironically, families in Boston's heavily Irish seventh ward cleaved more closely to the nuclear model celebrated in popular culture.) Yet a befuddled census taker described only a few of them as boardinghouses. Apply-ing this name to Samuel Taft's residence at 93 Summer Street made sense; after all, he and his wife Lucy kept nineteen boarders. On the other hand, Fanny Morse's "Boarding House" on Tileston Street included only six, fewer than Forbes's private family, far fewer than the twenty-nine assorted souls who made up teamster Alfred Whitney's presumably private family.[10]

Landladies like Susan Forbes were only giving boarders what they wanted. Throughout the nineteenth century and into the twentieth, people in search of lodging expressed their preference for private families: "BOARD WANTED—IN A RESPECTABLE PRIVATE family;" "A FAMILY OF FOUR PERSONS . . . want board in a strictly private family"; "WANTED . . . A NICELY furnished room, with board, in a strictly private, refined, American family (none other)." "Must be homelike," the "young lady" who placed the latter notice added.[11] Or, as one antebellum advertiser wrote, "No boardinghouse keepers need apply." Similarly, poten-tial boarders wished to live in a "house where there are but few other board-ers." Landladies obliged, describing their dwellings in identical terms.[12] Just as the size of a "private family" proved flexible, claiming to house "few" boarders or "no other boarders" was as much a shrewd marketing tactic as a statement of fact. Both were open to interpretation, as a satirist for *Harper's* made clear: "no other boarders except an old gentleman who'll die before January, three young ladies training to be ministers' wives, a couple of very nice families, and two young men in the pawnbroking business, and of serious turn of mind."[13]

Landladies who advertised private families or claimed to entertain no other boarders knew that they risked empty rooms if they stated otherwise. Yet they did not necessarily engage in conscious deception. Or, to put it another way, like boardinghouse keepers who claimed to host visiting friends, and like many boarders themselves, they engaged in a good deal of self-deception. Terming her residence a *private family* allowed Forbes—who never in a million years would have thought of herself as a boardinghouse keeper—to keep boarders yet rhetorically distance herself from the marketplace.

At the same time, she was hardly immune from the dictates of the very real market in boarding places. Even as she touted her private family, Forbes was careful to emphasize her house's convenient location: "within seven minutes walk of State st." What's more, her transition from boarder to housekeeper worked a subtle mental transformation. She socialized with her boarders much as she had with the family at 34, although she accepted their invitations to lectures and meetings far less frequently. She even revived the English grammar class, but it only lasted a short while. Forbes was simply too busy and too tired, even for moral uplift and respectable entertainment. Her private language betrays a sense of distancing. She knew better than to describe No. 6 as anything other than a private family when she advertised for lodgers. She used somewhat different terminology in the pages of her diary. Here—in contrast to "our family at 34."—she conceived of No. 6 as a "household" and of its inhabitants as "boarders." Both the trials of boardinghouse keeping and the maxims of the marketplace had taken their toll; boarders were no longer merely friends, companions, and potential mates; they were also mouths to feed, messes to clean up after, rent payments that she could only hope would materialize on time.[14]

Forbes's semantic confusion suggests that the boundaries between public and private, boarders and family, were constantly shifting, even in the mind of one individual. It also suggests that privacy had a market value—and one on which certain kinds of establishments claimed to hold monopolies. If No. 6 Waverly Place was "private," the combination boardinghouse/saloon Annie Maloney kept in Charlestown, just northeast of Boston, in the 1870s was not. Once again, the language of private and public had many meanings. On one hand, "public" boardinghouses literally were "public houses," which, like hotels and taverns, served food and beverages to anyone who walked in whether or not he spent the night. In this sense, Maloney's establishment would have qualified as public because it included a saloon; farther up on the social scale, so would Troy's Mansion House Hotel, which stood just across the street from Catherine Thorn's genteel boardinghouse. "Private" boarding-houses—sometimes synonymous with private families, other times not—accommodated only the needs of the people who lived in them. Yet the meaning of *private* went far beyond the literal. "Persons can be persuaded to admit that they live in, or even that they keep a private boarding-house; but that they have, or ever have had, anything to do with a boarding-house, simple and unqualified, nothing would induce them to confess," the *New York Times* explained. Dubbing an establishment "private" signaled its respectability and relative gentility, distinguishing it from the disreputable haunts frequented by working-class and immigrant lodgers—that is, places like Annie Maloney's. Almost no one would have described Maloney's house as a private establishment, even if it had not included a saloon, least of all Maloney herself.[15]

Fitting Up

People who kept boarders or entertained visiting friends needed places to put them, and they acquired their houses in many and various ways. Those who owned their homes outright had the most to make and the least to lose (unless they mortgaged their houses to make ends meet); keeping boarders proved an especially viable option for widows who inherited real estate. Yet most urban landlords and landladies, like most urbanites in general, rented rather than owned the houses they kept. For some city dwellers, taking in boarders was a necessary prerequisite to leasing a house; even middle-class families often needed the supplemental income boarders provided in order to pay the rent. And in an era of declining birthrates, many older residences, like the three-and-a-half-story brownstone at No. 6 Waverly Place, had room to spare.[16]

If some families took in boarders in order to afford a house, others searched the classifieds with the explicit intention of opening a boardinghouse. Newspapers advertised residences "suitable for genteel boarding-house[s]." "A House to let to a respectable family of color for a Boarding House in a respectable part of the city," read a notice placed in the *Colored American* in the 1830s. Sometimes landlords expected new tenants to take houses, furniture—and boarders. "A finely furnished lodging and boarding house, 16 rooms . . . ; nice set lodgers, paying well," a typical ad of this sort promised.[17] Occasionally, boarders in search of lodging offered to rent a house and employ someone to provide them with board; other times prospective boardinghouse keepers made sure to line up lodgers before they signed the lease, as did "a lady who is about to take a very desirable house, in a first-class neighborhood."[18]

Acquiring a desirable house was easier said than done. "The real estate agent gauges you at once and regards you as a questionable tenant. The landlord wants good security and rent in advance as soon as he find out your intended occupation," one boardinghouse keeper complained. For every ad that proclaimed "suitable for a genteel boarding house" there was one that stated the owner's intention to lease "to a small private family only" or "to strictly private family."[19] All was not necessarily lost; the definition of private family was, as always, ambiguous, and many housekeepers would have interpreted these caveats as tacit permission to keep "but few boarders." Still, landlords had reason for suspicion. Too many boardinghouses in a single locale heralded the arrival of a "boardinghouse district," a situation sure to lower neighborhood property values. Of more immediate concern was whether tenants who depended on boarders for their income would be able to pay the rent.

Interior arrangements counted for as much if not more than external appearances. Apart from the daily tasks of cooking, cleaning, and marketing, much of the labor of boardinghouse keeping involved managing interior space. How housekeepers allocated it depended on the size of their establishments, the scale of their enterprises, the importance they attributed to privacy, and their relative desperation. The proprietor of a large house could more easily separate family space from boarders' space, designating the former as off limits if she so desired. For those with more modest aspirations, a spare room, ordinarily used for nonpaying visitors, could easily be transformed into accommodations for lodgers; indeed, boarders who lived with "private families" expected to share their rooms and even their beds with visiting relatives—or to sleep on the parlor sofa. They did not always do so cheerfully. "Miss Hillman indignant because her room was occupied by Bess," Forbes noted.[20] Families eager or desperate for income reduced the confines of their own quarters, doubling up to make space for lodgers. "When the house is full the dining room is used for a bedroom and meals are served in the kitchen," one observer complained. At times, landladies literally slept with their boarders. Mary Surratt, a Washington, D.C., boardinghouse keeper, roomed with lodger Honora Fitzpatrick, and Mrs. Haskell stayed with her boarder Susan Brown.[21] The very poorest urban families simply set aside a bed, a portion of a bed, or a corner where a boarder could stretch out on a mattress, pallet, or the bare floor.

The desperately poor had no parlors, but a middle-class family fallen on hard times might reluctantly relinquish its parlor for boarders' sleeping quarters, indicating a true fall from grace. Such drastic action was a last resort, for a boardinghouse with any pretension to moral decency needed a parlor. No house that forced young women to entertain male suitors in their bedrooms could be deemed respectable. The parlor was where boarders received visitors, courted, gathered and socialized. "Boarders in parlor this eve . . . Popped corn and cider," Susan Forbes remarked in winter 1863. Even as more fashionable establishments increasingly rented out suites instead of single rooms, allowing boarders the privilege of "private" parlors, the "public parlor" as Catherine Thorn termed it, remained a necessity. "Found quite a party in the large parlor, so went in, & had quite a pleasant merry time, till 10 o'clk . . . Mrs Price seemed pleased to have her boarders so sociable."[22]

As the contrast between Thorn's Clark House and the crowded tenement rooms photographed by social reformer Jacob Riis suggests, space and privacy represented different things to different people, their definitions a combination of economic circumstances and cultural preferences. Both were flexible concepts that meant little to some housekeepers and their lodgers, everything to others. As Richard Barker's experiences (detailed in chapter 1) suggest, even the "private" boardinghouses populated by genteel urbanites were far from private in our twenty-first-century sense of the term. Despite fellow lodgers crossing his threshold to peek at family photographs and séances transpiring behind the curtain separating his room from the adjacent suite, Barker enjoyed a good deal more privacy than did many of his peers. A married man and an attorney of some means, Barker always had his own room—a relatively uncommon occurrence. Until at least midcentury and considerably later in frontier areas, travelers who stopped at inns and taverns expected to sleep with strangers; sharing a room or a bed with a fellow lodger or a landlord's son was a difference of degree, not kind. Out of both financial necessity and desire for companionship, the single young men who accounted for the vast majority of the nation's boarders typically shared rooms (and sometimes beds). Such was the case of twenty-one-year-old Henry Pierce and his "chum," fellow clerk William Patterson. "In my chum I have found *every thing* I could desire *more* than I could expect in any one. A whole-souled, generous, agreeable, lively, sensible fellow. I could expatiate on his many good qualities, but it is not necessary. May I be blest with his company for-ever." Not every boarder found his roommates so companionable, but in other respects Pierce was far from unique. "Would room with one or more gentlemen, if agreeable," one boarder in search of lodging wrote. Forbes advertised a "Room for gentlemen," not a "Room for a gentleman." "It is by no means uncommon to see four, or even five or six beds in the same room," grumbled British visitor James Boardman, writing of New York establishments that catered to "smaller shopkeepers and merchants' clerks."[23]

Roughly contemporaneous (Boardman wrote in the 1830s, Pierce in the 1840s), Pierce and Boardman attached different meanings to the same phenomenon. Their divergent attitudes reflected different perspectives (a young American clerk versus a cranky British aristocrat), different genres (a private diary versus a published travelers' account intended to illustrate American cultural inferiority), and different degrees of crowding (two to a room versus four, five, or six). Clearly influenced by the popular culture he encountered, Boardman echoed American criticisms of boardinghouse life, even reprinting a humorous account that appeared in a New York newspaper. In the end it was Boardman who evoked emerging domestic ideals; as advice literature and prescriptive fiction increasingly advocated setting aside particular rooms for specialized functions, residences that took in boarders fell short. To middle-class observers enthralled by floor plans of model cottages, boardinghouses appeared crowded and disorganized, not to mention immoral.

Humorists had field days describing the makeshift arrangements that prevailed in urban boardinghouses, many of them former mansions subdivided after their wealthy owners fled to greener pastures. They wrote of "attics constructed so that standing erect within them is only practicable in one spot," closets transformed into bedchambers, and imperfect partitions, "which afforded opportunity for interchange of small courtesies . . . with our neighbor." (As Barker's tale of the medium behind the curtain suggests, their accounts, however exaggerated, were grounded in boarders' experiences.) Comic portrayals of boarding life—especially the widespread practice of "cramming in"—evoked the contrast between boardinghouses and the spacious Italianate cottages and, later, Queen Anne houses of the increasingly suburban middle classes. The contrast, as most commentators saw it, was moral as well as spatial; by turning every square inch into a commodity, boardinghouse keepers transgressed the imaginary border that separated home from marketplace.[24]

However they apportioned the spaces in their houses, landladies had to furnish them—or in boardinghouse parlance—"fit them up." Genteel boarders, especially widows and widowers and married couples, often arrived with furniture in tow, but housekeepers who wished to attract the most common type of boarder, single young men, needed furnished rooms. The effort and expense involved depended on the quality of the residence and its clientele. Fashionable houses catering to the wealthy boasted "spacious and luxuriously-furnished parlors" that included "comfortably-padded rocking-chairs," "marble tables," and "thousand-dollar piano-fortes." Up "broad staircases" lay "handsome apartments" and "modern improvements" (a euphemism for indoor toilets.) The further one descended down the social ladder, the shabbier the furnishings and the more "imperfect" the "lavatory arrangements" became. "How a three-feet-by-sixteen inches strip of threadbare carpet, a twelve-and-a-half-cents-Chatham-square mirror, and a disjointed chair may, in the lively imagination of Boarding-House proprietresses, be considered *furniture*," Gunn exclaimed. Establishments that housed workingmen and the lowliest clerks, where "a chest of drawers is, indeed, a rara avis," dispensed with all but the barest necessities.[25] Even if boarders outfitted their own quarters or if boarders' fitted-up bedrooms were all but bare, the "public" parlor had to be furnished. As it typically was the first room a prospective boarder encountered, a sumptuously appointed parlor was itself a form of advertising. "It is part of my capital to have my parlor well furnished," one astute businesswoman explained.[26]

Lodgers quickly learned to view with suspicion advertisements that promised "handsome furnishings"; indeed, novelists, newspaper reporters, and magazine writers portrayed boardinghouse fixtures as inevitably shabby. Commentators who emphasized faded upholstery and threadbare carpets had axes to grind; their observations were part of a larger symbolic assault on boardinghouses—creatures of the marketplace. In the popular imagination, boardinghouse sofas, chairs, mirrors, and curtains were literally and figuratively shopworn.[27] Such images had long shaped boarders' expectations. The English visitor Mrs. Felton professed surprise when she entered her rooms at a "genteel" Manhattan boardinghouse for the first time; they were "much better furnished . . . than I expected to find" in "a mere boarding-house." Dingy carpets, mismatched furniture, and lumpy mattresses—more than mere figments of the popular imagination—reflected the relatively high cost of furnishings, the wear and tear transient lodgers inflicted, landladies' reluctance to replace outdated or dilapidated items in their never-ending quest to make ends meet. Felton and her husband paid one hundred dollars a month for their lodgings in the 1840s ("in this sum I have not included any thing connected with the children"), between a fifth and a third of a workingman's annual wages. More typical boarders—those who paid three or four dollars at midcentury and ten to fifteen dollars by 1900—could expect to live with the sort of furniture one found in "a mere boarding-house."[28]

New or used, sumptuous or shabby, furniture represented a boardinghouse keeper's most valuable asset and, apart from rent, her most significant expense.

Those not already well supplied with bedsteads, bureaus, and Brussels carpets had to purchase them. "I bot [*sic*] bureau for Mr. Hathorn's room," read Forbes's diary entry for December 2, 1863. Forbes seems to have paid cash, but boardinghouse keepers often purchased furniture on credit, hoping that their profits would cover the bill when it came due.[29] As the fate of Sarah Barrows suggests, the risks were substantial. Barrows, "a New-Jersey blonde, who came to New York with speculative ideas, an abundance of cheek, and very little stock in trade," rented a brick house on Twenty-First Street in the fall of 1887, buying parlor furniture on installment. She furnished the remainder of the house "in an original manner." Advertising for boarders, she struck a bargain with the first respondent, Arnold Ingraham, a stockbroker, who agreed to supply her with $260 worth of furniture, "payable in first-class board and lodging for himself and wife at the rate of $15 per week." All might have gone well if Barrows had kept her half of the bargain—or more accurately, had she been able to convince grocers and gas dealers to immediately extend credit as well. The Ingrahams lived at Barrows's boardinghouse for two weeks before they had heat and for nearly a month before they received meals. Other boarders arrived and, learning the deficiencies of their new home, just as quickly departed, as did servants, depriving the establishment of a steady source of income and a labor force. Exasperated, Ingraham decided to follow their example and to take his furniture with him; Barrows threatened to "smash it to kindling wood" if he did. As debts mounted and creditors clamored, she made plans to sell everything in the house including the Ingrahams' furniture and the still unpaid-for parlor pieces, only to be thwarted when Ingraham hired a lawyer and the furniture firm moved quickly to recover its property. "Mrs. Barrows will probably return to New-Jersey at once," the *New York Times* concluded. "It is said that she has a husband in Newark, but that they have been separated some time." Drawing on what were by then longstanding associations between boardinghouse keeping and vice (a theme that chapter 5 will explore), the *Times* reporter equated economic failure with moral failure; failure was exactly what a "New Jersey blonde" estranged from her husband deserved. Sarah Barrows's story also delineates the varied economic arrangements that landladies and boarders fashioned between them *and* the fragile links that bound together landlords, boardinghouse keepers, boarders, and servants, subjects to which we will return.[30] What's important here is that Barrows's dilemma illustrates that furniture represented, as the *Times* put it, a boardinghouse keeper's "stock in trade" and an expensive investment for one without means.

Furniture was also an asset that could be liquidated. When landladies were desperate for cash, they did what Barrows tried to do: sold their furniture. More commonly, they mortgaged it. "Considerably in debt to several [parties]," Jane Randolph, a Manhattan boardinghouse keeper, mortgaged the contents of the house she rented on West Twenty-Second Street. Even the relatively successful seized upon this tactic in times of need. Mary Fitch, one of Susan Forbes's neighbors, ran a boardinghouse on Dover Street for at least fifteen years. In 1875 an agent for the credit reporting firm R. G. Dun & Co. described her as "smart + capable," worth between ten and fifteen thousand dollars, and "considered good" for credit. Only two years later, however, the economy and Fitch's business prospects had soured, and Fitch resorted to mortgaging her furniture.[31] Fitch owned the Dover Street house and another nearby. For the vast majority of landladies, who rented the houses they kept, furniture was an asset and a liability. If a landlord grew tired of waiting for overdue rent payments, he placed a lien on his tenant's furniture. Savvy housekeepers quickly learned to "make over" their "stock" to trusted friends to prevent its seizure. Of course, as Barrows's case suggests, liens proved fruitful only if the boardinghouse keeper in question owned her furnishings outright. Like Barrows, landladies starting out in business often purchased furniture on credit, hoping that the rents they would eventually collect would pay the bill when it fell due.

Landladies determined board rates through a complex calculus comprised of equal parts location, season, demeanor, and relative desperation. The "class" of an establishment, its inhabitants, and its immediate environs set the range of rents its proprietor might charge. Within the confines of a single residence, rates varied. Large rooms with windows cost more than small, interior chambers; the "hall bed-room" was the cheapest and least desirable of rooms in boardinghouse lore. Boarders paid more for first-floor quarters than those on the second floor; rates decreased with each flight of stairs. Nettie Barker, contemplating her return to New York from a visit to her in-laws in Kentucky, wrote Richard in 1888: "I would just as soon have the front room on the top floor for many reasons—it would be five dollars a week less than we have been paying—but it would be a long trip to take up and down the stairs three times perhaps oftener, a day."[32] Attic rooms, on the fourth or fifth floor of most brownstones—sweltering in summer, freezing in winter—cost least of all.

Various exigencies undermined these basic rules. Urban housekeepers charged the highest rents at the beginning of the fall season but resorted to "summer prices" when genteel boarders abandoned stifling cities for seashore and countryside. Landladies afflicted by unexpected vacancies—all too common occurrences—were more than willing to bargain. And boarders whose deportment suggested responsible behavior and reliable rent payments got better deals than those whose appearance and conduct inspired suspicion. Last but not least, landladies' favorites—"pet" boarders—merited special consideration in this and other matters. The inhabitants of a typical nineteenth-century boardinghouse found themselves in a situation not unlike airline passengers today, victims of numerous petty and not-so-petty injustices. Boarders might be charged different rates for similar rooms; a pet lodger who inhabited a coveted first-floor chamber might pay less than the recent arrival who regularly trudged up two flights of stairs. Because such arrangements inspired a good deal of grumbling when they came to light, sometimes inducing aggrieved parties to decamp immediately, boardinghouse keepers were careful not to divulge them.

Keeping Boarders

In 1889, Carrie Abrams, a New York landlady, sued Isaac White for $744, claiming he had not paid his board since 1887.[33] Most landladies were not so tolerant, most boarders not so persistent. White saw the advantages of his situation, so he stayed put, but boarders in general were notoriously transient. "Keeping" boarders had a double meaning; boarders were easy enough to attract, but they were difficult to keep. If they did not like the conditions in one house, they moved to another. "Permanent if suited," boarders' advertisements frequently promised; all too often, they were not suited. "Even the law seems to be against you," one landlady complained. "In almost every other business written contracts are made, but when you take people to board it is extremely difficult to get them to make any definite arrangement with you." Boarders, too, could manipulate cultural meanings. If they scoffed at the idea that boardinghouses could be homes, they also refused to see them as businesses worthy of formal agreements. If terms such as *private family*, *private boardinghouse*, and *visiting friends* helped protect genteel landladies against the taint of association with the market, they also left them vulnerable to fraud.

Too many fickle lodgers realized the boardinghouse keeper's "worst nightmare—empty rooms." "I have seen so many of my craft, and we all look alike," the anonymous landlady explained. "There is a hall mark on us all. I meet my sisters everywhere, at the market, in the cars, on the street, and I can tell one as far as I can see her. Care, anxiety, suspense are always written on our faces. We are pale from sleepless nights, and unnourished from food eaten with no digestive lightheartedness; we are nervous with worry and worn with work." Boardinghouse keepers did form something akin to sisterhoods when times were good. Some, like those who housed politicians when state legislatures were in session, formed unofficial combinations and collectively set board rates. More commonly, a landlady whose rooms were full encouraged lodgers to patronize her less fortunate sisters. But when times were rough, boardinghouse keepers were ruthlessly competitive. "Mrs. Waterman left Boarding here—went to Mrs. Barnes; Mrs. Cole left us for Mrs. Holman's in Cambridge. Has been here two weeks last Thursday." Such were the weary litanies that Susan Forbes dutifully recorded in her diary.[34]

Adding insult to injury, boarders—dissatisfied with the services they received or short of funds themselves—frequently departed without paying what they owed. One morning in October 1865, two of Susan Forbes's lodgers, Mr. and Mrs. George French, "went out," carrying their caged birds with them. "They did come in again till 12½ o'clock in the night," only to leave "rather mysteriously" the following morning. Even though she kept a private family, Forbes was a shrewd enough businesswoman to send her husband to follow the Frenches to their new abode. Knowing where they lived made it easier to press them for their unpaid board bills. Even better, the Frenches left their trunk behind.[35]

The trunk was the literal centerpiece of boardinghouse relations. Typically containing the entirety of a lodger's possessions, it represented a badge of boarder identity, a symbol of the transience of boarding life. But like so many aspects of boardinghouse culture, the meaning of the trunk proved contradictory. For if boarders moved freely between boardinghouses, trunks—massive receptacles that required the services of cartmen to transport them—did not. It was easy to sneak out of a boardinghouse, but it was nearly impossible to sneak a trunk past a watchful landlady or her servants. Trunks and their contents, then, furnished collateral—sometimes freely offered by boarders who arrived without cash in hand; other times seized by boardinghouse keepers when promised payments failed to materialize.

The common law gave housekeepers no such right. Only an innkeeper, defined as a person who catered to transients and was obliged to "receive everyone applying for accommodation who conducts himself in a proper manner" (a duty frequently violated), could retain a trunk. Boardinghouse keepers, because they made "special contracts" (albeit rarely written or binding) for specific lengths of time with guests they selected, could not. In practice, these distinctions, like those between travelers and boarders, became blurred. And some states gave boardinghouse keepers the same statutory privileges as hotelkeepers. Landladies considered keeping a trunk their customary right regardless of what the law said. Even when confronted by policemen enlisted by aggrieved boarders, they stood their ground—and they often succeeded. The Protective Committee of the Boston Women's Educational and Industrial Union (WEIU)—an organization that provided education and assistance to the city's wage-earning women—devoted a good deal of its time to recovering the trunks of its clients. "Trunks involve difficulties," the organization's annual report for 1889 noted. "The girl leaves it when she should not, or the mistress claims it wrongfully." And even the WEIU, happy to recover a trunk that "meant warm and decent clothing" for a girl it considered deserving, upheld the right of landladies to evict the disreputable and keep their belongings. "Plaintiff's character being questioned it was decided not to help her."[36]

Not all boarders possessed trunks, and landladies who catered to the desperately poor resorted to desperate measures. One, Delia Martens, refused to turn over a boarder's three-year-old son until he paid the eighteen dollars he owed her. "A Baby Held as Collateral" merited mention in the *Times* because of its sensational character and because the case provided reporters with ample opportunity to poke fun at its Irish protagonists. "I always paid me bills faithful and honest," the aggrieved father, a brick maker named Thomas Finneran, maintained. While he admitted that "we didn't keep no accounts, except in our heads, which may not a' been clear enough at time," he insisted that he and his landlady ("as foine a woman as ye would want to see at the toime") remained on excellent terms until he went "off with me friends" to celebrate the Fourth of July, leaving young Willie in the care of his landlady, "and didn't come back till late that night or it might 'a' been the next morning." When Finneran stumbled into the front hall and asked, "How's the choild?" Martens told him to leave and hit him with her broom. He "pushed her away, not wishin' to hurt her, but not wishin' to get hurt mesilf" and hurried off to another boardinghouse. A policeman showed up at his new lodgings, charged him with assaulting Martens, and hauled him off to the jail that New Yorkers nicknamed "the boardinghouse." Released from a five-day stint in the Tombs after a judge dropped the charges, Finneran tried once again to reclaim his child but was chased off by Martens's "big son" who threatened to "club" him. He finally regained custody of little Willie through the courts but only after fighting another legal battle, this one with his estranged wife.[37]

Beneath the journalists' jocular accounts lay a more complicated story of an unhappy marriage, a bitter custody battle, alcoholism (each parent accused the other of intemperance), and female cooperation (Martens sided with Mrs. Finneran and testified that Thomas fed the child whiskey). Quite possibly Martens's summary eviction of Finneran was part of plot to help Mrs. Finneran regain custody of her child. The case also illuminates just how widely the custom of retaining nonpaying boarders' "possessions" circulated. While she had few qualms about resorting to extralegal measures, Martens exercised her lawful rights as a boardinghouse keeper as she understood them, placing a "lien" on Willie Finneran.

The Business of Boarding

According to the cultural logic that distinguished boardinghouses from homes, Delia Martens did nothing more than take boardinghouse keeping to its logical extreme. She transformed a child, the emotional center of middle-class domesticity, into collateral. As she appeared in city newspapers—a drunken Irishwoman quick to brandish brooms and clubs, a woman who would stop at nothing to get the money owed her—Martens was exactly the sort of woman who came to middle-class minds when they envisioned boardinghouse keepers. Landladies like Susan Forbes embraced *private family* and similar euphemisms precisely because they feared being identified with women of Martens's ilk. Although Forbes kept about the same number of boarders as Martens, they catered to different clienteles; with the exception of a single clerk, Martens's boarders were workingmen: laborers, masons, firemen, and smiths.[38] Forbes could charge higher rates because she housed clerks, not manual laborers, but she also would have paid a higher rent. What distinguished these two women was not so much class and ethnicity but the larger place of boardinghouse keeping in their lives. Forbes had a husband's salary to fall back on and a family in Epsom; Martens, apart from any financial assistance she received from her "big son," depended on her own exertions. Had Alexander Forbes met an untimely death, his widow might have found herself in much the same situation as Martens.

Women (and men) who kept boarders did so for a variety of reasons. They ranged from those who took in boarders in times of financial necessity to those who deliberately and self-consciously embraced boardinghouse keeping as an entrepreneurial endeavor. Miss Elvira Jamison, who appeared in Dorothy Richardson's semifictional account of the life of a "New York working girl" (like other characters in *The Long Day*, Richardson modeled her on people she encountered in real life), typified the latter. A former resident of "some up-State country town," Jamison came to the metropolis with moneymaking on her mind. Her "good natured face and air of motherly solicitude" disguised a "penny-for-penny and dollar-for-dollar business woman." (The possibility that a landlady could pinch pennies *and* be maternal never occurred to Richardson.) Jamison opened first one, then two, and eventually three boardinghouses, shrewdly christening them to appeal to specific clienteles. The "Calvin" attracted "homeless Presbyterians," the "Wesleyan," Methodists, and "All People's," the parishioners of a popular nondenominational church.[39]

At the other end of the spectrum were the genteel widows of boarding-house folklore, who took in boarders only as a last resort. Inevitably incapable of managing their meager resources, they engaged houses at exorbitant rents, paid too much for provisions, and charged too little for their rooms. They merited sympathy precisely because they failed, thereby remaining uncorrupted by their adventures in the marketplace. As easily transformed as their shrewder sisters into cultural stereotypes, such women, like newly widowed Mary Barrows Shepley, who "preserved, an impoverished gentility . . . though just barely" by taking in boarders in Gilded Age Boston, were more than figments of the popular imagination.[40]

Most of the people who kept boardinghouses, advertised lodgings in private families, or sheltered visiting friends fell somewhere between these two extremes. Their status did not necessarily remain fixed. Alexander Price, a dealer in provisions and fruit in Troy, New York, first proclaimed himself a boardinghouse keeper in 1870, though he had been taking in boarders at least since 1850. The income they generated likely helped Price to rise from teamster to merchant. Of course, it was his wife Martha and, after her death, his daughter Amelia who, with the assistance of a domestic servant, kept house for the family and two or three boarders. Sometime between 1860 and 1870 the widower remarried and opened a grocery store and what Thomas Butler Gunn would have called a boardinghouse "on a large scale." (Price described himself as "keeping hotel.") Price's new residence in the Hakes building on Fulton Street housed forty-six boarders. A census taker listed Price as the concern's proprietor, his new wife as "assisting," but it would have been thirty-nine-year-old Helen Price who did the work of providing board and supervising a staff of nine, which included a cook, a handyman, two laundresses, two waiters, and three chambermaids. Indeed, Alexander's ascension from keeping a few boarders to running a large establishment coincided with his marriage to

Helen, a native Vermonter who perhaps possessed the business acumen for which New Englanders were famous.

In the world of nineteenth-century boardinghouse keeping, the division of labor the Prices adopted made a good deal of sense. Because he was a retail grocer, Alexander could buy provisions at wholesale prices, thus reducing what, apart from rent and furnishing, was one of the key expenses of boardinghouse keeping. This represented a far from unusual combination, one that persisted throughout the nineteenth century and was discernable at all rungs of the social ladder. "The landlady's name is Mrs. Bowden and I believe her husband runs a grocery," Richard Barker explained to Nettie after returning to Manhattan in the winter of 1893. "So they ought to be able to supply the table at wholesale cost."[41]

Despite the twin advantages of wholesale prices and a hardworking wife, Alexander Price, like so many nineteenth-century businessmen, experienced only fleeting success. Over the next decade his career spiraled downward—from grocer to keeper of a meat stall at one of the city's markets to private watchman, charged with guarding the steamer *Thomas Powell*. But as Alexander's prospects dimmed, Helen's brightened. Perhaps it makes better sense to say that she rose to the occasion. Sometime in the late 1870s Alexander abandoned his family. In 1880, the same year that Helen told a census taker that she was married (even though her husband had been absent at least since 1877), she assumed the proprietorship of Clark House, located in the new Brown building on Broadway. Clark House was smaller than Helen's previous Fulton Street establishment, sheltering only twenty-seven boarders in 1880, and it never quite achieved the reputation of its across-the-street neighbor, the Mansion House Hotel. Nevertheless, it was a step up from the accommodations Helen had previously managed; as Catherine Thorn's residence there suggests, it attracted some of Troy's first citizens. Helen Price might well have been one of those "grass widows" who represented her husband as deceased in the service of enhancing her respectability and increasing her business. In any case, like the semifictional Elvira Jamison, she considered boardinghouse keeping her profession, publicly advertising in business directories, listing her occupation on the census not as "keeping house," but as "keeps boarders." She retired at the relatively early age of forty-nine (perhaps she had accumulated a tidy nest egg; perhaps her health had declined; perhaps she was simply tired of keeping boarders), turned the business over to one of her lodgers, and became a Clark House boarder herself.[42] Only two years later she succumbed to pneumonia, probably a side effect of the influenza epidemic that gripped the city in the winter of 1889–90. An obituary in the Troy *Daily Times* praised her "excellent management" and assured readers that she "was held in the highest esteem." It also noted that her husband survived her but declined to mention his whereabouts, quite possibly because no one knew where he had gone. (At the turn of the twentieth century a census taker found seventy-eight-year-old Alexander Price living with a younger brother in Waukegan, Illinois.)[43]

If Helen Price stepped out—or rather, was forced out—from the shadows of the family economy, Susan Forbes remained firmly ensconced within it. Whatever else it represented, her private family was part of a familial economic strategy. While Alexander Forbes's declarations of love to a woman ten years his senior may have been sincere, he also recognized Susan's earning potential. The spinsterish schoolteacher was by no means wealthy, but she was a shrewd and capable manager and, within limits, she was not afraid of hard work. Her earnings from teaching and boardinghouse keeping helped Alexander move from dry goods clerk in Boston to co-proprietor of a department store, Forbes and Wallace, in Springfield, and she kept boarders for several years even after the move to western Massachusetts. Yet through the economic partnership that was her marriage Susan Forbes also realized plans of her own. In 1881 the couple purchased Fatherland Farm in Essex County north of Boston, recovering what Susan considered her ancestral home, lost to her mother's family decades earlier. Social climbing had its costs; while Susan spent her summers restoring her estate, Alexander was chasing women back in Springfield. The couple managed to settle their differences, relocating permanently to Fatherland Farm when Alexander retired in 1895. Alexander raised horses; Susan joined the Daughters of the American Revolution and studied genealogy. By 1896 Mrs. Susan E. P. Forbes (as she signed herself to an article she published in the *New England Historical and Genealogical Register*), the daughter of a poor-to-middling New England farmer, a former Lowell mill girl, and (though she never would have admitted it) a former boardinghouse keeper, had become a member of the local aristocracy.[44]

For every Helen Price or Susan Forbes, there was a Rebecca Haskell. Forbes's widowed former landlady was not so fortunate as her boarder, and unlike Forbes she depended entirely on what she earned from keeping boarders. She managed to keep a full house for three years, but in the spring of 1860 things started to go wrong. First one boarder, then another, departed, leaving several weeks' board bills unpaid. For whatever reason—it could have been the food, the service, the prices, the company—others followed. Desperately trying to make ends meet, she borrowed money from Susan Brown (Forbes) and quite possibly from other boarders as well. She mortgaged her furniture. Neither action forestalled failure. In April, Haskell "consult[ed]" with her landlord and gave up boardinghouse keeping—and, like Helen Price, became a boarder herself, remaining so for the rest of her life.[45] How she supported herself is anyone's guess; she may have labored for the housekeepers with whom she lived; she may have taken in sewing or laundry. She "kept house" for Forbes when the latter journeyed "home" to Epsom and sometimes helped her bake pies; likely, she performed these favors for other friends and acquaintances. While a casual reader might interpret these gestures as evidence of one friend lending a hand to another, it is equally likely that Forbes—and others—paid Haskell for her services.[46]

Because boardinghouse keeping took so many forms and because boardinghouse economies left so few traces, questions of success and failure are difficult to answer. The ranks of boardinghouse keepers included dedicated businesswomen like the fictional Jamison, the real-life Morrill, and the larger-than-life Mary Ellen Pleasant, a former slave who literally turned boardinghouse keeping into gold in post–Civil War San Francisco. They included countless married women whose largely invisible labor bolstered family fortunes or tided over households during hard times. They included people like Richard and Nettie Barker's Brooklyn landlords, the Hegemans, who kept boarders in order to afford the rent on a new commodious suburban house. Then, again, they included widows like Mary Shepley, Rebecca Haskell, and Delia Martens, and never-married women like the Williams sisters, heads of household dependent on their own exertions. Business longevity did not necessarily connote success; many landladies, like Susan Forbes, took in boarders only so that they could one day live without them.[47]

Boardinghouse Economies

Stories of success and failure reveal that, like many other nineteenth-century Americans, boardinghouse keepers were immersed in complicated webs of credit relations that included furniture sellers, grocers, butchers, cutlery makers, and crockery dealers. Landladies often expected boarders to hire their own washerwomen and supply their own fuel; those who did not expanded their credit networks to encompass laundresses, lumber merchants, and coal dealers. These modest transactions rarely attracted the attention of credit investigators. When they did, the reports usually were less than favorable. "Can tell a plausible story . . . not worthy of credit." "A widow lady doing a very small business. Says she has no means, and is not considered desirable for credit." "Not known to have any property, her husband left none, but we are told she pays her bills."[48] Most often the workings of boardinghouse economies surfaced when they were breached, as in the case of S. D. Whitney, who tried to fit up a country establishment on the Hudson for vacationing boarders in the summer of 1874. He told "a plausible story," informing creditors that he owned the estate, which he in actuality leased, "and commenced obtaining supplies on an extensive scale." In addition to swindling a dairy farmer out of four cows, he defrauded butchers, grocers, and carpenters as well as his housekeeper, whom he paid in furniture that he subsequently tried to steal back.

Whitney's ultimately unsuccessful scheme came to light because he was caught. Yet, in its broad outlines it represented a more prosaic reality: boardinghouse economies rested on often uncertain relations of credit that at bottom depended on the uncertain prospect of attracting boarders who could be trusted to pay their rents promptly and reliably. One observer claimed that a boarder who failed to pay his weekly rent was summarily "requested to provide himself with fresh lodgings forthwith."[49] Too often, however, landladies had little choice but to hope that delinquents would eventually pay up—especially at times when potential lodgers were scarce. Some turned to the courts for relief, as did Carrie Abrams, the New York landlady who sued the ne'er-do-well Isaac White for two years of unpaid board. Most had neither the savvy nor the resources to sue, nor the fortitude to endure the ridicule that public exposure inevitably visited upon them. White, for his part, told the judge that Abrams made up the story to punish him for paying attention to female lodgers—a statement that undoubtedly amused courtroom spectators and readers of the *Times* city column.[50]

Not all boarders behaved dishonorably. Some acted heroically, pitching in to pay their landladies' butcher or landlord's bill. The proprietress of Gunn's "hand-to-mouth boardinghouse," a far more common type than his "physiology" implied, "solicit[ed] cash advances on your week's board." "It is politic, as well as good-natured to comply," Gunn advised, "as you will thereby secure a savory dish or so, as well as the good-will of your landlady." The "theatrical boarding-house" also operated hand-to-mouth; "as surely as rapidly, you glided into the anomalous and unnatural position of creditor to our landlady." In his testimony before a New York judge, the father of the "baby held for collateral" explained that before their falling out, his relationship with his landlady had been one of mutual assistance. "Sometimes whin I got short she didn't moind droppin' me a dollar nor did I moind droppin' her wan when it kem to that."[51]

Like many of the buildings that housed them, boardinghouse economies were rickety structures, liable to collapse without warning. If rooms did not fill or if a lodger failed to pay promptly, laundresses' and grocers' bills still came due and rent collectors came calling. Like the fictional Mrs. Baillie of T. S. Arthur's *Tired of Housekeeping*, boardinghouse keepers "in trouble" typically "economiz[ed] all we can," pawning or selling precious possessions (in the Baillies' case, a cherished piano, a "handsome silver tea service," and the family jewelry). Or, they might reduce the quality and quantity of the food they served—a risky strategy since underfed and dissatisfied boarders were likely to depart. Finally, they might postpone paying their servants—or dispense with their services all together.

Situated at the bottom rung of a flimsy ladder that stretched from landlords to boardinghouse keepers to boarders and finally to themselves, servants were most vulnerable of all. Their predicament suggests, once again, the difficulty of delineating tidy boundaries; whether they kept houses or homes, few mistresses paid their servants on time. Justly or not, boardinghouse keepers acquired a reputation for being especially lax. They accounted for a sizeable portion of the employers the WEIU's Protective Committee investigated for failing to pay promised wages. They "live from day to day, not knowing whether next week they will have any cash and yet as ready to hire labor as if they had a bank-book, [and they] are steady delinquents. They make over their household goods to an intimate friend lest we attach them," the organization's annual report for 1890 lamented. The Protective Committee minced few words in describing landladies' treatment of their servants: "selfish;" "wanting in moral integrity;" "third and fourth rate employers."[52] The WEIU's reasoning fell in line with conventional wisdom: creatures of a corrupt marketplace, boardinghouses keepers failed to pay their servants. What else could one expect from boardinghouse keepers? Yet, like working girls who wished to recover their trunks, unpaid servants needed to be deserving of the Protective Committee's services. The committee was initially willing to assist a chambermaid who had been summarily dismissed without the twenty-two dollars owed her. When its members learned that her employer "had found the girl in the room of a young man one of her boarders," they changed their minds. "The case not to be taken up." In this instance they recognized the economic rights of a morally upstanding landlady, who felt compelled to evict the errant boarder as well, "a great loss to her in a money way."[53]

"References Exchanged": The Business of Respectability

Allowing the young man to stay would have risked even greater loss. In an era in which virtue increasingly resided in the home, private families signified respectability, public boardinghouses potential licentiousness. Like describing one's household as a private family or a home, dubbing one's house *respectable* had economic and moral implications. A single disreputable boarder could ruin the reputation of an establishment, encourage other lodgers to flee to more reputable quarters, and eventually force an erstwhile respectable landlady to admit people of questionable character if she wanted to fill her rooms. Such people might insist on lower rents or, very likely, might not pay their rents at all. In the worst-case scenarios, neighboring residents complained to the building's owner or agent, and landladies were evicted along with their boarders. Hence, antebellum boardinghouse keepers advertised explicitly for "respectable" boarders—a code for white, at least vaguely middle-class, lodgers who did not drink (or not to excess) or engage in questionable liaisons and paid their bills on time. "A few respectable young men may be accommodated with Board," one ad placed in the *New York Sun* in the 1830s read. Boarders, too, like the "single gentleman of middle age . . . desirous of becoming an inmate in a respectable Boarding House," expressed their wishes for respectable abodes.

The requirement that boarders and housekeepers exchange letters of reference replaced these earnest if somewhat vague entreaties by midcentury, but their purpose remained the same. References meant nothing if a landlady did not like a potential boarder's looks. Veteran housekeepers learned how to size up applicants quickly. Landladies of all classes looked askance at particular types—especially single young women (though some reportedly admitted them because they were sure to attract young men). And they quickly evicted lodgers who behaved less than respectably; this was probably why Mrs. Haskell's boarder James Haining left "34." Moral policing enforced personal preferences, and it also made good business sense; most boardinghouse keepers would not have distinguished between them.

Like *privacy*, *respectability* had no fixed meaning. The keeper of Gunn's "serious boarding-house," who prohibited "cards, latch-keys, reading in bed,

Sunday papers, and smoking" had different standards than the proprietor of his "theatrical boarding-house" who kept a "true Liberty Hall." There "you could send out for beer at any seasonable or unseasonable hour. You could call fellow-boarders by their nick-names, cut jokes and fraternize with everybody." As Gunn's remark suggests, boarders as well as boardinghouse keepers played a role in maintaining an establishment's respectability; recall Susan Brown's "English grammar class." And when reliable boarders objected to newcomers, landladies who feared for their livelihoods speedily evicted them. Such was the fate of "a highly respectable, accomplished and intelligent young lady." After inquiring "as to her social standing" and learning that she was a mere school teacher, the other boarders informed the landlady that they would leave "unless 'that school-teacher' were turned out."[54]

Respectability was no guarantee of economic success. Sailors' boardinghouses reaped huge profits from exploiting the less than morally upright habits of their clientele; some of the most lucrative boardinghouses were brothels. Nor should we assume that middle-class landladies held a monopoly on respectability. Delia Martens tolerated more than a bit of imbibing but not fathers who abandoned their children for all-night benders. All boardinghouses—even those that white middle-class Americans considered the most disreputable—had unwritten codes of conduct.

Unwritten social rules governed the ever-fluctuating identities of particular houses, rules that reflected both boarders' preferences and landladies' inclinations. Susan Forbes hired Irish servants, but it is fair to say that she *never* would have admitted an Irish boarder. Nor is it likely that one would have applied. Nevertheless, boardinghouse keepers' ability to control the composition of their households depended on their location, reputation, economic circumstance—even the weather. Genteel boarders flocked to seashore and countryside in the summer months, creating brisk business for local landladies who specialized in "summer boarders," but leaving urban establishments desperate for lodgers with little choice except to advertise "summer prices."[55] Unexpected vacancies persuaded landladies to be less discriminating in their choice of boarders than they otherwise might. Yet, this was a risky business strategy; a single déclassé, rude, or disreputable lodger might encourage other boarders to flee—and encourage more of the same to seek shelter under the same roof, rapidly altering the "character" of an establishment. Some landladies clung to respectability at any cost, but the most desperate—the newly widowed, the recently deserted, the keepers of the most miserably impoverished households—could ill afford to be choosey.

Like their white counterparts, African American boardinghouse keepers affirmed, as did William Still of Philadelphia, that they "accommodate[d] respectable persons." Respectability meant much the same thing to the black bourgeoisie as it did to the white middle class. Joel M. Lewis assured readers of the *Colored American* that his Boston establishment was "a Temperance House"; John Mitchell announced that he was "prepared to accommodate . . . genteel Boarders" at his house on Leonard Street in New York; Mrs. Emily H. Stockton of Philadelphia appealed to boarders "who are fond of a select table and polite entertainment." Nevertheless, in an era when white writers portrayed "Negro boarding-houses" as "hot beds of filth and of the vilest degradation," respectability carried distinctive importance. In this context, African American boardinghouses, like other entrepreneurial efforts, assumed the work of racial uplift; enterprising boardinghouse keepers, like grocers and other businesspersons, figured prominently in newspaper reports that documented the "progress of the colored people." And in an era when segregation remained the norm—even in the North—boardinghouses "for the accommodation of our people" performed the vital function of offering respectable lodgings to travelers who might otherwise be consigned to disreputable dives—or to go without shelter at all. "In Pro-slavery places like New York and Philadelphia . . . colored people are universally excluded from places of entertainment for strangers," the *Provincial Freeman* explained.

Like the proprietors of temperance houses of both races, African American boardinghouses often furthered the cause of reform. Again, however, they played a distinctive role. Before the Civil War they sheltered fugitive slaves. Frederick Bailey—soon to rename himself Frederick Douglass—found refuge at the New York City boardinghouse kept by abolitionist and grocer David Ruggles. Harriet Hayden's lodgers included William and Ellen Craft, who would publish their narrative of enslavement and escape, *Running a Thousand Miles for Freedom*, ten years after an enumerator listed them in the 1850 census.[56]

Chapter 14, "On Economy in Expenses," of Catherine Beecher's *Treatise on Domestic Economy*, first published in 1841, praised a model housekeeper, "a lady who kept a large boarding-house in one of our cities." This unnamed lady kept careful track of "income, expenditures, and profits." In 1869 Beecher published a second version of her domestic advice book, coauthored with her sister Harriet Beecher Stowe. *The American Woman's Home* lifted a great deal of its text directly from the earlier volume and included a chapter with the same title, this time focusing less on making ends meet than on "Christian

economy" and benevolence. *The American Woman's Home* omitted the anec-
dote about the successful boardinghouse keeper, substituting instead the story
of "a young lady" who founded a "a home for homeless and unprotected
women."[57] Little wonder: boardinghouses had more than their share of detractors in the 1840s, but by the 1860s a chorus of voices routinely condemned
them because they were not homes. Paeans to domestic accounting may have
meshed poorly with celebrations of the very domesticity that Beecher helped
to create, but invoking a boardinghouse keeper as a model for housewives had
by that time become sheer heresy. Although the stereotype of the genteel
widow forced to enter a heartless marketplace persisted in nineteenth-century
popular culture, far more common in novels, short stories, and newspaper
accounts were the "penny for penny, dollar for dollar businesswomen," women
who would stoop to holding "a baby for collateral." Little wonder that women
like Susan Forbes gave up her "private family" as soon as she was able. Of
course, it was not just its lowly status that made boardinghouse keeping a less
than desirable occupation; there were the "sleepless nights" spent wondering
if delinquent lodgers would pay their bills, worrying about the questionable
pastimes of the dapper new boarder, and contemplating the "nightmare" of
empty rooms. And if the business of keeping boarders could be harrowing, the
labor proved even worse.

CHAPTER THREE

"The Most Cruel and Thankless Way a Woman Can Earn Her Living"

A veteran landlady interviewed by the *New York Times* in November 1889 pronounced boardinghouse keeping "the most cruel and thankless way a woman can earn her living." She ticked off a laundry list of grievances: "weary days and sleepless, anxious nights," suspicious landlords, boarders who treated her "as if she were a sort of an upper servant." Her advice to prospective boardinghouse keepers? "Don't do it." The "soft-voiced elderly lady with white hair and a face full of anxious lines" had this to say about the work of boarding: "I have worked harder physically than the Negro in the cottonfield."[1] Some readers probably scoffed; others may have questioned her choice of analogy. Nevertheless, her words, however exaggerated, make one fact abundantly clear: boardinghouse keeping was hard work—*very* hard work. Few landladies, even those lucky enough to employ servants, escaped its drudgery.

Boardinghouse keeping differed little from other sorts of housekeeping, but it often meant keeping house on a larger scale. It also involved considerable labor. Whether it took place in a boardinghouse, a home, or one of the many places best described as something in between, woman's work was never done. Like housewives and their servants, landladies and *their* servants washed, cooked, scrubbed, and swept. The difference between the two forms of labor rested mostly on perception. Just as boardinghouses could never be homes, boardinghouse keeping, tarnished by its association with the market, could never measure up to keeping house. Just as inevitably, this carefully constructed distinction easily collapsed under the weight of boarders' (and sometimes landladies') conflicting expectations. Homes could turn into metaphorical boardinghouses, and boardinghouses could turn into not-so-metaphorical homes.

Working "Like Trojans"

What was this work that allegedly rivaled Southern field labor? Details are sparse. Boarders paid more attention to the work landladies purportedly refused to perform than to the work that they actually did. Landladies, like the anonymous boardinghouse keeper interviewed by the *Times,* spoke more of general exhaustion than the particulars of housekeeping. "Very tired," Susan Forbes frequently noted in her diary. Forbes's diaries offer a rare glimpse of what it was like to keep a boardinghouse—or, as she termed it, a private family. "Kitchen work," "chamber work," and laundering routinely occurred at 6 Waverly Place. Less routine were the annual spring and fall cleanings— though Forbes did not use those terms—when she and her servant washed the walls ("cleaned paint"), laundered the curtains, refurbished the parlor ("cleaning shades, glass, ornaments, etc."), and took up carpets, beat them vigorously, and nailed them down again.[2] An old lodger's departure or a new one's imminent arrival produced the flurry of activity that surrounded the "fitting up" of a vacant chamber—thoroughly sweeping, putting down new carpet or oilcloth (sometimes varnishing the latter), and arranging furniture as the new occupant wished.[3]

Like many keepers of houses and homes, Forbes—who continued to teach for nearly a year after taking up boardinghouse keeping—delegated much of the work to a single servant. Forbes baked the weekly supply of pies and cakes herself; a good New Englander, she likely served her private family pie at every meal. What she called "kitchen work," the daily chores of preparing meals, tending the stove, and washing dishes, fell to one of the many "girls" she successively employed. Forbes "got" tea (what some called supper) twice a week; like most keepers of houses and homes she gave her domestics Thursday and Sunday afternoons off. She did the kitchen work herself only when she was without help. Unfortunately for Forbes, a childless woman who had married relatively late in life, this happened fairly frequently. She hired seven servants in the four years that she kept house; none stayed very long. Perhaps she was a particularly hard taskmistress. She dutifully recorded the subjects of her minister's Sunday sermons; "Be perfect—be symmetrical in Christian character—diligent, patient, long suffering, etc., etc." must have had special relevance. Forbes certainly saw herself as "long suffering;" whether servants Ann Quinn, Bridget Warren, or Ann Drury would have called her "patient" is anyone's guess. Like many a housekeeper Forbes vented her frustrations in the pages of her diary. It is easy enough to imagine her voicing them in person. Quinn "went to Worcester on a 'spree'"; Warren "did not get home till late"; Drury "seem[ed] stupid, and partially intoxicated."[4]

Many women complained of the "servant problem," a difficulty fraught with class, ethnic, and cultural tensions. Forbes proved no exception. She was staunchly antislavery and a faithful supporter of city missions, but she had little patience with "Irish Biddies." Turnover at No. 6 was no higher than in many "homes." Nevertheless, the demands of maintaining a household that sheltered several boarders probably contributed to successive departures. At least one of Forbes's hires, a young woman named Annie Ladd, simply was "not equal to the work." While landladies worked hard, servants worked harder. Fancy hotels and the most fashionable boardinghouses—bolstered by "first-class" rents—offered a modicum of social prestige and relatively good wages. The typical boardinghouse offered neither.[5]

The kitchen work at No. 6. Waverly Place should have been the least demanding of household labors, for the eight to ten "strangers" who resided there at any one time were a mix of boarders, who dined with the Forbeses, and lodgers, who ate their meals elsewhere. But the constant flood of visitors, most of them friends and family from New Hampshire, more than made up for the absence of three or four lodgers at daily meals. Bridget Warren might have agreed; she left Forbes for a job that involved only chamber work.[6] Perhaps she fancied the notion of being a chambermaid instead of a maid of all work; very likely, her new position offered slightly higher wages in addition to a slightly elevated status. In any case, chamber work, the weekly job of cleaning the bedrooms or "chambers," could be every bit as demanding as kitchen work. Forbes "fit up" rooms, but the routine tasks usually rested on her servant.

On a Saturday morning in December 1865, Ann Drury would have risen early to light the fire in the kitchen stove, a necessary prerequisite for "getting" breakfast. After preparing and serving the meal, and cleaning up after it (the famous educator Catharine Beecher, author of the widely read *Treatise on Domestic Economy*, suggested "scalding out" the sink every day, cleaning the kitchen walls "often," and washing "dishes not greasy," "greasy dishes," and "pots and kettles" separately), and after the boarders had vacated their rooms, she began the chamber work. But on this particular morning, Drury lay ill (in a few weeks her mistress would pack her off to a charity hospital). Forbes, assisted by Sarah Brown, a visiting relative, did the chamber work instead. They might have begun with the attic room occupied by Carrie Wiggin, a dressmaker, working their way down to the two third-story cham-

bers. Two of the "boys," John Smith and Alexander Kennedy, a clerk and salesman who worked in the same dry goods store as did Forbes's husband, occupied
the back room; another, Joseph Graham, shared with a Mr. Grant the front
room, which faced the street. Robert Hammerton, another dry goods salesman,
slept in one of the "side rooms" on this level or the one below, a Mr. Marshall
in the other. The next floor down included the back chamber in which Susan
and Alexander Forbes slept and the "bay window room," occupied by Georgine
Hillman, a teacher. One of the second-story side rooms probably provided temporary quarters for Brown and other visitors; the other might have been
Drury's. More likely she slept in the attic, near Wiggin's room, or on one of the
lower floors, nearer the kitchen.[7]

Altogether, Forbes and Brown tackled nine rooms, possibly ten. They
changed bed linens, aired mattresses, swept floors covered with oil cloth (the
nineteenth-century version of linoleum) and carpets with a broom or brush,
and dusted the furniture. "The ledges, mouldings, doors, and window sashes,
must not be omitted," Beecher advised. "Clean the plates of looking-glasses
with a sponge and pure water." Beecher recommended thoroughly cleaning
each bedroom once a week; her definition of thorough included moving all of
the furniture in order to sweep underneath it. Very likely furniture hefting
and window-sash dusting at No. 6 waited for special occasions like fittings up.
Chamber work also included daily chores that Forbes neglected to mention,
probably evidence of their ordinariness rather than her squeamishness. (She
was quite capable, for example, of noting one boarder's attack of diarrhea.)
Slop jars (which held the dirty water left over from boarders' morning sponge
baths) and chamber pots had to be emptied daily. No. 6 may have had an
indoor water closet, partially eliminating the need for chamber pots; equally
likely it did not. Chamber work at No. 6 may have encompassed the front and
back parlors—which Beecher also recommended be cleaned once a week.
Forbes's relatively infrequent mentions of "sweeping parlors" suggests that
in this, as in much else, No. 6 failed to live up to emerging domestic ideals.[8]

In addition to the sheer amount of square footage it covered, chamber work
relied on the least efficient of technologies. Removing dirt and dust from tacked-
down carpets with only the aid of brush or broom was backbreaking and often
futile labor. "Every housekeeper knows that they cannot be thoroughly swept,"
one analyst explained, "because the dust is forced downwards at each successive
effort, and protected from the action of the fibres of the broom."[9] (Forbes did not
hesitate to try available laborsaving devices; she purchased a "carpet sweeper"
but returned it, presumably because it failed to fulfill its promise.) Little won-

der that a boarder complained of rooms in which "every interstice of the carpet is filled with a gray dust, which threatens to strangle you when it is brushed";
very likely this was as true of Forbes's Boston boardinghouse as of the New York
establishment of which the complaining boarder wrote.[10] Little wonder, too, that
Forbes, who cleaned the chambers on the many occasions that servants quit,
fell ill, visited their families, or went on "sprees," found it exhausting. "I had a
hard day, doing the chamber work—had back . . . [ache] & took hot bath before
retiring." Even when she had help from young nieces and cousins from Epsom
(who in keeping with time-honored, albeit rapidly disappearing, rural traditions provided her with a flexible reserve labor force), Forbes was still exhausted.
"We worked like Trojans all day, very tired."[11]

Forbes refused to do one chore herself under any circumstances: washing.
(She did, rarely, stoop to ironing. And in one emergency her husband took in
the washing and helped her fold it.) Like many landladies, she expected her
boarders to hire their own washerwomen, although "the boys"—on whom
she doted—may have counted on laundry service.[12] At any rate, clothing
accounted for only a miniscule portion of the weekly laundry in a boardinghouse. Tablecloths, napkins, bed linens, towels—multiplied by the number of
residents—had to be washed, bleached, dried, and ironed. "There is nothing
which so much gives a table a neat and tasteful appearance as *clean* table-linen,"
Beecher observed; one doubts that the tables at No. 6 were consistently "neat
and tasteful." Perhaps Forbes's tablecloths looked more like the boardinghouse
specimen humorist Thomas Butler Gunn described as "resembl[ing] a map
of the United States, in consequence of the many parti-colored stains orna-
menting it."[13] Beecher allowed family members to reuse their napkins but
urged clean ones for guests. In this sense if not in any other, Forbes probably
treated her boarders just like members of the family.[14]

Even if she cut these corners, as many boardinghouse keepers purportedly
did, Forbes—or, more accurately, those she employed—still would have confronted a veritable mountain of laundry each washday. She found the prospect
of soaking, boiling, wringing, hanging out, and taking in the clothes so dis-
tasteful that she secured the more expensive services of a laundress, usually a
Mrs. Cronin, whenever she was without regular help. (Or perhaps Forbes, a
middle-aged woman subject to heart palpitations, like the unfortunate Annie
Ladd, was simply "not equal to the work.") Her notations give us a sense of the
time and labor involved: "Mrs. Cronin washed—here 7 hours." "Mrs. Cronin
here 7 hours, ironing etc." "Mrs. Cronin washed—6 hours."[15]

"There is no one thing, more necessary to a housekeeper, in performing her
varied duties, than a *habit of system and order*," Beecher's *Treatise* explained.

For Beecher, these duties encompassed not only housework but also "duties of a religious, intellectual, [and] social nature." Efficient housekeepers—those who labored according to "system"—found time to fulfill them all. She recommended a fixed regimen for achieving these goals: "preparing for the labors of the week" on Mondays, washing on Tuesdays, ironing on Wednesdays, folding, mending, and putting away clothes on Thursdays, cleaning and sweeping on Fridays.[16] Beecher's ideal schedule deviated only slightly from housewives' customary routine, which usually set aside "Blue Monday" for washing and Tuesday for ironing. Chamber work at No. 6 rarely proceeded according to any regular timetable, but Forbes tried to keep a semblance of "system" in regard to other chores. Washing usually took place on Mondays, ironing on Tuesdays. But all too often her plans collapsed under the weight of numerous contingencies. The ever-changing composition of Forbes's "private family" proved the most disruptive force. Boarders and lodgers came and went, necessitating constant fittings up. Some stayed for months, even years, occasionally leaving for brief vacations and then returning. Others used No. 6 more or less as a hotel, remaining for planned visits of a few days or weeks. Still others departed unexpectedly: "Mr. Bartlett left us without a farewell—has been here, rooming, a week tomorrow night."[17] Forbes, too, had to contend with the usual housekeeper's trials. Visitors arrived unexpectedly, "refrigerators" broke down, servants fell ill, or simply quit.[18]

Circumstances like these turned Forbes into one of those women whom Beecher pitied, "driven along by the daily occurrences of life, so that, instead of being the intelligent regulators of their own time, they are the mere sport of circumstances."[19] They often prevented her from accomplishing the "duties of a religious . . . [and] intellectual . . . nature" so near and dear to her heart. She occasionally skipped church because she was "tired," but intellectual pastimes were the most common casualties. Overseeing the management of No. 6 left her with little time for attending the public lectures she had previously enjoyed; Alexander often went without her to the sorts of entertainments they once attended together. One day in early 1866, Forbes turned down an invitation to hear Oliver Wendell Holmes. The new servant she expected had failed to report, and she had done the kitchen work herself. She was simply too tired to go out.[20]

"No Allowance for Little Difficulties"

Forbes's tribulations explain why boarders seldom expressed satisfaction with their accommodations. Home life was no less vulnerable to unexpected catastrophe, as anyone who has read *Little Women* will recall. But as the land-lady interviewed by the *Times* recognized, context was everything. "Irregu-larities" that happened in homes quickly became "the subject of laughter or sympathetic recital to understanding friends." "Any hitch" in a boarding-house's "domestic routine . . . becomes at once a mountain of offense."[21] Boarders did not hesitate to list real and imaginary offenses. Boardinghouses, to hear them tell it, were unspeakably dirty, quite unlike homes. Unemptied slop jars and dirty washing basins abounded. A "soiled cloth" and dingy doilies adorned the dining table of one fictional boardinghouse; upstairs, "vermin already occupied" the closet. Magazine writer Fannie Benedict described what she termed a typical experience in a "second-rate" boardinghouse. "You find the mattress stuffed with pigs' hair, on beds innocent of springs, the bed cloth-ing soiled, and of a peculiar odor." In a posthumously published essay, Lady Blanche Murphy, an Englishwoman who managed to visit New York before her demise, warned would-be boardinghouse residents of "fly-specked" mir-rors, "filthy basement dining room[s]," parlors decorated with "dirty artificial flowers," and beds "preoccupied by uninvited and most unpleasant neighbors." The humorist Mortimer Neal Thomson, writing under his pen name, Q. K. Philander Doesticks, seized on bedbugs' comic possibilities, claiming to have waged "sanguinary combat with an odoriferous band of determined cannibal insects" in his boardinghouse bedroom.[22]

Boarders without literary pretensions uttered similar complaints, some-times resorting to equally colorful prose. Julia du Pont Shubrick's boarding-house neighbors complained of a rat "promenading their room," a revelation that prompted her to sit up half the next night, fearing the same. "I think I should like to be at Dellwood again," Antoinette Barker wrote in 1890 of the boardinghouse in which she had stayed the previous summer, "but I wouldn't want to sleep on that same bed. I am sorry Mrs. S. & her daughter are such poor housekeepers." Barker did not elaborate; whether the bed was "innocent of springs," held a "mattress stuffed with pigs' hair," sported soiled bed cloth-ing, or included "uninvited neighbors," she did not say. A few years later, her husband, Richard, left his boarding place for another because "there were some little things I didn't like."[23]

Boarders rarely understood why there were "things" they didn't like. Per-haps they did not want to understand. Doing so would have revealed their complicity and their failures. They often wrote of "first-" "second-" and "third-rate" boardinghouses as if these were strictly moral categories that bore no relation to cost. But the rates boarders typically paid—kept low by intense competition and their own modest wages and salaries—purchased few amenities. Indeed, they usually purchased a labor force barely "equal to the work": the landlady, sometimes her daughters, and one or two servants. "The poor little thing is working herself nearly to death," Alice Simons (a would-be artist who supported herself as a teacher) wrote of her Washington, D.C., landlady in a rare expression of sympathy. Simons was a woman familiar with the rigors of housework. (Her compassion, however, did not extend to all of the landladies she encountered.)[24] Even crotchety bachelors, who presumably knew little of housekeeping, had moments of insight. Gunn betrayed a hint of comprehension when he complained that "the performance of fortnightly scrubbings-out" in an uncommonly clean boardinghouse banished lodgers to the back kitchen.[25] In this instance he grasped, as many boarders did not, the simple logic that underlay housekeeping in both boardinghouses and homes: getting one set of chores done meant postponing another.

Glimmerings of this sort were rare. More often than not, the landladies who populated nineteenth-century imaginations were "bad" housekeepers, not overworked ones. Like the proprietress of Gunn's "dirty boarding-house," one of the many varieties he included in his famous *Physiology,* they simply evinced a "stoical indifference . . . to what ordinary mortals affect to consider the decencies of daily life." "Indifference," in Gunn's opinion, sometimes reflected laziness. The keeper of the dirty boardinghouse "didn't waste time in washing plates, dishes and other gastronomic utensils." His tongue-in-cheek account had her washing towels only once a year, duping lodgers by ingeniously shifting linens from room to room.[26]

Boardinghouse lore more typically ignored exertion, however feeble, and ingenuity. Housekeeping chores simply happened—or, more often, failed to happen—tablecloths were "reversed—once a fortnight"; "in bed-making, one sheet only was changed at a time," or "sheets [were] changed once a month, and a towel [was provided] that wipes your hands and face for three weeks." These curiously passive descriptions mirrored contemporary understandings of housework performed in "homes." As Americans increasingly defined work as activity that produced cash, they rendered unpaid labor increasingly invisible, as not work at all. "Work" transpired in the marketplace, not in the home. Descriptions of household labor therefore usually omitted any mention of elbow grease.[27]

What then of boardinghouse keeping? Clearly, it was paid labor. That it subjected women's household labor to the marketplace was one of the primary reasons, as many nineteenth-century Americans saw it, that boardinghouses were not homes. Writers, novelists, and humorists never tired of repeating that landladies were out for the "main chance"; their motives stemmed from "interest," not "affection." "The word home is gradually going out of fashion, at least among those of us who are dependent on avaricious landladies for food and lodging," Benedict complained.[28] Seen in this light, boarding-houses—however well kept or industriously managed—could never equal or even approach the comforts of home—because they were creatures of the marketplace. Even landladies' best efforts could never satisfy, for avarice tarnished everything it touched. Stealing across an imaginary cultural threshold, the market invaded what should have been a home.

Still, if boardinghouse keeping was not housework, its residential character meant that it was not quite labor either. If homes effortlessly radiated cleanliness and order, boardinghouses sported "mixed-up arrangement[s] of pots and pans, babies, crockery, cradles, cooking stoves, and blankets."[29] If home fires magically tended themselves, boardinghouse chores magically remained neglected. Boardinghouses exuded a particularly malevolent magic: dust accumulated, mildew sprouted, noxious odors wafted unchecked through dim and dirty hallways. Boardinghouses, in other words, were dirty *because* they were boardinghouses.

Other reports plainly documented landladies' shortcomings, deficiencies often underscored by unflattering references to their class or ethnic origins. Declaring "the use of soap and water" an American national characteristic, the English-born Gunn offered his readers a scale of "comparative dirtiness": "Frenchman, *dirty;* German, *dirtier;* Irishman, *dirtiest.*" National character extended to "persons" and "Establishments;" a glimpse of its keeper revealed the cleanliness of the boardinghouse. Gunn found an Irish landlady's "hydrophobia . . . equally manifest in her person, children, and Establishment—the former being large, loose, oleaginous and black-worsted stockinged; the second, unkempt, inodorous, and ragged; and the three emphatically dirty . . . No good man could look at her without a wish to put her under a pump." Benedict offered her readers a similar typology, less explicitly linked to ethnicity and race. "There is the fleshy, greasy faced one, there is the vinegar faced, slip-shod matron, with a ragged dress and the snuffles . . . Occasionally you meet a jolly, neat, old fashioned, motherly body, in a nice calico. If she possesses any sort of accommodations in her house secure them, for such a treasure of a hostess is difficult to find."[30] Even here exertion (or lack thereof) was not the point. Dirty or ragged clothes could have been interpreted as evidence that their wearer had been washing pots or scrubbing floors when the doorbell rang.

But the authors of these accounts did not intend a landlady's appearance to reveal whether she labored industriously or refused to lift a greasy finger. Rather, through some mysterious alchemy, her "person" simply was an extension of her "Establishment."

Gunn, Benedict, and numerous other observers inhabited a wider moral universe that astute readers would have recognized. The industrious housewife of domestic fiction, both in "person" and "Establishment," radiated sparkling cleanliness and perfect order. The "neat, old fashioned, motherly body" was her all too rare boardinghouse counterpart; the keeper of the dirty boarding-house was her foil. The landlady "who receives you in fashionable apparel" (Benedict) and the proprietor of "the fashionable boarding-house where you don't get enough to eat" (Gunn) lavished attention on their persons at the expense of their establishments. They had their homely counterparts as well, the "selfish" young wives who appeared in numerous morality tales. (In fact, these were the very sorts of women who were likely to prefer boarding to housekeeping.) Addicted to extravagance and luxury, they neglected their husbands and children, spending their days shopping and gossiping until well-deserved catastrophe effected their reformations. The boardinghouse keeper who kept her curtains drawn so that prospective lodgers noticed neither the accumulated dust nor the "state of the upholstery" embodied the hypocrisy that nineteenth-century popular literature delighted in exposing.[31] The solution to all of these cultural problems lay in the well-ordered home—tastefully but not ostentatiously furnished—which achieved its neatness and cleanliness as if by magic.

Indeed, contemporary impressions of boardinghouses, however accurate, depended on implicit—and often explicit—comparisons with idealized homes. If boardinghouses were dirty, homes were clean; if boardinghouses were crowded, homes were spacious; if boardinghouses were public, homes were private. "And so you feel no reluctance, wife, to giving up this convenient house, with its finely-warmed apartments; the bathing apparatus; the library, with its shelves so laden with books to amuse, to instruct, and divert you; the conveniences of good closet-room, and those spare chambers, where your friends are so well accommodated; the commodious yard, the fine prospect of the surrounding country, and all the many advantages which this residence possesses . . . ?" the hero of Sarah Josepha Hale's *Boarding Out* (1855) asks his wife, when she contemplates abandoning her self-described "home" for a fashionable boardinghouse. To underscore the lesson—which the errant spouse learns only through sad experience—Hale takes the reader on a tour of cramped, vermin-infested dwellings, operated by boardinghouse keepers of uncertain character and questionable taste.[32]

Writers like Hale meant something quite specific when they spoke of *home:* a single-family dwelling that placed a premium on privacy, space, and cleanliness—all markers of emerging middle-class identities. It was no coincidence that the home her heroine inhabited and abandoned featured "bathing apparatus"; predictably the boardinghouses to which she relocated did not. Were "homes" really cleaner than boardinghouses? The question is impossible to answer. Some homes must have been cleaner than some boardinghouses; some boardinghouses must have been cleaner than some homes. It would be a mistake to take boarders' complaints literally; boardinghouses, whatever their dirt and disarray, helped to define the meaning of home. It would also be a mistake to interpret contemporary descriptions as mere figments of boarders' imaginations. Rising standards of cleanliness posed challenges that few establishments were equipped to meet. Cockroaches and bedbugs moved from house to house, hidden in the recesses of boarders' trunks. Boarders themselves arrived with less tangible baggage, bringing varied habits and standards of personal cleanliness with them.

Yet, in many respects—dirtiness among them—homes resembled boardinghouses more closely than many observers cared to admit. Even few middle-class residences measured up to the ideal. (Only the very wealthiest Americans could have afforded the "convenient house" that Hale's protagonist so blithely leaves behind.) "Americans" perhaps were not nearly so addicted to soap and water as Gunn suggested. "To wash the face, feet, hands, and neck, is the extent of the ablutions practiced by perhaps the majority of our people," Beecher lamented in 1841. She expressed less alarm three decades later, evidence that her middle-class readers had incorporated bathing into their routines. Nevertheless, she continued to underscore its necessity. Other problems were not so easily remedied. Critics wrote as if roaches, flies, mosquitoes, and bedbugs—mysteriously capable of distinguishing between houses and "homes"—inhabited only boardinghouses. Most "homes" suffered similar afflictions; window screens, running water, and indoor toilets remained rarities until the end of the century. Beecher's *Domestic Economy* (1841) and *The American Woman's Home* (1869), which she co-authored with her more famous sister Harriet Beecher Stowe, included recipes for killing roaches, bedbugs, fleas, flies, mosquitoes, crickets, mice, and rats. When commentators conjured up images of immaculate homes in contrast to dirty, vermin-infested boardinghouses, they invoked unattainable ideals, not real residences.[33]

Not all boarders were dissatisfied. "I . . . ask myself ten times a day if there is anything in the world more comfortable and more magnificent than Miss Boyd's boarding house," the British visitor Margaret Hall wrote in 1828. Some seventy years later Richard Barker praised the cleanliness of his new Manhattan boardinghouse and the diligence of its chambermaid: "And don't she keep the bath room & tub in order! I take glorious baths in the morning & no matter how late at night any one else uses the tub when I get there the next morning I can't discover the least sign that any one even used the tub before. It looks brand new, and the rugs are arranged in artistic order over the floor. The window has been opened & the room aired." Barker wrote in 1894, at a time when well-to-do urban dwellers could expect such amenities as running water. Expectation and fulfillment were two different things. Barker's previous situation with a "private family" in Brooklyn (where "there were some things that weren't quite right") did not include a bathtub, forcing him to rely on public baths.[34]

Money bought cleanliness; boarders grudgingly admitted as much. But even the residents of elite institutions did not always get their money's worth. Shubrick made her home in a fashionable Philadelphia boardinghouse on Spruce Street. That a rat dared "promenade" in such close proximity to a du Pont suggested that vermin were no respecters of social distinction. Similarly, when Antoinette Barker grumbled about "Mrs. S's" housekeeping, she targeted no second-rate establishment, but a boardinghouse in Brooklyn's exclusive Bay Ridge district.[35]

Nettie Barker may have had reason to complain. Then again, complaining about one's boardinghouse was only natural. In the larger scheme of things, money in the abstract—not real currency that purchased particular amenities—often shaped boarders' expectations. Boardinghouse keepers labored for money, not love; dirtiness was a byproduct not of conscientious labor saving but of the mere fact of boardinghouses' association with the marketplace. Bonds of affection ensured cleanliness and order; "stoical indifference" resulted in chaos and filth. Beneath these cultural certainties lurked a fair amount of confusion. Boarders should have known better, but they expected their landladies to be philanthropists. They learned to their inevitable disappointment that boardinghouse keepers economized, often ruthlessly, in order to turn small profits or merely make ends meet. All too often, boarders' logic collapsed. They attributed boardinghouse dirt to their keepers' preoccupation with the "main chance." But it was precisely because landladies were paid for their services that boarders expected so much.

"The Great, Yet Most Necessary, Evil—the Boarders Themselves"

Boardinghouses were not always dirty; boarders occasionally grumbled of all things about establishments that were *too* clean. Gunn complained that a temperance-minded landlady's infatuation with cold water encouraged a more generalized "hydropathic condition." "Her house, her person, her very cat was overwashed." Both her "establishment" and her "person" provided a dramatic contrast to the keeper of his "dirty boardinghouse." Cleanliness in this instance was no cause for celebration. An occasional tippler, Gunn viewed cold-water boarding places where cleanliness was next to godliness as threats to his bachelor freedom, a bit *too* much like home. While none of his idiosyncratically classified boardinghouses escaped his comic scalpel (he left blank the chapter titled "The Boarding-House which Gives Satisfaction to Every Body"), Gunn, like many of his readers, did not really want to go home. Enduring the inconveniences of boarding life—dirty wash basins, cramped quarters, and less-than-delectable food—made one a member of the "fraternity," the imagined community of "single young men" to whom Gunn dedicated his *Physiology.*[36]

Literal not symbolic cleanliness troubled Alice Simons. "Some horrible *housecleaning* has been turning me out of my room and robbing me of my night's read," she informed her sister in 1877. "I hear a threat of having my carpet scoured with beef gall and ammonia. If I see any beef gall coming this way I shall take my stand at the door with a loaded pistol and make a gallant defense." Although she wrote for a private audience, Simons had mastered the art of boardinghouse humor. Equal parts resentment, indignation, and anxiety lurked beneath the laughter. Simons did not appreciate being "turned out" of her room; temporary eviction was a painful reminder that the room literally was not hers. She had little affection for beef gall and ammonia, substances she seems to have considered boardinghouse chemicals, distinct from the more benign solutions that cleansed homes. Perhaps, she feared, her landlady suspected that *she* was less than clean. Certainly this was no worse than what Simons believed of other boarders. "I would, very much, like to come for Christmas," she wrote her sister some years later from another New York boardinghouse, "but think it best not to leave my room, as I do not know what dirty creature will be put in it, during my absence."[37]

Just as boarders rarely seem to have understood that boardinghouse keeping involved cruel and thankless labor, they seldom acknowledged that they created work. They dirtied dishes, tablecloths, and bed linens; they filled slop jars and chamber pots; they muddied carpets; they introduced "determined cannibal insects" to previously unsullied bed cushions. Susan Forbes spent a July morning "hunt[ing] bed-bugs" in a boarder's room. Perhaps the fault was hers; she was not above buying at auction "old mattresses" that might have harbored "uninvited neighbors." Yet Forbes described her quest as a special mission, distinct from ordinary chamber work; evidently blaming her lodger, the aptly named Mr. Sleeper, for their presence. If Forbes believed her boarders dirty, she was not alone. "I never saw such a young man as that Brown," the proprietor of a fashionable New York boardinghouse complained. "He shan't stay in my house. I never come into this room that I don't find his boots in the wash-basin, and his washing on the floor. No wonder the women can't get the dirt out of his shirts."[38]

Boarders also did their share of property damage. The keeper of a sailors' boardinghouse in early nineteenth-century Providence meticulously documented broken knives and forks, "pitchers cups and Saucers." Sailors were a rowdy lot and their behavior in this instance confirmed their reputation. Boarders far higher on the social scale wreaked equal havoc. "Our handsome French china dinner set . . . is completely ruined," one fictional landlady lamented. On deciding that she wanted a lodger's room for her own, Forbes "took a survey of matters." We can only guess at the results; as she made no further comment, perhaps all was well. Or perhaps she found something akin to what the fictional landlady discovered upon opening a chamber door: "The elegant rosewood washstand is completely ruined. Two knobs are off of the dressing-bureau, the veneering stripped from the edge of one of the drawers, and the whole surface marked over in a thousand lines . . . Three chairs are broken. And the new carpet we put on the floor looks as if it had been used for ten years."[39]

Fictional descriptions like these reflected a very real problem: damaged furnishings represented loss of capital, which landladies only rarely recovered. Yet, peeling veneer and scratched finishes, broken chairs and threadbare carpets also functioned as metaphors for the moral damage that was sure to ensue whenever homes turned into boardinghouses. Indeed, boardinghouse keepers were no less enamored of home than were their critics. Taking in boarders, the veteran landlady explained to the *Times*, turned one's home into "a house invaded by strangers."[40]

"Everything Is Expected of Her and Nothing Is Appreciated"

Invading strangers took many sorts of spoils; they plundered hearts as well as houses. Boarders paid for more than food and lodging, a fact of which they were uncomfortably aware. Indeed, the task of distinguishing "interest" from "affection" in practice proved difficult for boarders and landladies alike. Was boarding a purely economic relationship? A familial one? Both? This dilemma troubled Julia du Pont Shubrick, who reproached herself for not "liking" the keeper of her Philadelphia boardinghouse. Yet, returning after a brief journey and finding its proprietor absent, she complained that the establishment "had a forlorn look without Miss Smith." "One realizes the *boarding house,* at seeing no one ready to welcome you." Even the presence of an unlikable landlady could make a boardinghouse seem more like home. In feeling that she *should* like her hostess, Shubrick, a lonely widow, betrayed her discomfort with a relationship based purely on "interest" and her reluctance to admit that she paid for the services, including the emotional support that made a house a home, that Smith provided. As Shubrick's quandary demonstrates, determining what could be bought and what could not be sold was no easy matter.[41]

Here was one of boardinghouse-keeping's more problematic features. For while numerous observers strenuously argued that boardinghouses were *not* homes, in at least one respect they resembled their supposed antitheses; like "private" households, they sheltered both economic and noneconomic relationships. The work of boarding involved more than simply cooking and cleaning; it also included the intangible—if unachievable—charge of providing lodgers with surrogate homes, a task that required emotional labor as well as physical effort. As Benedict's notion of the ideal boardinghouse keeper ("a jolly, neat, old fashioned, motherly body, in a nice calico") suggests, boarders far from "home" expected mothering. They wanted landladies to listen to their troubles, advise them on matters of romance, and protect them from the evils of urban life. Different sorts of boarders, of course, wanted different sorts of mothers. Some young men and, increasingly, young women resented landladies who scrutinized their visitors, snooped in their rooms, and enforced strict curfews. Others were all too happy to make their homes in establishments that adhered to "temperance principles," forbade tobacco, and scrupulously observed the Sabbath. "Motherly bodies" walked a fine line, for male boarders and cultural commentators easily misinterpreted their maternal solicitude as "matrimonial ambition." No wonder that the landlady interviewed by the *Times* found solace in the cold-hearted maxims of the rational marketplace. "Remember always," she advised prospective boardinghouse keepers, "while you can be polite and civil; that you are not entertaining guests, but are serving strangers for a money consideration."[42]

Boarders of all ages expected another sort of mothering. If the *Times'* "experienced housekeeper" was at all representative, nothing caused landladies greater irritation than the unspoken requirement that they nurse sick boarders. "If one of the boarders is sick the landlady must accord her every courtesy and care, must get up little dishes for her special delectation and betray in every way a lively interest in her illness, or be called hard-hearted and selfish," she complained. Sickness certainly added to Susan Forbes's already considerable workload. "Mr. Young, lodger sick at home. Gave him meals," she noted one March day in 1864. Illness transformed this lodger, who ate his meals at restaurants, into a boarder whom Forbes had to feed. "Feel rather miserably," she reported of herself a few days later, "*dyspepsia.*"[43] Illness struck No. 6 again on the first day of the following February. First, "colic" afflicted Miss Hillman. Forbes fetched the doctor on several occasions (once, but only once, her husband did so instead), adding real and metaphorical miles to her usual rounds. Alexander's limited help notwithstanding, Forbes did not bear this burden entirely alone; Hillman's mother moved in until her daughter recovered some three weeks later. Mrs. Hillman's presence was a mixed blessing; she took over much of the nursing, but she was another mouth to feed and another boarder to clean up after. Forbes seems not to have charged her room and board; to do so, perhaps, would have been "hard-hearted and selfish." Just two days later, as Hillman was "gaining slowly" but still unable to leave her room, Miss Wiggin, the dressmaker who lived in the attic, fell ill. She, too, turned from a lodger into a boarder: "took two meals here—lay on sofa all day." That very afternoon, "Mr. Smith came home sick, & did not sit up." " I ran up & down all day," Forbes concluded her diary entry, and "got very tired indeed." A few days later, while Hillman and Wiggin were still convalescing, Mr. Finlay "came home sick."[44] Forbes might have rejoiced that February was the shortest month, for she spent much of it calling on doctors, preparing special meals, and running them up to lodgers' rooms.

As Forbes and the "experienced housekeeper" attested, boarders expected bedside services for free. The author of *Miss Slimmens' Boarding House* poked fun at her penny-pinching protagonist for adding the cost of a pigeon—a favorite delicacy for the ailing—to a boarder's weekly bill. Landladies who failed to act as proper nursemaids risked boarders' scorn. Alice Simons, a frail woman who would soon succumb (probably to tuberculosis), resented what she perceived as her landlady's hardheartedness. "I detest the wench so, since my last illness that I never bring myself in contact with her." Yet boarders could be equally cold-hearted. "I have had women board with me who were prominent in some of the city's charitable organizations, who spent much of the time visiting hospitals . . . who let me lie ill in my room for a week without so much as asking a servant about my condition, much less paying a moment's visit of sympathy to my bedside," the landlady interviewed by the *Times* complained.[45] Boarders wanted it both ways. They wanted "affection" when they were sick but stopped at "interest" when their landladies fell ill.

These were the sorts of unconscious mental bargains boarders might make with themselves as they confronted the moral ambiguities of a marketplace that insistently transgressed tidy boundaries between love and money, boardinghouse and home. Cleanliness and dirt, sickness and health constituted the mundane realities of daily life. At the same time they served larger cultural purposes, helping to define the always-elusive meaning of home. So, too, did food, which provided additional critical fodder for those who argued that boardinghouses could never be homes.

"Scene in a Fashionable Boarding House." This lithograph from the 1830s depicts the age and sex composition typical of middle-class boardinghouses. Most of the boarders gathered in the parlor are young men, but one, perhaps a widower, is much older. In keeping with properly run boardinghouses' reputations as places for respectable courtship, one of the young men flirts with a young woman—who may or may not be his wife. Courtesy of the American Antiquarian Society.

Humorist Thomas Butler Gunn's conception of the deficiencies of typical boardinghouse accommodations. A slovenly landlady shows a cramped, sparsely furnished attic room to a prospective boarder. *The Physiology of New York Boarding-Houses* (New York: Mason Brothers, 1857), 19. Courtesy of Rare Books and Manuscripts, The Ohio State University Library.

"Mrs. Flintskinn," proprietress of a "mean boarding-house." A potent symbol of landladies' incessant and—as popular commentary saw it—unwarranted economizing and the personification of a corrupt marketplace, the angular Mrs. Flintskinn starves her boarders but, Gunn's text tells us, reserves a roast turkey for herself. Thomas Butler Gunn, *The Physiology of New York Boarding-Houses* (New York: Mason Brothers, 1857), 156. Courtesy of Rare Books and Manuscripts, The Ohio State University Library.

The proprietor of "the boarding-house where you're expected to make love to the landlady," another of Gunn's types. A stereotypically rotund landlady displays her collection of male boarders' hearts on a skewer. This depiction and its accompanying text implicitly acknowledged the real difficulty of defining proper relationships between landladies and male boarders. Thomas Butler Gunn, *The Physiology of New York Boarding-Houses* (New York: Mason Brothers, 1857), 147. Courtesy of Rare Books and Manuscripts, The Ohio State University Library.

"Bad Manners at the Table" and "Gentility in the Dining Room." These paired illustrations from a popular etiquette book visually equate bad table manners with boardinghouses and good ones with "homes." The numbers over the heads of the unruly boarders correspond to various offenses against social propriety—feeding a dog, elbows on the table, picking one's teeth with finger or fork, and neglecting silverware altogether. The guests at a dinner party in a middle-class home commit no such sins. Thomas E. Hill, *Hill's Manual of Social and Business Forms* (Chicago: Hill Standard Book Co., 1882), 152–53. Courtesy of Special Collections Library, University of Kentucky.

"How My Maiden Neighbors Learned My Secrets." A cartoon published in *Harper's* lampooned boardinghouses' lack of privacy. *Harper's Weekly*, January 9, 1858, 21. Courtesy of Herman B Wells Library, Indiana University, Bloomington.

LODGING HOUSES PRIOR TO 1854

THE NEWSBOYS' LODGING HOUSE, 1854

A typical "cheap" lodging house indiscriminately lumped together homeless men, women, and children, charging them a few cents for a spot on the floor, while the Newsboys' Lodging House boasts a clean, comfortable, orderly, and moral atmosphere. Intended to celebrate the work of the Children's Aid Society and encourage donations, these illustrations undoubtedly exaggerated the differences between the two types of establishment but were far from inaccurate. *The Crusade for Children: A Review of Child Life in New York during 75 Years, 1853–1928* (The Children's Aid Society of the City of New York, 1928), 18–19. Courtesy of Herman B Wells Library, Indiana University.

A frame from Gene Ahern's long-running syndicated comic strip, *Our Boarding House*. Major Hoople is a "boarding-house betty" who lives off the earnings of his wife, Martha, rarely lifting a finger to help. His frequent get-rich-quick schemes never bear fruit. Note the misspelling of *convention* in the second balloon. *Our Boarding House*, June 6, 1928. Courtesy of Special Collections, Michigan State University Libraries.

CHAPTER FOUR

Boarders' Beefs

A BOARDING-HOUSE COLLOQUY:—

Landlady (deferentially). Mr. Smith, do you not suppose that
the first steamboat created much surprise among the fish when
it was first launched?

Smith (curtly). I can't say, marm, whether it did or not.

Landlady. Oh, I thought from the way you eyed the fish before
you, that you might acquire some information on that point.

Smith (the malicious villain). Very likely, marm, very likely; but
it's my opinion, marm, that this fish left its native element
before steamboats were invented.

Godey's Lady's Book (April 1873)

At the boarding house where I live
Everything is growing old
Long grey hairs upon the butter
Everything is green with mold

When the dog died, we had sausage
When the cat died, catnip tea
When the landlord died, I left there
Spareribs were too much for me

*"At the Boarding House," anonymous, undated song, sung
to the tune of "Silver Threads among the Gold"* (1873)

Boarders suffered numerous indignities. They endured cramped bedchambers, soiled linens, and dirty carpets. Rats and "determined cannibal insects"
"promenaded" through their rooms at night.[1] But worst of all was the food.
The real and imagined deficiencies of boardinghouse fare—immortalized in
innumerable stories, jokes, and even songs—inspired a colorful folklore and
an equally colorful vocabulary: "hirsute butter," "damaged coffee," "ancient

bread," "azure milk," "antediluvian pies." One satirist claimed to have been served "the fossil remains of an omnibus horse." Others wrote of apple dumplings with "crusts so tough" they "require[d] . . . axe[s] or cleaver[s] to cut" them, watery soup, over-salted butter, dry toast, and "apple-pie with crust like sole leather." Still another suggested that boardinghouse potatoes might make good "cannon-ball substitutes."[2]

Social commentators spilled more ink on food than on any other aspect of boardinghouse life. Perhaps food, with its intrinsic variety, offered humorists greater latitude and creativity (for discussions of boardinghouse food were almost always comic); even writers who admitted that boardinghouses generally served good plain food could rarely resist descending into parody. Perhaps jaded bachelors, who might be expected to overlook faulty housekeeping, cared more about their stomachs than their surroundings. Perhaps, more important, food—"board"—stood at the heart of boardinghouse experience; daily meals at a common table distinguished boarding from lodging and other living arrangements. Perhaps, most important of all, food, its quantity and quality, reflected landladies' real and perceived obsession with economy. And *economy* underscored boardinghouses' association with the market, reminding residents that they lived in houses, not homes. As with other aspects of boarding life, the story was not so simple. Home and work, love and money proved not inseparable but hopelessly intertwined.

Cuisine

"Our chief objection applies all most universally to the *cuisine* of Boarding-Houses," explained Thomas Butler Gunn in his *Physiology of New York Boarding-Houses*. Gunn made his point by intentionally employing what he considered an oxymoron. Boardinghouses might serve eats, vittles, or simply food but never anything approximating *cuisine*. And according to nineteenth-century cultural logic, they could not. Presided over by "avaricious" landladies motivated by "interest," not affection," boardinghouses sheltered strangers, not private families. Interest tarnished everything it touched, turning cleanliness into filth, order into disorder, and exposing otherwise private homes to the glare of publicity. If boardinghouses offered unappealing victuals, homes—in theory at least—served delectable meals. Claims to the superiority of home cooking—a term that seems not to come into general usage until the twentieth century—rested on especially shaky ground. European travelers routinely commented on the mediocrity of American food; Americans themselves rarely admired their national cuisine.[3] If boardinghouses bore a closer resemblance to homes than many analysts cared to admit, there is good reason to believe that the vittles dished up in boardinghouses were not so very different from the food served in homes.

Nevertheless, nineteenth-century commentators considered boardinghouse food a distinct species. They wrote of "boarder's beef" as if the beef served to boarders came from an entirely different type of cow. They evoked the "painfully intense . . . odor of boarding-house vegetables." They pondered the mysterious contents of boardinghouse hash and the unidentifiable "Sunday vegetable."[4] Yet, the extent to which boardinghouse "cuisine" deviated from all but the most refined American diets is open to question. Most urban boardinghouses, like most homes—at least until the end of the century—served "plain" food. Meat—usually beef—appeared three times a day; cakes and pies—the mainstay of "a real Yankee meal"—at least two. Boardinghouse diets, like typical nineteenth-century "home-cooked" meals, were at least as notable for what they excluded. "The invariable beef-steak" was a staple, but poultry, lamb, "chops" of any sort, and eggs were usually absent. Vegetables, other than cabbage and potatoes, and fresh fruit appeared only rarely. When fruit was in season, boarders might find "a couple of apples, or pears or a slice of melon, or two or three small peaches" in place of their pie; strawberries and blueberries, served in "very small saucer[s]," were special treats.[5] The composition (and deficiencies) of the typical boardinghouse meal remained remarkably stable over time. In the early 1830s the anonymous author of "Picture of a New York Boarding-house" complained that "no fowls ever make their way to the breakfast table." Fifty years later, feeling sick and "dreadfully dejected," Alice Simons nevertheless "plucked up spirit" to come to the table because "we had cold chicken for supper."[6]

Comic depictions of boardinghouse food resonated broadly, crossing class, gender, ethnic, and even racial lines.[7] Writers focused most commonly, however, on establishments that catered to clerks, skilled workers, and, occasionally, "the better sort of clerks." *New York Tribune* reporter Junius Browne, for example, divided boardinghouses "into two great classes—those that aspire to be genteel or fashionable, and those that do not. Having gone through the former, few persons would have energy or curiosity enough to continue the experience."[8] Like Browne, most who commented on the state of boardinghouse food assumed the persona of the young male clerk fresh from the countryside, eager to make his fortune in the city. His meager earnings condemned him to gastronomic disappointment; the higher the rent, the greater variety of foodstuffs available. Simply put, the food at the "best" boardinghouses offered "the best that the market affords"—and few clerks could afford the best. A landlady who kept house on Boston's fashionable Beacon Street boasted that her "menu embraces everything in season, well-cooked, neatly served, and in abundance." A correspondent for the *Dublin University Magazine* explained that "in the very highest class of family boarding-houses . . . the table is often as abundantly and as well supplied as that of a first-class hotel." He described a veritable cornucopia: fresh sweet potatoes, eggplants, pumpkin, squash, lima beans, corn, parsnips, beet-roots, tomatoes, peaches, bananas, avocados, oranges, and limes. His list exemplified *neither* typical nineteenth-century boardinghouse fare *nor* typical home-cooked meals. Rather, it described the diet of wealthy urbanites.[9] Young clerks who criticized the monotony of boardinghouse meals may have fondly recalled their rural homes, but it was not home cooking for which they pined. Denied the varied and exotic diets that increasingly characterized upper middle-class urban cookery, they displaced their resentments onto boardinghouse keepers. Just as their prospects for upward mobility dimmed during the latter years of the nineteenth century, so, too, did their diets confirm their lowly status. Their meals served as daily reminders that "a deal of commonplace talk" at the boardinghouse table must substitute for "the dainty abundance of Delmonico."[10]

As remarks about "leather steaks" and "indigestible pies and doughnuts" suggest, boarders grumbled more about their food's quality than its variety. As Timothy O'Donovan put it, "ugh!" *Was* boardinghouse food really worse than "home" cooking? The question is impossible to answer. And as the nineteenth century drew to a close, the gap between what one twentieth-century physician would term "the boardinghouse diet" and the foods consumed by the prosperous middle and upper classes widened. (That boarders' complaints incorporated an increasing variety—"wilted eggplants" by the end of the nineteenth century, for example—suggests that what one historian terms the "revolution at the table" did not bypass boardinghouses entirely.)[11] In the end, the answer does not really matter; the important point is that most nineteenth-century Americans believed that boardinghouse fare was inferior. How food tastes is at least partly culturally conditioned, as varying evaluations of various national and regional cuisines suggest. If nothing else, depictions of boardinghouse "cuisine"—invariably served in dingy dining rooms—demonstrate that the environment in which food is served affects its taste. For, in the end, most commentators resorted to something of a circular argument: boardinghouse food was bad *because* it was served in boardinghouses.

"In the Kitchen"

If boardinghouse eats were not quite distinct from home cooking, cooking in a boardinghouse was virtually identical to cooking in a home. Any difference in the actual labor involved usually was a matter of scale. Like other aspects of housekeeping in the nineteenth century, food preparation was hard work. Even a meal that featured "boarder's beef," "hirsute butter," and "apple-pie with crust like sole leather"—easily explained as the product of laziness, indifference, or simply the boardinghouse itself—represented considerable expenditure of time and energy.

All meals began with a trip to market. Urban dwellers might patronize street vendors, grocery stores, or provision dealers, but they did much of their shopping at vast, open-air markets. Easily misconstrued as a leisure activity or one involving only minimal labor, shopping was time-consuming and exhausting. Because they lacked refrigerators and even sometimes iceboxes, nineteenth-century keepers of houses and homes needed to shop frequently to avoid spoilage, especially during the summer. "Went to market A.M.—bot beef, veg's. sug, flour, salt. etc.," Susan Forbes noted in her diary in October 1865. For Forbes, shopping meant rising early; taking the streetcars to market; carefully assessing the available wares (in an era when one could take the quality of nothing for granted); haggling with butchers, fruit vendors, green grocers, and dairymen; and lugging her purchases home.[12]

An unsuspecting modern reader of Forbes's terse prose could easily underestimate the time and labor marketing involved. That she purchased meat, vegetables, flour, and salt meant that she dealt with at least three different vendors, probably more, while trudging through a crowded marketplace. Her concluding remark—"In the kitchen A.M."—is equally subject to misinterpretation. City living transformed Americans from producers into consumers—or so conventional historical wisdom tells us. Consuming, however, required a good deal of work, for few foods went directly from market to oven or stovetop. Today's shoppers are accustomed to granulated sugar, shrink-wrapped meats and poultry, and finely ground flour. From the vantage point of the nineteenth century, however, such prepared foods lay far in the future. City markets sold chickens, which customers sometimes had to kill and always had to pluck, rabbits still in their skins, and dead fish not yet divested of their scales. Unlike her country cousin, a city shopper could buy a ham without butchering a pig, but she could not cook it until she had soaked it for several hours to remove the salt that preserved it. She purchased coffee beans green, then roasted and ground them at home. Sugar came in lumps or loafs that had to be pounded into granules. Flour had to be sifted—often several times—in order to obtain the fine texture that cakes, pie crusts, and like delicacies required; first, however, the cook needed to remove dirt, insects, remnants of chaff and bran, and other impurities.[13]

Cooking was hot, backbreaking, and even dangerous work. Most urban dwellings had cast-iron stoves by the end of the Civil War, although the poorest working-class housewives continued to cook over open hearths until the end of the century. Indeed, technological innovations explain competing definitions of boarder's beef. The version that had been "dried, not browned, over the coals" (described in the 1830s) was cooked over an open hearth after flames had yielded to coals; the meat that had been baked "for not less than seven hours in an oven" (described in the late 1850s) was the product of a cast iron stove.[14] Stoves reduced some of the hazards associated with open hearths (although they still could cause fires and inflict nasty burns). They also made it possible to cook a greater variety of foods at the same time and using varying methods—boiling, simmering, frying, and baking. Foods that households once went without or purchased from local bakers—foods difficult to cook in hearths, such as yeast breads, cakes, and pies—could now be made at home.[15] Forbes was a convert to the new technology; in August 1864 she "had stove put in pd 31 dolls for it—tea kettle & boiler." Her purchase was less than an immediate success: "Stove burner leaks—got to be fixed."[16]

As Forbes's experience suggests, stoves were a mixed blessing. Just as housewives had to keep hearth fires going, stove fires—whether generated by wood or coal—needed frequent tending. Stoves generated greater heat with greater efficiency, an advantage in winter, a distinct disadvantage in summer. With no means of calibrating temperatures (period recipes directed cooks to bake in "hot," "warm," or "moderate" ovens), baking remained a particularly unpredictable enterprise. Water for boiling had to be obtained at outdoor pumps until midcentury (later in poorer neighborhoods) and lugged to the kitchen. Stovetop cooking required heavy cast-iron pots and pans, sized to fit burner openings. And because stoves *could* cook foods not easily produced in kitchens powered by open hearths, expectations rose, hastening the decline of soups and stews and the ascendancy of what the anthropologist Mary Douglas terms the "A + 2B" meal, usually consisting of a sizable portion of meat accompanied by side dishes of bread and vegetables. Similarly, they accelerated the cultural supremacy of yeast or "white" bread, which required rising, kneading, another round of rising, and carefully supervised baking. "White bread" quickly became a symbol of middle-class cookery—and a synonym for middle-class status.[17]

Housekeepers and boardinghouse keepers alike had to balance marketing, food preparation, and cooking with myriad other tasks—sweeping parlors, cleaning chambers, washing, and ironing. Which one got the shortest end of the proverbial stick depended on many factors—family size and composition (especially the presence of daughters who could assume some of the labor), the numbers of boarders, and the respective ability to hire "help." All things considered, the burdens of housekeeping probably weighed more heavily on boardinghouse keepers, who only rarely commanded a labor force sufficient to accomplish the tasks at hand. Food might scorch or fires wane while landladies and their servants "hunted bed-bugs" or "did the chamber work."[18] Beef might overcook while distracted landladies hurriedly took in laundry soaked by an unexpected storm. Alternatively, indigestible meat might not have been cooked long enough, snatched from the oven by a harried servant who needed to get it on the table in time for the noonday dinner.

Lodgers only dimly understood that boardinghouse keeping meant work. Occasionally, they lamented what they perceived as landladies' laziness or indifference to their welfare. They wrote of dried-out roasts that "never felt the softening and savouring influence of the basting spoon," silently evoking idealized homes in which loving wives and mothers affectionately wielded domestic utensils. Gunn complained of a boardinghouse keeper who leavened her pastries with "soda, saleratus, and cream of tartar" instead of making more desirable—and labor-intensive—yeast breads. Most commentators, writing from the vantage point of crusty bachelorhood, had little firsthand knowledge of cookery and even less of the labor it involved. Slovenly servants and bedraggled landladies were somehow responsible for the mediocrity of their meals; exactly how they were not always quite sure. Many accounts read as if their authors believed that the poisonous atmosphere of the boardinghouse simply worked a kind of malevolent magic, toughening beefsteaks, souring bread, adulterating butter.

Viewing food preparation as labor—one chore among many—goes far toward explaining boarders' complaints. Roasts "never felt the softening . . . influence of the basting spoon" because landladies and servants were busy with the chamber work. (Meat was more prone to drying out in ovens than over open fires; as late as 1869, the Beecher sisters lamented the passing of the open hearth for precisely this reason.)[19] Few landladies had the leisure to bake time-consuming yeast breads. Indeed, observers commented on the prevalence of "Indian corn bread" at boardinghouse tables. Friday's pies might appear "antediluvian" because boardinghouse keepers, like most house-keepers baked once a week, usually on Saturdays. Susan Forbes's short-lived adoption of condensed milk, cheaper and easier to store than fresh milk, may have yielded a beverage with an "azure" tinge.[20] Landladies rarely served chickens because they were expensive and because plucking them took time and effort. Boardinghouse keeping favored slow-cooking roasts and stews over fancy dishes that required frequent attention. Landladies, in short, were caught between rising expectations regarding the quality and variety of food, the rents they received, and their ability to command the necessary labor. A "cultured and refined landlady" made this equation exceedingly clear. She boasted that her establishment offered food "well-cooked, neatly served, and in abundance." She employed "five or six attendants to see to the wants of my patrons." She could well afford to do so. She charged her wealthy "guests" $80 to $110 per week at a time when the average boarder paid between five and ten dollars.[21]

Boarders seem seldom to have made such calculations themselves. They preferred vague abstractions to meticulous tallies—even though many urban boarders were clerks and salesmen who in their working lives were in the business of doing such close accounting. Just as discussions of cleanliness might ignore pesky matters of rent and wages, so too did complaints about cuisine overlook the fact that board bills typically purchased few delicacies.

"Domestic Parsimony"

Like the early-twentieth-century readers of Upton Sinclair's *The Jungle,* nineteenth-century boarders cared about their stomachs. Most expressed little interest in their landladies' welfare and were convinced that landladies economized at boarders' expense. For evidence they needed to go no further than the food on their plates. Yet, unlike Sinclair's readers, boarders cared about hearts—*their* hearts. For food revealed landladies' assiduous efforts at economy. It revealed that landladies cared only for money—*their* money. If indeed the way to a man's heart was through his stomach, boardinghouse vittles symbolized the cold calculating hearts of boardinghouse keepers.

Sometimes economy asserted itself in quantity, sometimes quality, sometimes both. Even in the nicest establishments, if boardinghouse lore is to be believed, boarders never got enough to eat. In this respect, boardinghouses probably did fail to replicate the fabled abundance of rural tables. Examples were legion. Boarders, one observer claimed, rushed to the table at the first ring of the dinner bell, "having learned by familiar hunger that to him who has an appetite delays are dangerous." Humorous accounts lampooned landladies' obsession with economy. Recounting the workings of what he termed "another mean boarding-house," Gunn explained, "We will endeavor to describe its domestic—not—economy—but parsimony." A newspaper account satirically recommended that landladies school their boarders in the art of fasting, as practiced through "spirit power" in India. Another waxed philosophic about the possibility of providing as "many radishes as boarders."

A reporter for the *New York Tribune* created the fictional Mrs. Codhooker. Her name evoked Yankee thriftiness gone awry. To *cod* meant "to hoax . . . to humbug, impose on"; to *hook*, according to John Russell Bartlett's *Dictionary of Americanisms*, was a "common vulgarism" meaning "to steal." Mrs. Codhooker did all these things. She deliberately served her boarders clams so tough that their jaws were too tired to eat anything else. She ordered hard rolls "with a crease down the middle" so she could easily give half to each boarder. She quickly warmed to a salesman hawking "a little book entitled 'Appetite Breakers, or the Landlady's Friend.'"[22]

Supposedly because of such treatment lodgers considered what would become known as the boardinghouse reach a necessity rather than a sign of boorish behavior. More often, landladies insisted on serving, lest hungry boarders help themselves. They doled out miniscule portions, rewarding with withering glances boarders who asked for seconds. They were more generous with tea, reportedly because of repeated dilutions. "How so large a quantity of the beverage could be made with so small a quantity of the Chinese herb would be a matter of marvel to anyone not acquainted with the economy of a New York boarding-house," noted the anonymous author of "Picture of a New York Boarding-house."[23]

The contents of the "boardinghouse diet" also reflected economy. The only fruits reportedly served at the boardinghouse table were prunes and the only dessert was rice pudding, both chosen for their cheapness. A boarder claimed to have forgotten what chickens looked like; having been served "only legs and pin-feathers," he had "sort of lost the shape of the bird." Lamb seldom appeared, but "roasted mutton, reeking in its own grease, is seldom wanted to grace the table."[24]

As the "reeking" mutton indicated, economy also affected quality. Landladies of boardinghouse folklore added extra salt to the butter and water to the milk to make them last longer. They sent their servants to collect the "refuse of . . . [hotel] dining-table[s]." They haunted urban markets, searching for "bargains in wilted eggplants," "leather steaks, highly perfumed butter, limed eggs, green fruit and unsavory vegetables," and flounder, "which boarding-house keepers like, because they are cheap." "The latest and hardest customer" at any New York market, Junius Browne claimed, "is the cheap boarding-house keeper" who "is resolved on buying much for little." Deliberately wait-ing until all but the least desirable items had been purchased, she drove hard bargains with butchers, greengrocers, and dairymen eager to unload their remaining wares. (Predictably, in this telling, young married couples who occupied their own homes did their marketing earlier.) "It's the best hour for going to market," the fictional boardinghouse keeper Alvira Slimmens announced, "all the choice things are taken, and, of course, I have to put up with the cheap pieces, whether I want to or not. You won't catch me giving my boarders sirloin roasts and porterhouse steaks; it isn't what I keep board-ers for."[25] Accounts like these, which neatly connected boardinghouse keep-ing quite literally to the "market," were not entirely fictional. Like other city dwellers, landladies timed their excursions to what they were willing and able to pay. Susan Forbes was well on her way to membership in the res-pectable middle classes, a journey that boardinghouse keeping helped her to underwrite. Nevertheless, she "went out at 11½ to fish market."[26]

"Domestic parsimony" meant that boarders could never be quite sure what they were eating. Humorists exploited the comic possibilities, dramatizing the gulf between the known (home cooking) and the unknown (boarding-house cooking). A tale from the *Philadelphia Mercury*, reprinted in an African American expatriate newspaper published in Toronto, offered a tongue-in-cheek "useful hint to those ladies who undertake to provide nutriment for boarders with strong stomachs and weak purses." At first the landlady of a "$2 and 50c. boarding house" berated her cook for using "too much of the shin of beef" when the dinner soup turned out "uncommonly rich and unctuous." The servant's explanation exonerated her: a kitten had fallen into the soup ket-tle. The landlady's response: "Cook, have we any more kittens? We might drop in one you know, every time we have a soup dinner." Pestered by boarders who demanded turkey for Christmas dinner, the keeper of a fictional actors' board-inghouse promised them "sumpin' better'n turkey" and tried to pass off mut-ton and common rabbits as rare beasts from Australia.[27] Q. K. Philander Doe-sticks imagined boardinghouse tables as sites of comic warfare that pitted devious landladies against canny boarders.

There appeared at breakfast a dish of beef . . . it was not molested; at dinner it made its appearance again, still it was not disturbed; at tea fragments of it were visible, but it yet remained untouched; in the morning a tempting looking stew made its appearance, but alas! it was only a weak invention of the enemy to conceal the ubiquitous beef; at dinner a meat-pie enshrined a portion of the aforesaid beef; it went away unharmed.

For a week, every day, at every meal, in every subtle form, in some ingenious disguise, still was forced upon our notice this omnipresent beef; it went through more changes than Harlequin in the Pantomime, and like that nimble individual came always out unharmed.[28]

Anecdotes like these assumed the status of urban legend (and point us, perhaps, to the origins of the term *mystery meat*). They also served as early indictments of leftovers, although that term—a pejorative from the beginning—seems not to have entered the popular vocabulary until the 1890s. The general idea appeared much earlier; Beecher's *Treatise on Domestic Economy* (1841) warned against "mixtures" and declared soup "hard of Digestion." As Beecher's misgivings suggested, leftovers, imaginatively—or unimaginatively—prepared, were as likely to be found in homes as in boardinghouses; repeated servings of rancid mutton may have helped drive Lizzie Borden over the edge. Nevertheless, boardinghouse concoctions like those Doesticks described drew their comic punch from their blatant parody of the "ordered" and knowable meat-and-potatoes meal cooked, of course, in homes. Soups flavored with kitten meat and ingeniously disguised week-old beef strayed far from "A + 2B."[29]

Humorists naturally exaggerated. Still, they expected the culinary experiences they described to resonate, if only faintly, with their readers. Resonate they did, for ordinary boarders incorporated the conventions of boardinghouse folklore into their unpublished private writings, and, conversely, folklore drew on ordinary boarders' experiences. Jacob Deterly's diary periodically noted the "State of Boarding" in Cincinnati in the 1820s. "This evening supper I had a roasted SPIDER! Along with my Beef stake—Not long since ate part of a baked one!! In bread, Drowned, baked or roasted FLIES we get in abundance—hair & Dirt add greatly to quantity—to analyze the coffee would puzzle a great chymist." More than half a century later, Alice Simons wrote her sister that she very much wished her to visit but feared the effect of "the mysterious chemical ingredients of New York boarding house cookery" on her young nieces and nephews. A year later, in 1878, nothing had changed. "This is now the ninth

(9th) day that I have eaten no meat. The horrible chunks of shoe leather that they dole out to me here would try the digestion of an alligator; and I have been living on bread and butter, occasionally varied by hominy and butter, and ice cream. I must say I begin to feel the effects of the *ethereal* diet."[30]

Serious concerns lurked beneath comic depictions of boardinghouse fare. Denunciations of economy, however exaggerated, reflected landladies' very real efforts to make ends meet. Boarders seldom understood just how difficult this task was to accomplish. (Simons, we have seen, was an exception: "She has all her rooms filled but one, now, but only the prices are *so low* for her latest boarders that I know she finds it difficult to make both ends meet," she wrote of her New York landlady in 1889.)[31] Even if they did, it was far easier to blame unscrupulous landladies than to ponder the vagaries of an economic system based on high house rents, prevailing rates of board, and their own uncertain wages. The market in the abstract, not the actual cost of provisions in real urban marketplaces, often shaped boarders' expectations. Boarders resented being cheated, and perhaps they were. In the end, the question of what was fair was impossible to answer, for boarders and landladies relied on different notions of fairness. Increasingly accustomed to thinking of house-keeping as something other than work, it is not surprising that young men who made up the majority of urban boarders little valued the labor of boarding-house keepers. Increasingly accustomed to thinking of housework as a labor of love, they resented landladies' obsession with the "main chance."

In a literary culture in which physical appearance provided a ready indica-tion of character, boardinghouse keepers in fact and fiction personified econ-omy. "Any cosmopolite knows a boarding-house proprietress at a single glance . . . She is generally very thin and haggard, in worn and threadbare attire, with a cold, yet nervous and anxious manner, as if all her blood and sym-pathy had gone out of her with the last payment of rent. Or she is large and fleshy, tawdry in dress, with . . . sharp gimlet eyes."[32] The first sort, this typol-ogy implied, shared her boarders' adversity; the second literally swallowed their rent payments. Gunn's "Mrs. Flintskinn" typified the former; Mrs. Codhooker, "a stout old woman, with a red face and two wisps of gray hair that were draped back over each ear from the sprouting place, like hawsers," the latter.[33]

Mrs. Codhooker and her companions were the nightmare opposites, the evil twins of the industrious, frugal housewives celebrated in domestic fiction. But wasn't this exactly what housewives who lived in "homes" were supposed to do: economize? Wasn't that the message of numerous prescriptive tales that fea-tured the ill-fated exploits of extravagant wives? Yet, the model housewives of prescriptive fiction avoided untoward extravagance and "false economy."[34] (As most inhabitants of Fall River recognized, the Borden household and its excessive miserliness fell far short of an ideal home.) Once again, the circumstances under which one economized mattered a good deal. Surely, economical housewives ventured to market as the sun rose high overhead. But housewives economized to better their families' fortunes; boardinghouse keepers economized at boarders' expense. Thus, economical home cooking tasted better than economical boardinghouse fare. Still, the very fact that at least a third of all "homes" took in boarders, their keepers no doubt practicing the most careful economy, complicates any simple distinction between boardinghouse and home.

So, too, in the end did boarders' complaints. They inadvertently revealed that the boundaries between home and work, love and money, house and home were porous and indeterminate indeed. Boarders wanted the most for their money; when they muttered about exorbitant rents, they recognized the pecuniary realities of their circumstances. At the same time, they yearned for the comforts of home—qualities that included material conditions as well as less tangible emotional and psychological benefits. They reacted bitterly when boardinghouse keepers cut wafer-thin slices of cake, doled out thimblefuls of tea, or served only the cheapest cuts of meat—in part because they feared they were getting less than their money's worth, in part because assiduous frugality exposed the economic underpinnings of the relationships in which they were enmeshed. Paying a clandestine midnight visit to their landlady's kitchen, one group of underfed lodgers discovered a roast turkey that she had reserved for her own domestic circle. In the process, they also discovered that whatever her pretenses to the contrary, the boarders were not truly part of her family. "Let all boarders notice whether their landlady dines with them, *and eats a good dinner. Let them watch whether she only tastes a mouthful, and afterwards dines in her own private apartment," one irate lodger complained.[35] As with their expectations regarding cleanliness, boarders anticipated less *and* more from boardinghouses because they paid for the services provided them.

Considerable evidence suggests how complicated and fraught with moral ambiguity the politics of boardinghouse keeping really were. The fictional Miss Slimmens recalled in one of her many monologues a conversation with a boarder. "When Mr. Little was in one of his funny tantrums yesterday, I told him I thought he found a great deal to amuse him. 'Yes,' he said, 'he laughed to grow fat! He'd as soon get fat by laughing as by eating.' 'Miss Slimmens,' said he, looking at me as solemn as the grave, 'we pay six dollars a week apiece for the inestimable privilege of being members of your family.

What we *eat* is a secondary consideration.'"[36] The oblivious Slimmens (her name itself meant to evoke parsimony) missed Little's sarcasm. Still, the imaginary conversation suggests that landladies might invoke "family"—sometimes disingenuously, sometimes sincerely—and that boarders, for all their lively humor, longed for the comforts of home. Sometimes they got them; in fact and fiction, "pet" or "star" boarders always received second helpings. Kentuckian Richard Barker learned this firsthand, when the African American cook at his Manhattan boardinghouse, declaring herself a "Southern woman," served him fried potato cakes for breakfast. Barker got more than home cooking out of these exchanges. His meals recalled the tastes and the racial hierarchies of "home."[37]

Money purchased these amenities. Barker considered himself on the brink of poverty, but compared to his fellow New Yorkers and the residents of his native state, he was relatively well off. He seems never to have patronized anything but "genteel" boardinghouses. His letters often described the food he ate, and he only occasionally expressed dissatisfaction. Never was he served "chunks of shoe leather" or "the fossil remains of an omnibus horse." (His fellow boarders did occasionally complain about the quality of their breakfasts.) Even the most fantastic tales of boardinghouse food betrayed resentment, to be sure, but also affection and grudging admiration for landladies' creativity. Perhaps more so than any other experience, food bound boarders to Gunn's imagined "fraternity" of young male boarders. Stories that featured boardinghouse food differed in content and tone from the shrill warnings of moralists who feared—sometimes for good reason—that boardinghouses were sites of crime and vice.[38] In comic tales that featured *cuisine*, boardinghouses posed threats to unwary kittens and sensitive stomachs but offered little moral danger. Boarder's beef and boardinghouse hash by virtue of their qualifiers implicitly expressed longings for "home." But they also celebrated bachelor freedom.

The Boardinghouse Reach

Boarders dined together at a common—or what one observer termed a "public"—table. They gathered at breakfast each morning. They came "home" for the midday meal, dinner, and returned at the end of the workday for supper or tea. Times varied according to the reputation of the establishment; the more fashionable the boardinghouse, the later the meals. Most operated according to a fairly predictable schedule: breakfast between six and seven, dinner between noon and one, supper or tea between five and six. "The regulation which specifies certain settled hours for meals is almost religiously adhered to throughout the United States, whether in hotels or boarding-houses," the writer for the *Dublin University Magazine* advised his audience.[39]

Boarders sometimes resented the regimens imposed on them. "There is no such thing as coming down to a late breakfast," the anonymous Irish traveler explained. "Meals are served at a certain specified hour . . . and when the hour comes round—sure as inexorable fate—the gong resounds through the house, and the boarder who does not appear at the table must expect to wait, no mat-ter how craving his appetite, until the next meal is served." Having rushed home from their work places, boarders assembled before dinner, "waiting impatiently for the sound of the gong, at the first stroke of which they rush, pell-mell, into the eating-room, and take their seats at the table."[40] Meal-times did shape boarders' routines. While a boarder at Mrs. Haskell's, Susan Brown (soon to be Forbes) found the fact that "Dinner hour changed to 1 o'clock" worth noting in her diary. "The lunch bell has rung, so I will say goodby[e]," Alice Simons closed a letter to her sister.[41] "I . . . shall begin a lit-tle letter to you before the dinner-bell rings," Richard Barker wrote to Nettie in 1893. A few paragraphs later, "There goes the bell." "There goes the tea bell and so I shall close for the present," he signed off on another occasion. On still another: "It not yet being quite dinner I thought I would begin before the bell rang." His letter ended predictably: "There goes the dinner bell."[42]

Timetables like these sometimes provoked resentment because their rela-tive rigidity reminded residents that they inhabited only "substitutes for home." Home dwellers who missed breakfast could expect to be fed anyway; late risers in all but the very best boardinghouses went hungry. Neither mas-ters nor mistresses of their own households, boarders depended on the whims of others. Young men who had only recently left "home" behind did not care to have their wings clipped by substitute mothers who insisted that they appear at the table on time. This was precisely the bone of contention between Forbes and two of her "boys," William Finlay and John Smith. Whether or how she solved the problem she did not say; whether the dispute contributed to Finlay and Smith's decision to move to another boardinghouse the follow-ing year is equally uncertain. (They would eventually return to the Forbe-ses'.)[43] We have reason to suspect, though, that the "boys"—temporarily at least—grew tired of being treated like "boys."

Like boardinghouse food itself, "certain settled hours" served as daily reminders of boarders' own small failures. Breakfast and dinner bells (more fashionable boardinghouses relied on gongs) turned even white-collar men and women into symbolic factory workers, forced to obey their summons.[44] They compelled clerks, salesmen, stenographers, and teachers to recognize, at least implicitly, that their time was not their own, for boardinghouse regimens merely mirrored work schedules. (The lowlier one's position, the more important punctuality was to keeping it.) Time was money, but time also represented social status. Fashionable boardinghouses, as every urbanite knew, served breakfast late.

The behavior of boarders themselves, especially those who inhabited less-than-genteel establishments, magnified social insecurities and reminded them that they were far from "home"—at least in the sense that home increasingly connoted middle-class standards of gentility and taste. The *boardinghouse reach* seems not to have been coined until the early twentieth century, but if nineteenth-century Americans were unfamiliar with the term, they recognized the behavior. "A man that habitually rises on his feet to reach across the table for a dish, and pulls it to himself . . . is unworthy the appellation of a gentleman" declared *Miss Leslie's Behaviour Book* (1859). Significantly, this description appeared in Leslie's chapter on "Hotel Dinner." By the mid-nineteenth century, boardinghouses—even more so than their fancier counterparts—had acquired reputations for bad table manners as well as bad food. It is unlikely that the boardinghouse reach—or its equivalent—was unique to the institution that bore its name. The manners (or lack thereof) of boarders who "rushed, pell-mell" into dining rooms were probably not so different from the dinnertime behavior of families and farm hands who gathered around rural tables. But as civility became increasingly essential to middle-class life, what contemporaries classified as boardinghouse manners modeled how *not* to behave.[45]

A matched pair of illustrations published in *Hill's Manual of Social and Business Forms* (1882) made this abundantly clear. *Hill's* did not explicitly identify "Bad Manners at the Table" as a boardinghouse scene, but the overwhelming presence of young men at the table suggests that they are not in a "home." The diners commit a variety of social sins. They tilt back their chairs; they gesticulate wildly; they eat with their hands; they feed a waiting dog scraps from the table. The boardinghouse keeper struggles in vain to control a screaming, kicking baby. If chaos reigns in "Bad Manners at the Table," "Gentility in the Dining-Room" is an oasis of decorum and tranquility. A uniformed maid waits upon a well-dressed group of mixed-sex diners, each of whom exhibits perfect posture and impeccable manners.

These paired illustrations tell us much about perceptions of social class in nineteenth-century America. "Bad Manners at the Table" depicts a working-class residence. The room is bereft of adornments; lunch pails perch on the mantel; a diner wears a leather apron, a badge of mechanic status. "Gentility in the Dining Room" portrays an upper-middle-class dinner party that, true to its title, takes place in a tastefully furnished, eminently genteel, dining room. The two illustrations offered a quintessentially middle-class moral: poverty was little more than the result of bad table manners. The presence of so many unattached men warned of moral danger and also explained the uncivilized behavior. Men, *Hill's* implied, needed the civilizing influence of women.[46]

But not just any women. Adding more women like the boardinghouse keeper of "Bad Manners at the Table" would simply multiply the social offenses. Few of the landladies in boardinghouse lore possessed the gentility necessary to model proper conduct. Those who did—usually women who had seen better days—rarely succeeded in controlling their boarders' boorish behavior. And many boarders, even middle-class ones, did not want to mind their manners. The freedom to behave badly (and, we shall see, in a variety of ways) was one of the rewards of bachelorhood, a benefit of being away from home.

"Bad Manners at the Table" and "Gentility in the Dining Room" offered Hill's readers the sharpest possible contrast between boardinghouse and ideal home (albeit one in which the children were already safely in bed), neatly paralleling distinctions between uncouth behavior and impeccable manners, working-class squalor and middle-class comfort, unregulated masculinity and womanly oversight. Real life rarely offered such clarity. Not all homes were middle-class; not all boardinghouses were working-class. Indeed, the paired illustrations offered reassurance and provoked anxiety. Transforming class into a matter of acquiring the "right" manners partly assuaged such concerns. But the two engravings conveyed another, less heartening message: if bad manners explained poverty, middle-class people who failed the test of gentility deserved social and economic failure. In the midst of the ill-mannered men who clearly work with their hands sits a diner who wears a white collar.

Most important, Hill's pairing reversed the customary associations between "private" homes and "public" boardinghouses. "Gentility in the Dining Room" does not portray a private family but genteel sociability, the sort of sociability a well-heeled urbanite might find at someone's "home"— or at a fashionable boardinghouse table. It would have made little sense, of course, for *Hill's* to depict a "private" family; it was a "manual for business and *social* forms," a guide to behavior in the presence of others. Yet, if "Gentility in the Dining Room" modeled proper social behavior as formal, "Bad

Manners at the Table" unwittingly suggested that landladies and boarders constituted a sort of "private" family whose members felt little need to stand—or sit—on ceremony.

Rather than erecting barriers between home and marketplace, private and public, the vicissitudes of boardinghouse life created confusion about where those boundaries were to be found. "Now that there is . . . so much living in public," Leslie's *Behaviour Book* found it necessary to include instructions for "deportment at a hotel, or at a large boarding-house." How then was one supposed to behave in a small boardinghouse? Which residences qualified as large, which as small? Which were private; which were public? Nineteenth-century Americans, we have seen, tried to solve the problem by creating often flimsy distinctions between public and private boardinghouses and between living in a boardinghouse and boarding with a private family. Leslie implied that these differences could be readily perceived, noting for example that at a hotel dinner, "your dress need not be more showy than you would wear when dining at a private house, particularly if you are a permanent boarder."[47] Yet, in an era when the differences between private and public, even permanent and transient were always shifting, recognizing these distinctions and behaving accordingly was easier said than done.

The problem was nowhere clearer than when boarders who fancied themselves genteel complained that their neighbors were too familiar. In other words, they were complaining that boardinghouses were too much like homes. Here the boardinghouse table assumed special importance. Boarders could avoid each other most of the time if they wished. They could retire to the relative privacy of their rooms instead of sitting in the common parlor. They could go for walks or (depending on their sex or class) patronize shops, saloons, or other public amusements. But, unless they were ill (and we can imagine much malingering) or could afford to add the cost of eating at restaurants to the price of their rent, they had to face their adversaries at breakfast, dinner, and tea. Daily mealtime dramas in which boarders eagerly awaited their housemates' arrival or coldly snubbed them show how difficult it was to navigate the imaginary boundaries that separated public and private, familiars and others, boardinghouse and home. By the latter part of the century, some "first-class" establishments had come up with a solution, offering "private tables" to their wealthy clientele.[48]

Boarder's beef probably tasted better when it was served at a private table, more like food served at "home." Charlotte Perkins Gilman would have understood the reasoning behind this assumption—and quickly dismissed it. "We are all reared in a traditional belief that what we get to eat at home is, by virtue of that location, better than what we get to eat anywhere else," she complained in 1903. "Economy, comfort, and health are supposed to accompany our domestic food supply, and danger to follow the footsteps of those who eat in a hotel, a restaurant, or a boarding house. Is this long-accepted theory correct?" For Gilman, the answer was *no*. An advocate of "kitchenless houses" (and a former boardinghouse keeper herself), she believed that preparing food in individual kitchens was hopelessly wasteful, unscientific, and inefficient. Because housewives were not trained professionals but only amateurs guided "by the habits of a dark, untutored past," they invariably produced meals that were neither nutritious nor healthful.[49] Gilman's indictment of home cooking, like her vision of entrusting cooking and other housework to trained professionals, fell mostly on deaf ears. If anything, the reputation of home cooking only improved. Home cooking, in fact, may not have reached its apotheosis until the twentieth century, for its maturation as an ideal depended on the departure of servants (who often did much of the actual cooking) from middle-class households.[50] Gilman's perceptive insights aside, the belief that boardinghouse fare was distinctly unsavory continued unchecked at least into the 1930s. Just as the boardinghouse served as a useful counterpoint that helped nineteenth-century Americans construct the idea of home, boardinghouse "cuisine" helped create the concept of "home cooking."

CHAPTER FIVE

Nests of Crime and Dens of Vice

In many respects Mary Surratt was a typical boardinghouse keeper. Her husband, less than competent in business affairs, died in 1862, leaving behind a Maryland plantation, a house in Washington, D.C., and numerous debts. The Civil War wreaked further havoc. Maryland abolished slavery in 1864, but by that time most of Mrs. Surratt's slaves had already freed themselves. Surratt had little choice but to rent the plantation, move to Washington, and do what many women in similar situations would have done: open a boardinghouse. Like many landladies, she relied on circles of acquaintance; several of her lodgers were friends of her son, John. Others visited the house on H Street, and she received them graciously. She was especially gracious to a handsome actor. Perhaps he simply charmed her; perhaps she saw him as a potential suitor for her daughter, to whom he was quite attentive (though rumor had it he was engaged to someone else). Perhaps, as some accounts suggest, the forty-five-year-old landlady, variously described as "stout," "large, Amazonian . . . [and] square built," and "still a woman of fine presence and form," was infatuated with him herself. Perhaps Surratt, a former slaveholder and a Confederate sympathizer, actively supported his goals and abetted his plans.[1]

The handsome actor was none other than John Wilkes Booth. And on July 7, 1865, less than a year after launching her boardinghouse career, Mary Surratt found herself at the end of a noose. Convicted as a member of the conspiracy that plotted the assassination of Abraham Lincoln, she holds the dubious distinction of being the first woman executed by the federal government. Questions regarding the legality of the military tribunal that tried her persist, as do debates concerning the justice of the verdict and the fairness of her sentence, hopelessly caught in the tangled threads of Civil War memory.[2] Whether she was guilty or innocent—and most likely she was neither entirely guilty nor wholly innocent—Surratt died because she was a boardinghouse keeper, charged with knowingly "receiv[ing], entertain[ing], harbor[ing], and conceal[ing]" the conspirators, one of them her own son. Or, as the newly inaugurated president Andrew Johnson put it, "she kept the nest that hatched the egg."[3]

Beyond the specific evidence marshaled against her, Surratt's prosecution made sense according to the conventional wisdoms of nineteenth-century culture. By the time of her trial, boardinghouses had acquired reputations as places of crime and vice. Neither the lowest sorts of residences nor their genteel counterparts escaped these associations. Fashionable establishments, located in the best neighborhoods, as well as "dens," most commonly found in urban slums, sheltered gamblers, prostitutes, and confidence men. Indeed, in an era when nests connoted comfortable homes and dens (not yet the cozy retreats of suburban dads) dangerous lairs, tainted "nests" like Surratt's H Street house, which bore the outward signs of respectability, arguably posed the graver danger.

The Surratt case included, at least implicitly, many motifs of boardinghouse lore: nefarious strangers, dangerous intimacies—even murder. Surratt's fate, moreover, underscored a commonplace peril. Landladies might never learn the true identities, occupations, and intentions of those they boarded; there was always the possibility they would be held legally or morally accountable for their lodgers' behavior. Boardinghouse keepers' predicament exemplified the central dilemma with which nineteenth-century urbanites wrestled: how to distinguish truly respectable people from those who only appeared respectable.[4] If reports that conflated boardinghouses with crime and vice exposed unpleasant social realities—many of which flourished quite independently of particular residential configurations—they also revealed deep anxieties about the meaning of women's domestic labor. Sometimes in reality, more often symbolically, boardinghouses easily dissolved into brothels. Like brothels, they sold women's services, bringing housewifery into the marketplace.

Smooth Talkers and Well-Dressed Adventurers

Before the Surratt affair and long after, boardinghouses were sites of real and imaginary crime. But they attracted particular types of criminals. Most common was the "boardinghouse thief," carefully distinguished in crime reports from the "house thief" who burglarized private residences.[5] This difference was more than semantic; stealing from boardinghouses required special skills. House thieves and even hotel thieves depended on stealth and detailed knowledge of the internal workings of locks and bolts. Boardinghouse thieves, on the other hand, relied on social graces. Rather than sneak into homes or hotel rooms in the dead of night, they insinuated themselves—however briefly—into boardinghouse communities.

Boardinghouse thievery, like much else, was a hierarchical profession; not everyone possessed the clothing, bearing, or manners to gain admission to fashionable establishments. Some had to settle for slimmer pickings. Thomas Ward lodged for a night at an "emigrant" (Irish) boardinghouse in New York City's fourth ward, where he divested his roommate of a pocketbook containing "sixty-six sovereigns." The most celebrated practitioners, however, targeted the well-to-do. Confidence men and women par excellence, they skillfully disguised themselves as "Professors of German," traveling salesmen, and genteel socialites. Invariably "well-dressed" and "exceedingly polite," they easily gained the trust of ordinarily suspicious landladies, often paying their rent in advance (small change compared to the loot with which they absconded). One woman sought lodgings at a New York boardinghouse, promising to furnish references if the proprietress wished. "As she was handsomely dressed, wearing a long seal-skin sack over a rich silk dress, a fashionable bonnet, and jewelry that appeared to be expensive, it was considered safe to allow her to engage the rooms, with the understanding that they were to be paid for in advance." The handsomely dressed newcomer departed before she had even passed a night under the landlady's roof, taking the clothing and jewelry of another boarder with her. Boardinghouse thieves typically arrived empty-handed; the absence of a trunk (a receptacle of massive proportions that required the services of a cart man to move it) should have been a dead giveaway, for it signaled the ability to depart silently and quickly, without leaving any collateral behind. But they were so charming that landladies believed them when they said their luggage was at the railroad station and would be delivered the next day. The typical boardinghouse thief, as the *New York Tribune* described him, was a "well-dressed adventurer, whose baggage is always just one day behind him."[6]

Well-dressed adventurers—and adventuresses—sometimes victimized landladies, too, making off with their silver or china. Just as often, they preyed on fellow lodgers. While other boarders were at breakfast, dinner, or work, they "plundered the inmates," an easy enough thing to do since boarders' doors, unlike hotel room doors, seldom had locks. They purloined bank notes, stocks and bonds, diamonds, "roll[s] of handsome silk," "cashmere wrap[s]," "valuable gold chain[s] and earrings," and vanished quickly. "Before his victims have finished their morning or evening chat the thief's work is complete, and with well filled valise, unnoticed he slips out of the house," explained New York police detective Thomas Byrnes. "Probably before the robbery is discovered, the professional criminal is aboard of a train and on his way to some other city to dispose of his plunder and resume his profitable exploits."[7]

Boardinghouse thieves ranged from hardened professionals (one notable was still plying his trade at the age of sixty-five) whose photographs graced police department "rogue galleries" to the seventeen-year-old son of a Cleveland doctor who took lodgings under an assumed name at a fashionable New York boardinghouse and broke "open the trunks of all the boarders . . . taking over $400 worth of valuables."[8] Their demeanors and modus operandi changed little over time. The same story, with only minor variations, continually appeared in police blotters over the course of the nineteenth century. Boardinghouse thieves' ubiquity suggests that they posed real threats to the property of middle- and upper-class urbanities. They also functioned as stock characters in Victorian melodramas. Their exploits made for interesting reading and served as cautionary tales to those who abandoned countryside for city, home for boardinghouse. In a world of strangers—assembled in microcosm in boardinghouse parlors and at boardinghouse tables—who could be trusted? Landladies who boasted of their ability to ascertain the character of potential boarders offered only false assurances. Worst of all, these scenarios made clear, boarders and boardinghouse keepers alike judged newcomers on the basis of appearance—especially the quality of their apparel—not character, substituting the calculations of the marketplace for moral judgment.

Boardinghouse thieves unwittingly advertised the superiority of homes (at least those that featured strong locks), where kin, not strangers, gathered. Yet, they also thrived on the very qualities that numerous observers claimed boardinghouses lacked: sociability, intimacy, and trust. Accounts of cash, cashmere, and jewels left lying about—quickly disappearing into thieves' valises—gratified the curiosity of plebian readers by providing voyeuristic glimpses into the habits, possessions, and indiscriminate carelessness of wealthy boarders. Similarly, Police Inspector Byrnes disparaged women's "foolish fondness of making a display of their jewels and valuables in the parlor or dining-room of the fashionable boarding-house" in plain view of the "covetous eyes" of "astute robber[s]." Even more foolish, according to Byrnes, were the foolish women's companions, who readily divulged the authenticity and worth of their diamonds to the charming new arrival.[9] Unlocked doors, unconcealed valuables, and "foolish fondness" reveal carelessness or simple stupidity, but they also show that boarders tended to trust each other. (Recall Richard Barker's readiness to store his possessions in another lodger's room.) If boardinghouse residents did not see themselves as collectively constituting families, they did see themselves as part of exclusive communities to which only people of similar status and affinity could gain admission.

Other swindlers stayed longer, perpetrating more elaborate hoaxes. Some, like "Charles H.," who represented himself as "William Aspinwall, of the 'Howland and Aspinwall branch,'" simply wanted a place to live without the inconvenience of paying for it. This smooth talker engaged a desirable second-floor room in a Lexington Avenue boardinghouse, "constantly 'promising' the lady of the house money, but as constantly 'being disappointed in his remittances from his friends.'" After three weeks he disappeared, leaving behind his trunk filled with rags and bricks. Others sought additional spoils, as did the notorious Johnny McAlpine, a man of many aliases. "Captivating" his landlady, he managed to live rent free for several months in a "fashionable boarding-house in a genteel quarter in the city of New York."[10] Assuming the alias of "Doctor Thorne," another swindler made the rounds of New York boardinghouses "support[ing] at their expense not only himself, but his wife and children." He engaged "first-class rooms at first class prices," pledging his "valuable baggage" as security. Suddenly and unavoidably called out of town on business, he left his family behind, promising to settle his accounts on his return. "He accordingly departs, but not to St. Louis or Chicago—oh dear, no." Instead, he rented a cheap room in the same city. His wife and sons (aged ten and twelve) visited him daily, bringing him meals purloined from the boardinghouse table. Also concealed in each day's dinner basket were various items the trio had stolen from the boardinghouse and their "valuable baggage," which they slowly transported to the "doctor's" humble abode. Back at the boardinghouse, "Mrs. Thorne" continued to play the game, receiving "daily letters from her husband, but no money, though money is always expected by the next mail." The landlady's suspicions aroused, the remaining members of the family silently departed, leaving behind only empty trunks.

"Agnes S." pulled off another "genteel swindle," exploiting the sympathies of her lonely landlady, fast becoming her "inseparable companion and intimate." "Although she never paid her board, she was never requested to do so." Confessing that she was not the "maiden" she had represented herself to be, but a married woman whose husband "had been obliged to conceal himself from the gaze of the public owing to some 'unfortunate' business transactions," she persuaded her landlady to shelter her putative spouse as well. The pair "lived for several weeks in luxury at the widow's expense," a scandalous state of affairs that encouraged several of the "better" boarders to depart. When the boardinghouse keeper fell ill, Agnes and her "husband" took over the management of the establishment, collecting boarders' rent and keeping the money for themselves.[11]

Sometimes the tables turned; landladies, too, could play confidence games. Byrnes's *Professional Criminals of America* featured the story of "a lady, a little *passé*, but still pretty, who keeps a popular boarding-house, and who has in her time kept several boarding-houses, all of them 'popular' while they lasted, but none of them last very long." Using her "ingratiating nature," she persuaded "some favorite boarder—generally some rich old bachelor or widower" to pay an exorbitant sum—reportedly as much as one thousand dollars—in advance for room and board. "Then, suddenly, somehow or other, her affairs become 'entangled,' and she is unexpectedly obliged to 'give up' her house. The house is accordingly given up, and the landlady temporarily disappears till the former favorite lodger 'gives up' all hope of ever getting his advanced money back again." Like other boardinghouse swindlers, she did not remain idle for long. "Then she reappears in a new street, occasionally in a new name, and the routine of 'borrowing' from a lodger and then 'giving up' the house again is gone through with once more." "As a rule lodgers generally victimize their landladies," the report concluded, "but this instance shows that sometimes the rule is reversed and the biters are bit."[12]

Breathtaking in their boldness and creativity, schemes like these capitalized on the conflicting impulses that animated boardinghouse life—sociability and intimacy on one hand, transience and anonymity on the other. Like run-of-the-mill boardinghouse thieves, less transient swindlers relied on their "ingratiating" personalities and their ability to assume the appearance and demeanor of the respectable middle classes. (Many probably *did* hail from the respectable middle classes, resorting to confidence games when they fell on hard times or found bourgeois prescriptions for hard work and delayed gratification tedious to follow.) Such schemes flourished not only because their victims were gullible but because they mimicked common boardinghouse scenarios. Landladies and lodgers expected certain losses to come with the territory. Ordinary lodgers—people who would never have considered themselves thieves—fell behind on their rents; some might even steal away in the middle of the night, leaving empty trunks. (This is precisely what happened to Susan Forbes, who witnessed two of her boarders leaving the premises at two in the morning, birdcage in hand.)[13] Landladies who suffered financial "embarrassments," an all too-common occurrence, borrowed money from their boarders, loans that might—or might not—be repaid. Those who could not make ends meet gave up their houses, leaving boarders with little choice except to find new quarters, even if they had already paid the next week's or month's rent. Adventurers' genius rested on their ability to take commonplace circumstances to their logical extremes. The line between adventurers and respectable people caught in difficult circumstances was thin indeed.

"Lady Boarders" and "Female Boardinghouses"

Boardinghouse thieves often stole more than money. Many schemers—like "Colonel" McAlpine and the "passé but still pretty" boardinghouse keeper—relied on their sexual charms to achieve their ends. And if anything rendered boardinghouses suspect, it was the specter of illicit sexuality. In contrast to idealized middle-class homes, inhabited by self-controlled husbands and passionless wives, boardinghouses threw together "promiscuous" assortments of men and women, sheltering them in close and dangerous proximity. The possibilities for sexual shenanigans—even in the most scrupulously respectable households—were endless. Worse yet, not all boarding establishments were respectable. And in the end, it did not really matter. Many commentators believed that "respectable boardinghouse" was an oxymoron anyway.

The most extreme scenarios conflated boardinghouses with brothels, a supposition supported by language and fact. A "female boardinghouse" or a "first-class boarding-house for young ladies" meant a brothel in the parlance of nineteenth-century New York; savvy urbanites knew that the term *lady boarder* denoted a prostitute and that a notice for "rooms to let, with board for the lady only" advertised a house of assignation.[14]

Boardinghouses could indeed become houses of prostitution, and in a number of ways. For one thing, brothels *were* boardinghouses. They provided their inmates with room and board, albeit at exorbitant rates, usually extracted by madams from prostitutes' earnings. Other bordellos, especially high-class ones, disguised themselves as fashionable boardinghouses. Deceptions of this sort offered a modicum of protection to their inmates and a veneer of gentility to their patrons. "The lady boarders in these houses never walk the streets nor solicit company," the reformer Matthew Hale Smith explained in *Sunshine and Shadow in New York*. What went on inside bore no little resemblance to parlor life in a genteel boardinghouse. "The visitor is received by the madam in whose name the mansion is kept. One by one the lady boarders drop in. Conversation becomes general and spirited. Some remarks are rather broad. There is little to dispel the illusion that one is on a call at a first-class boarding-school or seminary." Only "as the evening wanes, and wine flows," did "the talk" (and presumably the action) "become bolder."[15]

Little wonder that advice writers counseled newcomers, especially young women, to search for lodgings with care. Unable to decipher the terminology of newspaper advertisements, country bumpkins in search of boardinghouses might find themselves in brothels or houses of assignation, consigned to lives of "infamy." "Families from the country frequently stumble across these places by accident," the author of *Secrets of the Great City* warned. "If the female members are young and handsome, they are received, and the mistake is not found out, perhaps, until it is too late."[16] Other establishments became de facto brothels when naïve landladies unwittingly rented rooms to prostitutes. Arrested in a police raid, Mary Bennett, the keeper of an actresses' boardinghouse—already a suspect residential category—insisted "that she did not know of anything wrong going on in her house." Alternatively, a boardinghouse keeper who fared poorly in a highly competitive marketplace knowingly rented to women of ill repute as a last resort. Still others—"women who have tried to keep respectable boarding-houses"—abandoned boardinghouse keeping for the more lucrative pursuit of brothel keeping.[17]

The plots and characters that animated lurid novels and urban exposés included associations between boarding and brothels that stretched well beyond the literal. Avaricious boardinghouse keepers, madams in all but name, wittingly or unwittingly encouraged young women to take up lives of shame. Denied her rightful earnings by one "beast of prey," a poor sewing woman confronts another. She "dares not to return to her miserable boarding-place in Delancey street, for her Irish landlady is clamorous for the two weeks' board now due . . . Despair settles down upon her. Hunger is its companion, for she has had no supper. Where shall she go?"[18] The ending to this melodrama was all too obvious. Often lampooned for their excessive nosiness, landladies could just as easily be condemned for failing to exercise adequate moral supervision. "Her parents knew not of her whereabouts, nor did the widow with whom she boarded know that she was leading a life of infamy." "Miss Marston left my house three days ago with a young gentleman who has been waiting on her," a fictional Boston boardinghouse keeper wrote a distraught father. "Have heard nothing from her since and don't know the name of her fellow."[19]

"Boarding-House Episodes"

Accusations of impropriety dogged even the most respectable boarding establishments; concerns about prostitution melded easily into concerns about other, less obviously commercialized, forms of sexual misbehavior. The mere fact that boardinghouses potentially released their inhabitants from the restraints of home and family rendered them suspect. As the example of the wayward Boston boarder suggests, suspicions especially centered on women lodgers. Whether they appeared as innocent victims or worldly practitioners of urban vice depended in large part on their age and marital status. "No one ever saw an adventuress under the age of thirty-five," explained pulp writer George Ellington. "No woman could possibly play any very desperate or dangerous game which required forethought, discrimination and shrewdness who was under that age."[20] In contrast, moral ruin was an ever-present possibility for "single young ladies" who exchanged rural homes for urban boardinghouses, as their new abodes brought "them into contact with men of unknown, and perhaps not irreproachable characters."[21]

Divorcees and "California widows" reportedly accounted for many female boardinghouse inhabitants—identities that automatically cast doubt on the character of both boarder and residence. "It may be safely affirmed that there are not ten boarding houses in the city, which do not contain improper characters," wrote Edward Winslow Martin in *The Secrets of the Great City*. "Observers have been struck with the number of handsome young widows who frequent these places. Sometimes these women claim to be the wives of men absent in the distant Territories, or in Europe, and pretend to receive letters and remittances from them. In nine cases out of ten such women make their living in a manner they do not care to have known." These concerns—however exaggerated—had real consequences, for they affected the housing choices of all women, respectable or disreputable. Throughout the nineteenth century, boardinghouse keepers in search of lodgers advertised for single men or married couples, almost never single women; they accepted female boarders only as a last resort—in part because women's wages were low (thus rendering them less than reliable payers of rent), in part because any woman adrift— that is, away from home—was potentially a woman on the town.[22]

Or, she was simply trouble. This was true of one Miss Van Derven, who in the summer of 1884 engaged rooms in a Long Island boardinghouse run by a German couple named Gustave and Clara Wolf. "A very attractive young woman," she "became a great favorite, especially with the gentlemen boarders." Van Derven's sojourn came to an abrupt end when she was seen riding in a carriage with one of these gentlemen, his wife and children conspicuously absent. United in "unreasoning jealously," Mrs. Wolf and the other female boarders decided she had to go. The landlady's "fat husband" reluctantly acquiesced. Meeting resistance (Van Derven had, after all, paid her rent for the week), he allegedly attempted to evict her by force, encouraged by his wife, who, "with profane and indecent language ordered her husband to throw the fractious boarder down the stairs." "Pitched out" along with her trunks, Van Derven returned to Manhattan, retained a lawyer, and sued the Wolfs for assault and defamation of character. Mr. Wolf denied "having struck Miss Van Derven," instead "lay[ing] all the trouble on his wife."

An account of the affair published in the *Times* drew on familiar themes (even disparaging the probable quality of Mrs. Wolf's food). Scratching the veneer of respectability, it revealed foul-mouthed, "fat Germans"; "unreasoning jealousy"; and marital discord. It also exemplified an increasingly popular journalistic genre. Articles with titles like "A Boardinghouse Episode," "Revelations Succeeding a Boarding House Scandal," and "A Row in a Fashionable Boarding House" appeared frequently in the 1880s and 1890s, their authors delighting in exposing the true character of boardinghouses of "some pretensions" inhabited "by people of more or less fashionable proclivities." While their casts of characters varied, they collectively suggested that middle-class establishments—far from being the respectable habitations they claimed to be—harbored disreputable people and questionable social practices. The Van Derven case in particular suggested that young single women could be perpetrators as well as victims of vice—or at least not entirely blameless for the domestic havoc they wreaked.[23]

Similarly, young men appeared in fictional and journalistic accounts as rogues who exploited boardinghouses' moral laxity and as victims of their tainted environments. In T. S. Arthur's "Taking Boarders" (1851), a widow's decision to take up boardinghouse keeping begets near ruin for her twenty-year-old son Henry. Introduced to various vices by two boarding clerks, Mason and Barling, the once-promising law student takes to drinking, gambling, and staying out late at night. Writing a few years earlier for the *Brooklyn Eagle*, Walt Whitman articulated what Arthur could only imply in the pages of the genteel *Godey's Lady's Book*. Whitman deemed boardinghouses a species of "wicked architecture," a term he employed to describe all habitations that were not single-family, owner-occupied dwellings. Prevented by steep New York real estate prices from acquiring homes—a prerequisite, Whitman believed, for marriage—young men indulged in "either the constant practice of visiting houses of ill-fame or are living in a quasi household with a kept mistress." Whitman's conception of the relationship between marital status and residential arrangements offered at best a simplistic explanation for the existence of vice. Nevertheless, he had reason for concern, for "wicked architecture" did indeed facilitate premarital liaisons—although not in quite the way he predicted. The revelations surrounding the famous murder of Helen Jewett, a high-class prostitute, suggest that, by the 1830s, the increasing popularity of boardinghouse life attracted real-life Masons and Barlings, who self-consciously rejected the middle-class virtues of piety, sobriety, and sexual self-control. Freed from parental oversight and subject to employers' supervision only during working hours, young clerks who resided in boardinghouses enthusiastically embraced the very pastimes Whitman feared, frequently "visiting houses of ill-fame."[24]

Other boarders pursued less sensational vices. "The bible says the wages of sin are death—I have seen it illustrated. I hope to profit by my observation," Henry Pierce, a twenty-one-year-old clerk in a Boston hat store, solemnly recorded in his diary (which he marked "Not intended for perusal") in the early 1840s. Nevertheless, he went on to report that "I have contracted partially the 'awful,' 'disgusting,' 'lowlived,' loaferish, etc., etc. habit of smoking—this though the 'most decent' of loafers' graces meets with some disapprobation from several who are much interested in my welfare but in consideration of my total depravity will not of course expect much better things. Though not a teetotaler I have not drunk more than would be requisite for them as medicine."[25] Pierce expressed confidence in his ability to set his own moral limits, devising a personal code more restrictive than the one followed by brothel-goers but considerably more lax than people "much interested in his welfare" would have liked. Boarding granted him a degree of independence and access to pleasures he never could have enjoyed at home. Far from pining for unattainable homes, some lodgers preferred the relative freedoms of boarding life.

Boardinghouses' reputations were more than figments of reformers' imaginations. Because they housed lodgers in close proximity, they provided opportunities for respectable courtship as well as dangerous intimacies. Indeed, the distinction between the two was often in the eyes of the beholder. Timothy O'Donovan was annoyed if not quite scandalized at the behavior of his landlady and landlord's granddaughter, who allowed the "small headed hang dog looking" Dr. Hoagland to "fondle" her; his housemates, or so he implied, seemed unconcerned. Whether he realized it or not, O'Donovan invoked—with minor variations—a common cultural theme, what Thomas Butler Gunn called "The Boardinghouse Where There are Marriageable Daughters." "Single lodgers preponderate in . . . [this] Establishment, of which . . . daughters constitute the main feature and attraction." Each of the three daughters at

Gunn's hypothetical boardinghouse—aged thirty, twenty-five, and sixteen—played her part "with that vigor of which only a woman in quest of a husband is capable." In this humorous telling the quest predictably failed; boarders *"do not stop long."* "Perhaps the young ladies rather *over-do* the Art of Fascination," Gunn mused; "perhaps the prospect of such a mother-in-law terrifies the gentlemen." His tongue-in-cheek account nevertheless hinted at complex calculations that stood at the tangled intersections of love and money, calculations that O'Donovan's landlords, the Tafts, may have banked on. On one hand, marriageable daughters—or granddaughters—attracted boarders; on the other, marriage to an upwardly mobile young bachelor, whatever its romantic satisfactions, promised escape from boarding's grim routines and uncertain rewards. From a landlady's vantage point, daughters were desirable because they typically assumed much of the labor of boarding. One daughter too many, however, was one too many mouths to feed and bodies to clothe. Besides, a successful son-in-law might relieve his mother-in-law as well as his wife from the drudgery of keeping house.[26]

This, of course, was just the sort of bargain that moralists feared. If boardinghouse life promised ready introductions to eligible bachelors, it also posed it own set of dangers, as Arthur's morality tale made all too clear. Not satisfied with exposing the threats disreputable boarders posed to previously upright young men, he introduces a charming but mysterious gentleman lodger, Mr. Burton, who romances the landlady's youngest daughter Miriam, a "quiet, gentle, retiring, almost timid girl." Corrupted by the degraded environment of the boardinghouse, Arthur's shrinking heroine confuses love with money, conflating a marriage contract with a business contract. She agrees to a dangerous transaction, eloping with Burton in exchange for his promise to support her beleaguered mother—to the tune of two thousand dollars per year. He turns out to a gambler and a bigamist; luckily, a wise uncle rescues her before the wedding takes place.[27]

Unlike woman's rights advocates, Arthur failed to criticize the "marriage market" that resulted from women's limited employment prospects. Instead, he endorsed another overcrowded and increasingly female-dominated profession—teaching—(his characters, to be sure, open a private school that caters only to the best people) as a more genteel and lucrative pursuit than boardinghouse keeping. In doing so, Arthur unwittingly revealed the difficulty of delineating the boundaries of home and marketplace, public and private. Mrs. Darlington initially pursues boardinghouse keeping as a means of avoiding the "dreadful exposure" that teaching or shop keeping would surely demand. "In taking boarders we only increase our family, and all goes on as usual," she reasons. Chastened by sad experience, she belatedly agrees with her brother Mr. Ellis (who speaks for Arthur) that overseeing a private school entails "less exposure" than boardinghouse keeping. School teaching, Ellis explains, is morally superior to taking boarders; "In the one case, you feed only the body, but now you are dispensing food to the immortal mind." More important, teaching, unlike boardinghouse keeping, allows the Darlingtons to "come together as one family, and shut out the intruding world . . . when the day's work is done." In effect, they exchanged one form of privacy—concealing gainful employment within the home—for another—maintaining the integrity of their family circle, uncorrupted by strangers.[28]

For Arthur, the sentimental moralist, landladies' daughters, placed in harm's way, were prey; for Gunn, the urbane humorist, they were predators, players of "coarse games" and makers of "bold advances," who had only themselves to blame. Both scenarios revealed their vulnerability. Their ambiguous status (somewhere between respectable young ladies and servants), their presumed—and sometimes actual—desperation, and, at times, their relative youth made them easy targets for sexual advances, welcome and unwelcome. Novelist Frank Harris numbered several women among his conquests during his brief tenure as a university student in Lawrence, Kansas, in the 1870s—including his landlady's sixteen-year-old daughter Kate. Kate, as Harris told it, seems to have been a willing accomplice and suffered no permanent damage. Less happy results are easy enough to imagine. Gunn's bold daughters, who boldly kissed favored boarders "in the passage" were merely abandoned, in part because their slightly questionable reputations preceded them, the favored boarder discovering that "others have enjoyed, are enjoying, or may enjoy, the same privileges." But landladies' daughters and granddaughters also might be seduced and abandoned. Or, like Mary Rogers, pregnant by a boarder and victim of a botched abortion, they might end up dead.[29]

Boardinghouse servants were most vulnerable of all. Just like those who toiled in "homes," they were fair game for men looking for a bit of fun. Boardinghouse chambermaids, the sporting paper *The Whip* proclaimed, "are used to licentious conversation and shamelessness is a second nature to them."[30]

For moralists like Arthur and even humorists like Gunn, the solution to these problems—given the century-long silence regarding homeowners' "seductions" of female servants—was to embrace home life instead of boarding life. For real-life boardinghouse keepers, the answer was a bit more complicated. Maintaining respectability was the key to protecting the virtue of all who resided under their roofs, ensuring that their establishments and inhabitants avoided the slippery slope that led to the brothel. Assessing the character of potential boarders, carefully monitoring their behavior once they arrived, evicting those who failed the test—all were essential to success. What lodgers often interpreted as landladies' excessive nosiness or selectiveness was a crucial part of keeping house. A witness testified that George Atzerodt, who failed to muster the nerve to carry out his planned assassination of Vice President Johnson, stayed only one night at the infamous H Street boardinghouse because "Miss Anna and Mrs. Surratt . . . did not care about having him brought to the house." Or, as twenty-two-year-old Anna reportedly put it, "she didn't care about having such sticks brought to the house; they were not company for her."[31]

Only meticulous moral policing made it possible for boardinghouses to exclude "sticks" and shelter respectable courtships, like that of Susan Brown and Alexander Forbes or the fictional Jo March and Professor Bhaer of *Little Women*. The educational reformer Horace Mann was a grieving widower when he arrived in the early 1830s at the genteel Boston boardinghouse kept by Rebecca Freeman, the widowed mother of James Freeman Clarke, a residence Gunn might have dubbed "the boardinghouse frequented by Transcendentalists." There he met two of the famous Peabody sisters, Elizabeth and Mary. Both sisters set their sights on Mann; he would soon tell Elizabeth that they could never be more than friends. He eventually married Mary but only a decade after he had abandoned Mrs. Clarke's boardinghouse in a fit of renewed grief. Despite its complications and comic possibilities ("whoever marries a Peabody must look after the *housekeeping*," one observer remarked), Boston society perceived this relationship, like Clarke's boardinghouse, as eccentric but in no way disreputable. On the other hand, tongues wagged when sociologist Lester Ward and his "friend" Mrs. Emily Palmer Cape occupied adjacent rooms in a Madison, Wisconsin, boardinghouse. (Both were married to other people.) Respectability was an unstable compound, perennially open to interpretation, liable to explode at any moment. As the case of Miss Van Derven suggests, "boardinghouse episodes" revealed the disreputable natures of "boarding house[s] of some pretensions." The trick was to keep up the pretensions.[32]

"Vergin'" Landladies and Pet Boarders

Commentators focused a good deal of their attention on "sticks," "lady boarders," and landladies' daughters, but relationships between landladies and male boarders loomed largest in boardinghouse lore. Newspapers enjoyed reporting the marital discord boarders caused, especially in working-class and immigrant families. Liaisons involving ostensibly middle-class—and usually middle-aged—widows and spinsters took up equal space. Active predators, they merited none of the sympathy their daughters might have garnered. *Harper's Weekly* defined boarding as the "ceaseless and subtle persecution of men by women," a kind of revenge for the denial of suffrage and property rights. "When a woman has lost health, and youth, and honesty; when her heart has been ossified and her blood dried up, she has then reached the proper condition for being a boarding-house keeper."[33] The "tyranny" to which *Harper's* referred took a particular form. Such women painstakingly cheated their lodgers out of their hard-earned money—after all, their hearts had turned to stone. They also treated them as sexual prey. They lavished special attentions on "pet boarders," lodgers who received special culinary, sanitary, and financial privileges at the expense of their fellows. Sometimes pet boarders received maternal affection; more often—at least in boardinghouse folklore—they were objects of landladies' "matrimonial ambitions."[34] It was this confusion of maternal with sexual affection—typical scenarios featured landladies who pursued lodgers several years their junior—that commentators found most disturbing.

The middle-aged widow or spinster desperate for a husband was a favorite stock character. Miss Slimmens, a resident of the fictional town of Pennyville (a none-too-subtle reference that makes clear her relationship to the market), turns to boardinghouse keeping when her millinery shop fails. Aping familiar conventions, she places a "card" advertising for boarders in the *Pennyville Eagle:* "Single gentlemen preferred." "Matrimonial ambition" rather than suspicion of unattached female lodgers explains her preferences; perceptive readers might have noticed that "by a lady without family, who has more room than she requires" aped the language of advertisements for houses of assignation. "Our chances for receiving the attentions of the opposite sex are so much better," she confided to her servant Dora.

Miss Slimmens makes a fool of herself recklessly pursuing her young lodgers. "Surely you must have noticed that I am accosted by the prognostic of *Miss* Slimmens," she announces at the dinner table. "My affections are virgin as the unkissed bloom upon the grape." One boarder offers a speedy retort: "*Vergin'* upon fifty." Miss Slimmens can never succeed, not only because her age disqualifies her but also because she foolishly combines love and money, home and marketplace. "My object in establishing this boarding-house has not been simply to make money—to feed, like a coroner, on the hearts of my victims, charging them a high price, and giving them cheap provisions in return, while I withhold that sympathy and intimacy which is more precious than bread and meat. My *principal* object has been to establish a *home*—a place where young men, away from their mothers, may find, for a moderate reimbursement, the comforts of which they were accustomed before they left the shelter of their childhood's roof." This is a fraudulent claim; Slimmens does indeed "feed like a coroner." She cuts corners at every opportunity, gleefully calculates her weekly profits, and never forgets "worldly prudence." Once again, her boarders see through her. One anonymously pens a satirical love poem. (Miss Slimmens, of course, fails to recognize the satire.)

> Sweet maiden Alvira, how calm could I rest
> In thy bo-door of sweets, with the one I love best;
> Where the storms which we feel in this cold world should cease,
> And where love and economy mingle in peace.[35]

Love and economy, as Miss Slimmens's subsequent adventures make clear—at least to everyone except the hapless spinster—can never mingle. Thwarted in her misguided attempts to secure her boarders' affection, Slimmens decides to buy a husband: "If I can't make love, I can make money, and I will. Maybe money will buy what female charms won't." She succeeds, all too fleetingly, in attracting the attentions of a new boarder, "Professor" Lankton. Ever calculating, she refuses to lend him money until after the wedding—though she does agree to pay the minister's fee. Like the nefarious Mr. Burton of Arthur's "Taking Boarders," Lankton is a bigamist. His wife shows up shortly after the ceremony, and the crestfallen but still "vergin'" Slimmens learns that the "Professor" "makes his living out of his successes with women."[36] In contrast to Arthur's eighteen-year-old Miriam, the spinster "vergin' on fifty" remained a figure of fun.

Matilda McClusky, one of the many women that the boardinghouse thief Johnny McAlpine managed to dupe, bore no little resemblance to fictional Miss Slimmens. Her story, as presented by former policeman Philip Farley, echoed many of the same themes. Farley's *Criminals of America* offered an entertaining mix of real criminals, true crimes, and invented dialogue. Farley took his cues from boardinghouse folklore, turning McClusky, the real-life victim of a real crime, into the butt of a joke. Like Slimmens, the widowed McClusky reportedly housed only single young men. Like Slimmens her motives were a confusing mixture of love and money. Single men expected to share their rooms; by limiting her clientele thus, she could "cram" a greater number of boarders into her "fashionable" New York house, increasing her profits. Some slept six to a room, an arrangement made possible by her "most original and fantastic designs" for bedroom furnishing. As for the fictional Miss Slimmens, single men also aided "matrimonial ambitions." McClusky set her sights on McAlpine, who quickly became her pet boarder, hinting that he "would some day be raised to the dignity of the back parlor—Mrs. McClusky's boudoir of bliss—and the mastership of the mansion." McClusky, like her fictional counterpart, was doomed to disappointment: "the 'Colonel' was making love to the widow and half-a-dozen other women besides, outside the house, and running up a bill."[37]

Accounts like these rarely noted that women turned to boardinghouse keeping because they needed the money. Rather, they silently reproached them for not having husbands to support them—that is, the right sorts of husbands. For sometimes boardinghouse thieves and pet boarders—the distinction between the two was often a difficult one to make—came to stay. Gunn's depiction of a "cheap boarding-house" described "the mistress of the establishment" as "a bulky English-woman of (certainly) five and fifty, in possession of a third husband," the latter evidently a former lodger who had settled his back rent by marrying his landlady.[38] Again, the story featured an unattractive woman, middle-aged and "bulky." This scenario was common enough that men, like the third husband, who let their wives house and support them, had a name. Nineteenth-century Americans called them "boardinghouse betties."[39]

Beneath humorous and sensational accounts we can discern people shrewdly negotiating the interstices between love and money. We can also see people trying to work out the terms and meanings of their relationships. Read according to a cultural script that sharply distinguished home from market, even the mundane details of boardinghouse keeping took on questionable meanings. Sexuality pervaded even the most scrupulously proper establishments, for boarding placed landladies and male tenants on terms of physical intimacy. Acting in many respects as surrogate (and paid) wives, boardinghouse keepers emptied men's chamber pots, changed their bed linens, and washed their clothes. Boarders' proximity to housekeepers, coupled with the nature of the labor that the latter performed, helps to explain why observers of city life identified boardinghouses with brothels. Indeed, *brothel* served as a metaphor, invoked to describe arrangements by which a wide array of women's services—including but by no means limited to sex—entered the world of cash exchange. If commercialized sex quite literally placed women on the market, boardinghouses seemed to do so in more subtle ways.[40]

Landladies were never passive bystanders in this cultural war. Some, especially those who represented themselves as genteel, were well aware of the moral concerns that their calling aroused and acted accordingly. They disguised the pecuniary nature of their businesses by refusing to advertise, personally collect rent, or explicitly discuss terms. One boardinghouse keeper Gunn described "professed a more than *Mrs. General-like* contempt for money, making her sister collect the bills"; another placed envelopes outside her lodgers' doors to ensure that money never literally changed hands. Distressed gentlewomen who owned houses on Boston's fashionable Beacon Street verbally camouflaged paying boarders as "visiting friends."[41]

Nevertheless, the home set the terms of the conversation, providing a standard by which all other social arrangements could be measured. If the middle-class home furnished a setting for the proper expression of a carefully regulated sexuality, the malignant environment of the boardinghouse fostered dangerous intimacies and unrestrained passion. Sometimes, too, horror overrode humor, even when the usual characters were involved. Declaring that "home and its virtues" represented the nation's "security against anarchical disorder," an 1857 *Harper's Weekly* editorial blamed a particularly sensational murder and, indeed, "all of the great crimes" on the poisoned atmospheres of the boardinghouses in which they took place.[42]

The Burdell case confirmed boardinghouse critics' worst fears, supplying proof that illicit sex and violent crime resided in the best of neighborhoods. "A wealthy, but eccentric dentist," Harvey Burdell lived in "quiet, aristocratic Bond Street." Something of a miser, he apparently rented the greater part of his house to Emma Cunningham, a "buxom widow" who kept two boarders "who were on very intimate terms with . . . [her] family." Other accounts describe Burdell as the proprietor of the boardinghouse and Cunningham as its housekeeper. Whether Burdell acted as employer or landlord—or both—it is clear that Cunningham managed the daily business of the household. If women's work ideally included the maintenance of sexual propriety in addition to more prosaic household chores, Cunningham failed miserably. She "divided her affections" between Dr. Burdell and another boarder—a state of affairs that led to "frequent uproars in the house." Soon after threatening his paramour with eviction, Burdell was brutally murdered. The postmortem examination revealed that he had been "strangled by a ligature applied round the throat, and that no less than fifteen deep wounds, almost any of which would cause death, had been inflicted with some sharp instrument on his person."[43] Suspicion quickly centered on Cunningham, who had uttered incriminating threats; she was tried for the crime but speedily acquitted. Freed from prison, she produced a marriage certificate of dubious validity, presented herself as Burdell's widow and successfully claimed her dower rights. A subsequent attempt to gain outright possession of Burdell's estate, which involved "borrowing" a baby from a lying-in ward and attempting to pass him off as Burdell's rightful heir, failed.[44] The case quickly entered the popular vocabulary; a boarder housed by a particularly intimidating landlady feared she would "Burdell" him if he fell behind on his rent.[45]

To the author of the *Harper's* editorial, the Burdell case offered a scathing indictment of boardinghouses and a staunch defense of the home. Homes, in this instance, needed defending; he presented them as an endangered species, threatened by the nefarious—but popular—practice of boarding out. "Keeping a boarding house is an office that will give to one of a kind and benevolent nature a good opportunity of exercising her native qualities," labor reformer Virginia Penny's *Employments of Women* explained. "Sympathy closely binds such to the unfortunate, and pleasures are doubled by participating with others."[46] In practice, the limits of "sympathy," "benevolence," and "participating with others" must have been difficult to determine. The precise terms of boarder/housekeeper relationships—and the extent of their sexual meaning—were always negotiable, with ample room for misunderstanding on both sides. Gunn's satirical *Physiology* provided comic but uncommonly perceptive discussions of this very issue. Recognizing the psychological and sexual tensions that boardinghouse keeping involved, he devoted entire chapters to "The Boardinghouse Where You're Expected to Make Love to the Landlady" and "The Boardinghouse Whose Landlady Likes to be Ill-Used."[47] Gunn's analysis raised questions that confronted landlady and lodger alike. Which behaviors expressed an innocent desire to "participate with others" and which smacked of sexual impropriety? Where did sympathy end and economic interest begin? When did the concerns of "home" enter the marketplace, and, conversely, when did the market enter the home? If self-appointed cultural spokespeople claimed to tell the difference between the home and the marketplace, the boardinghouse and the home, it was often far more difficult to make these distinctions in practice.

The contrasts between *Harper's* solemn coverage of the Burdell case and the more humorous accounts that appeared in publications like *Criminals of*

America were partly matters of chronology. As the nineteenth century drew to a close, fictional and journalistic accounts (often barely distinguishable) poked fun at "respectable" boardinghouses, invoking a jocular style previously reserved for truly disreputable establishments. Authentic moral danger seemed less likely and fear less pronounced. Returning to his Manhattan boarding-house late one night in 1888, Richard Barker stumbled upon his landlady's daughter standing in the hall in her nightgown. No lurid encounter this; "Miss Laura" reacted with horror, Barker with amusement. "She jumped up & down like a rabbit & screamed like a bird. Altogether 'twere a beautiful sight to behold," Barker wrote his wife. "If she hadn't made so much noise maybe I shouldn't have seen her at all." Just a few days later, Barker made the mistake of coming down to breakfast too early. "Again surprised Miss Laura who was standing at back parlor door in light embellishments."[48] To be sure, Barker was a respectable married man, unlikely to misbehave, and Mrs. and Miss Brown, respectable boardinghouse keepers, were not likely to tolerate misbehavior. Placed beside Barker's matter-of-fact account, the admonitions of earlier moralists and the continued dire warnings of organizations like the Young Women's Christian Association, sound increasingly shrill. As middle-class Americans adjusted to urban life, as they abandoned piety for sophistication, descriptions of boardinghouse life lost some of their alarmist tone. Or, to put it another way, commentators became more adept at distinguishing between different degrees and kinds of danger.

Yet humor had never been far from the surface. And humor should not be discounted; jokes are serious business, means of dealing with very real anxi-eties. The crowds that gathered during Mrs. Cunningham's courtroom appear-ances chanted, "Where is my darling baby?" mocking the words Cunning-ham was supposed to have uttered. Even P. T. Barnum got in on the act, displaying the "sham-baby" and his real mother as an exhibit at his famous museum. The Burdell case, *Leslie's Illustrated Newspaper* could only conclude, was an "extraordinary comic-tragedy."[49]

Mary Surratt's case was merely tragic. As she learned to her dismay, pet boarders could be betrayers. She "nurtured" Louis Weichmann, a War Department clerk, "as a son." Her maternal solicitude did not stop him from testifying against her. Weichmann was the prosecution's star witness.[50]

CHAPTER SIX

"Will They Board, or Keep House?"

"Will they board, or keep house?" For Eunice Beecher, wife of the famous—soon to be infamous—preacher Henry Ward Beecher, this was the momentous choice newly married couples faced. Beecher's domestic advice books, compilations of the columns she published in the *Christian Union*, counseled newlyweds to avoid boardinghouses at all costs. Hers was only one voice in a larger chorus that lamented the evils boarding visited on marriage. Advice writers, novelists, short story authors, newspaper reporters, magazine commentators, legal theorists, and home economists almost always weighed in on the side of keeping house. Boarding, they reasoned, was uneconomical, undesirable, and a threat to marriage itself. Or, as Judge John A. Jameson wrote in an article on "Divorce" published in the *North American Review* in 1883, "Boarding-house life is especially fatal to permanence of the marital relation."[1]

Why did boarding threaten marriage? The answers varied. Some observers invoked privacy, others economy. Some worried about wayward husbands, others about delayed childbearing and spoiled children. Perhaps they worried most about the effects of boarding on married women's labor—though they danced around the question of whether housekeeping was indeed work. Defending housekeeping, which numerous analysts deemed fundamental "to the marriage relation," had unintended consequences. In opposing boarding, commentators of various stripes offered increasingly flexible definitions of *home*, helping to pave the way for grudging acceptance of "French flats" and apartments. Demonstrating the superiority of housekeeping over boarding, moreover, meant plunging into mundane details that often revolved around real costs: rents, household budgets, food and fuel prices, and servants' wages. Advocates of housekeeping won one cultural battle, for their efforts surely hastened boardinghouses' slow demise. At the same time, they lost another, for they revealed the home's intricate relationship to the marketplace.

"High Rents and Pretentious Habits"

"One of the peculiarities in the lives of Americans consists in the practice of boarding," German traveler Francis Grund wrote in 1837. "Single and married men, and whole families, prefer this mode of life, to taking lodgings by themselves, or going to the expense of housekeeping." Like many foreign visitors, Grund considered boarding a peculiarly American practice and the boardinghouse a peculiarly American institution. He was one of few observers, foreign or domestic, who condemned neither. "Whatever inconvenience may be attached to this habit, it is, nevertheless, commendable on the score of economy . . . Many young men, who cannot afford renting a house, (which in America is very expensive,) are in this manner enabled to marry a little sooner than their means would otherwise allow them."[2]

As Grund's matter-of-fact statement suggests, home life in nineteenth-century America did not necessarily imply home ownership. The vast majority of urban dwellers, whether they boarded or kept house, lived in rented quarters; renting was common practice even in towns and villages. Even a rented house was beyond the reach of many middle-class Americans. To be sure, couples had almost as many reasons for choosing the American institution as detractors had for condemning it. Some preferred hotel and boardinghouse sociability to domestic isolation.[3] Others wished to escape the burdens of housekeeping. Still others preferred transience to permanence, freedom to attachment. But urban couples most commonly chose boarding because they could not afford "homes." Given this fact, social commentators might have railed against low wages and salaries, the high cost of housing, or, more generally, the high cost of living.[4] They might have heaped scorn on boarding husbands, chiding them for inadequate breadwinning or insufficient ambition. In general, they did neither. Men did not always emerge blameless from the pages of popular commentary, but it was their willingness to indulge their spoiled spouses rather than their economic failures that usually engaged critics' attention. Women shouldered the heaviest symbolic burdens, shoring up their husbands' masculinity and deflecting attention from exploitative real estate markets. Married couples boarded, so numerous stories went, because wives were selfish, lazy, extravagant, and poorly trained in the art of domestic management.[5]

"If the tastes of our people were better regulated, and mere show was not preferred to substance, there would be less resort to the hotel or boardinghouse on the plea of moneysaving," *Harper's Weekly* complained in 1857. "The tastes of our people" usually translated into the misguided inclinations of extravagant wives, though *Harper's* satirical account of the Nincompoop family chastened parents and husbands for failing to regulate feminine behavior. "Young Nincompoop marries a wife out of a family which, with its expansive ideas of style, is living to the full stretch of its means. Mrs. N. has been brought up in luxury, of course; her tender feet have never pressed any thing less soft than velvet, and her delicate hands have never been roughed with a kitchen implement." Mr. Nincompoop is eager to protect his wife from kitchen implements, "fashionable sneers," and "household duty," but his income "will not suffice to secure a fashionable establishment of his own, so he provides the next best, and not very dissimilar, thing—a fashionable boarding-house." The Nincompoops could easily afford a home of their own, the *Harper's* editorialist insisted, if only Mrs. Nincompoop would forego "gentilities" in favor of modesty and simplicity. To be sure, she was not the only villain in this republican morality tale. Her weak-willed husband refused to stand up to his wife and in-laws; her parents erred by bringing "her up in luxury." But ultimately the Mrs. Nincompoops of the world bore the responsibility for choosing home life over boarding life.[6]

Thirty years later the terms of the debate remained much the same, although its participants had expanded to include some of the more prominent voices in the emerging field of home economics. In February 1889 the *North American Review* published a forum titled "Is Housekeeping a Failure?" "No; emphatically, no," answered cooking instructor Maria Parloa. The *Review* might just as well have called the piece "Is Boarding a Success?" The answer would have been the same. The five participants—Parloa, Marion Harland, Rose Terry Cooke, Catherine Owen, and Shirley Dare—were renowned for their expertise in domestic economy. Like Eunice Beecher, they claimed that families had two choices: board or keep house. Like Beecher, they unequivocally endorsed keeping house. Doing so meant mounting a successful challenge to arguments that favored boarding. Chief among these was economy.[7]

Best known to modern readers for her New England regionalist fiction, Cooke launched a spirited attack on "the most urgent argument" in favor of boarding: that it "is cheaper than keeping house." She recognized that economy was an elastic concept. While she praised the importance of "investigation and experience"—formalities she accused her imagined opponents of ignoring—she staked her claims on a less tangible calculus that accorded equal measure to moral, physical, and monetary costs. She acknowledged that "boarding, as far as mere board and lodging go, is cheaper than a house of one's own." But, Cooke argued, reckoning true economy meant going beyond "mere board and lodging." Proponents of erstwhile economy failed to consider "the unwholesomeness of air and food in boarding." "Bad air and improper food entail illness, a doctor, perhaps death; none of them economical but the last," she concluded.[8]

It took more than bad air and poor food to prove boarding a false economy. As Cooke saw it, the hypocrisy and insincerity of boardinghouse society required additional investments. "In a boarding-house, women are obliged to dress better than in their homes." Marion Harland concurred, pronouncing the economy of boardinghouse life "more than doubtful" when one took into account certain "obligations," including "the increased cost of dress [and] the temptation to divers forms of extravagance not encountered in the quiet home-circle."[9]

All five contributors identified extravagance—the flip side of economy—as the enemy of home life. Novice housekeepers who confused the "elegancies of life" with "necessaries"—as Dare put it—unwisely concluded that housekeeping was indeed a failure and exchanged their homes for boardinghouses. "High rents" posed no obstacle when "pretentious habits" were abandoned. If only women would "put pretension and imitation of other people aside," Dare insisted, they could comfortably keep house and avoid boardinghouses. Much like the imaginary Nincompoops, other newlyweds, unable to afford "elegancies" from the start, flocked to boardinghouses, Owen noted, because they offered "a semblance of luxury" and the ability to "live in a home of more pretension and in a better location than they otherwise could."[10]

Luxury, of course, was in the eye of the beholder; even the contributors to the *North American Review*'s forum implicitly acknowledged that the line between "elegancies" and "necessities" was difficult to draw. In an age of unprecedented material abundance, nobody expected middle-class families to forsake worldly goods. The trick lay in tasteful consumption. Eunice Beecher believed that avoiding boardinghouses was only one of the young housekeeper's duties; in addition, she must "study to make home attractive." For Beecher, this meant choosing "true taste" over "*style*" and "arrang[ing] a home for comfort, not for a temple of fashion." Beecher's instructions for "making a sitting-room peculiarly attractive" included no Brussels carpets or damask curtains, typical indicators of fashionable decor. But they did include "neat, white shades," a piano, "the easiest and most comfortable lounges and chairs," "a commodious table for books"—amenities that required comfortable and commodious incomes.[11]

Just as no one suggested that respectable people in search of homes live in true poverty, almost no one publicly suggested that wives subsidize home life by engaging in gainful employment or even in hidden market labor such as taking in sewing, washing—or boarders. (Beecher, who had once taken in boarders herself, reluctantly endorsed teaching and "fine sewing" as last resorts.) Indeed, "The Two Homes," a cautionary tale published in the African American *National Era,* suggested that cause and effect ran in the opposite direction, for it argued that extravagant wives who drove their husbands to financial ruin suffered the sad fate of having to turn their homes into "genteel boardinghouses" to make ends meet. Yet, in the view of numerous advice writers, novelists, and cultural critics, wives bore the responsibility for keeping house—and keeping their families out of boardinghouses—no matter how high their house rents or how small their husbands' incomes. Recipes for domestic management steered clear of female breadwinning, but they came perilously close to countenancing the shrewdly calculating behavior that contemporaries condemned in boardinghouse keepers. "One must be prompt and careful enough to extort the consideration of cool landlords, able to cope with plumbers, and provision dealers, quite hardened to decline paying dishonest charges, and to return goods which are not what they pretend to be," Dare advised.[12]

Much of the advice proffered to would-be housekeepers was maddeningly vague. How could one tell the difference between a comfortable home and a "temple of fashion"? How exactly *could* one keep house on a husband's modest income? In the latter years of the nineteenth century, however, books with titles like *Six Hundred Dollars a Year* and *How to Live on a Small Income* appeared with increasing rapidity. First published as a series of articles in *Good Housekeeping,* Catherine Owen's *Ten Dollars Enough: Keeping House Well on Ten Dollars a Week* went through eleven editions between 1886 and 1893. It's easy to see why. A cookbook and advice book packaged as an engaging novel, *Ten Dollars Enough* offered practical suggestions for people who wished to avoid boardinghouses. The book's main characters, Mr. and Mrs. Bishop, begin married life as boarders. In contrast to the extravagant wives who populated so much domestic fiction, Molly Bishop longs to try housekeeping. By chance an acquaintance decides to take his family to Europe for a year and offers to sublet his cottage in suburban New Jersey to the Bishops for a modest twenty dollars a month. Successive chapters, including "Molly and Mrs. Lennox—Economical Buying Makes Good Living," "To Boil and Prepare Lobster—Sandwiches—Clearing Soup—Omelet Soufflé," and "What To Do With a Soup-Bone," chronicle Molly's failures and triumphs. As their titles suggest, they contain menus, recipes, cooking advice, and carefully detailed budgets—all wrapped up in an appealing series of anecdotes. "There!" Molly concludes the chapter on "Veal Cutlets, Breaded," "here is an account of our expenditure."[13]

Monday—	Meat and sundries	$2.90
	Cream	.10
	Yeast	.02
Tuesday—	Oysters	.12
	Steak	.30
	Lima Beans	.05
Wednesday—	Extra milk for soup	.04
Thursday—	Smelts	.10
	3 pounds beef	.35
	Pork	.10
	Lettuce	.05
Friday	Cauliflower	.10
	Milk for soup	.04
	Clams	.15
	Soup bone	.15
Saturday	Veal cutlets, 1½ pounds	.27
	Chicken	.50
	Bacon	.14
	Extra butter	.25
	Milk for week	.56
	Ice, 100 pounds	.40
	Fuel	.50
		————
		$7.19

Some readers took Owen a bit too literally. "To those who questioned the cost of articles I would say: they forgot, reading in *December,* when they were doubtless paying higher prices, that the prices quoted were for *September.*" Noting that her intended audience included "readers in widely different parts of the country," she explained that the sums she quoted were "average New York retail prices." By the standards of a worldview that sought to distinguish the home from the market, Owen's acknowledgments—in addition to her content and her very title—represented a capitulation of sorts. *Ten Dollars Enough* paid lip service to the standard themes of sentimental fiction. But, on the whole, it was decidedly unsentimental. In order to promote home over house, Owen's manual quite literally engaged the marketplace, unintentionally revealing that homes were small businesses.[14]

"The Grave, Solemn Responsibilities That Enter into the Relation"

In the eyes of cultural critics, boarding represented nothing less than wifely insubordination. The cookbook author Marion Harland believed that keeping house was one "of the grave, solemn responsibilities that enter into the [marriage] relation"; shirking those responsibilities was tantamount to breaking one's wedding vows. To a certain extent, she was correct. By refusing to perform the labor that transformed a house into a home, boarding wives *did* violate their marriage contracts—or at least the common law tradition by which women exchanged their unremunerated work for protection and economic security. Yet, legal doctrine, which implicitly defined housework as labor, clashed with newer popular conceptions of housekeeping as something other than work. In characterizing boarding wives as lazy, most champions of housekeeping affirmed the latter argument; after all, if housekeeping was not really work, only the truly indolent and truly decadent would choose boardinghouses over homes.[15]

"Is leisure the best thing for women?" asked Harland. Of course it was not. Neither Harland's question nor her answer was particularly original; both drew on decades of criticism of lazy boardinghouse wives. "I have heard many ladies declare that it is 'just quite the perfection of comfort to have nothing to fix for oneself,'" the English visitor Frances Trollope wrote of the female boarders she encountered in antebellum Philadelphia. Trollope viewed these women with a mixture of "pity and contempt." "As to what they do . . . it is not very easy to say; but I believe they clear-starch a little, and iron a little, and sit in a rocking-chair, and sew a great deal." Trollope could not "easily imagine a life of more uniform dulness." But her remarks also betrayed traces of anxiety. What if boardinghouse life indeed proved superior to domestic drudgery?[16]

Despite a mountain of antiboardinghouse rhetoric, many people did prefer "uniform dulness" to housework. In fact, a good deal of evidence suggests that women turned to boarding not necessarily because they were lazy but because they were exhausted. Mark Twain feared the effects of the "wearing and wearying slavery of house-keeping" on his wife. "When the evening comes and the gas is lit and the wear and tear of life ceases, we want to keep the house always; but next morning we wish, once more, that we were free and irresponsible boarders." Richard Barker's friend, the decidedly less famous Mr. Hines, shared Twain's sentiments. "We are going to board again . . . as Papa says Mama has to work too hard," two-year-old Walter Hines reported (whether Papa or Mama penned Walter's missive is unclear). Stating what most popular discussions of boarding left unsaid, one magazine writer observed, "Your life knows no blue Mondays" in a boardinghouse. "Every day may be that blessed Thursday, that interregnum of peace which every woman understands; when washing day and ironing day and baking day are passed, and sewing day and cleaning day have not yet dawned." Boarding wives aroused controversy partly because their preferences had the potential to reveal that housework was backbreaking labor. But popular portrayals of women who abandoned homes for houses stepped back from this cultural brink. They invariably trivialized housewives' complaints, defining house-keeping as the proper supervision of servants, defining housework not as labor but as "duty." They turned a problem of labor into one of management.[17]

Duty represented something of a compromise between rosy visions, in which love magically produced darned socks, wholesome meals, and sparkling cleanliness, and the reality of grueling toil. Ideally, *duty* meant learning the fundamentals of housework—not so that middle-class housewives could do their own cooking and cleaning but so they could delegate those tasks to others responsibly. Wives who rejected duty left servants to their own, usually inept, devices, and left husbands to pine in vain for clean, orderly houses and palatable dinners. One of T. S. Arthur's fictional malcontents complains that her husband "wanted to persuade me that it was my duty to go into the kitchen everyday, and see that the cook attended to her business." "It is evident that you did *not* superintend the dinner to-day," a character in an 1866 *Godey's* short story tells his wife, after finding an "extra nice roast" served up as a "burnt mass." Even servants—at least in fiction—complained of inadequate supervision. "If she would look after things a little, and tell me how she wanted them done, I could get along well enough," a soon-to-depart cook grumbled. "But while it is all left to me, I am never sure that I am going right or wrong." Reluctant or unable to manage, mistresses like these dragged their families into boardinghouses—moves that resulted in certain disaster.[18]

The authors of prescriptive fiction and advice literature touted good management as the key to keeping house—and keeping out of the boardinghouse. Eunice Beecher advised brides to do without household help—but only until they were well enough versed in household labor to "detect any mistake or blunder in a servant." "If bread is brought to the table that is not satisfactory, it is wise to be able to say to your cook, with confidence, 'Your bread should have risen longer before being put into the oven. It is not exactly heavy; but feels solid, and bites tough.' Or, 'Your bread is full of holes. You have not kneaded it sufficiently.'"[19] One suspects that Beecher was about as successful at managing servants as she was at marriage; it's difficult to imagine real-life cooks responding gracefully to such criticism. More to the point, Beecher's counsel offered little comfort to the vast majority of housewives who had no servants.

Theoretically, Beecher believed that lacking help posed no problem; theoretically, wives should choose housekeeping over boarding, even if they had to do their own housework. "Let us say to every young couple, *Go to housekeeping by all means.*" But her underlying message revealed an all-too-familiar ambivalence toward household labor. *All Around the House; Or, How to Make Homes Happy* included her advice to a young wife whose husband's income was so "diminished by the reduction of wages" that "they could no longer pay what they had been doing for their board." Learning that they had "furniture sufficient for one room," Beecher advised her not to move to cheaper lodgings but to "take one room," "go to housekeeping," and do her own washing. To stem her correspondent's growing incredulity ("Do my own washing!"), Beecher told her own story of newlywed life in Indiana. Unable to afford a house, the Beechers rented "two small rooms" previously "occupied by laboring men" and thus "exceedingly dirty." Undaunted, aided by many pails of soap and hot water and the exertions of Henry Ward Beecher himself, who "with as willing hands, and a much stronger arm, lightened the labors wonderfully," cleanliness soon triumphed. The Beechers furnished their rooms with a hodgepodge of makeshift furniture—Beecher's "college study table, chair, single bedstead," the "remnant of an old bookcase," "a cooking or ironing table" fashioned from two boards originally intended for firewood, and "a curtain of four-cent calico."[20]

Apart from the vision it conjured of a young Henry Ward Beecher scrubbing walls and cheerfully chopping firewood, this inspirational tale has a certain poignancy. Only a year after the publication of *Motherly Talks with Young Housekeepers* (1873) and three years before the publication of *All Around the House* (1878), Mr. Beecher's suspected affair with a parishioner landed him in both church and civil courts, tarnishing his reputation even though he was acquitted in both. The Beecher-Tilton affair called into question Eunice Beecher's authority as an advisor on "how to make homes happy." Certainly, in the Beechers' case, forsaking boarding for housekeeping did not guarantee a happy home; their marriage had been unhappy long before the famous scandal erupted. Pressured by her husband to reduce household expenses in the wake of mounting legal costs, Eunice Beecher self-consciously entered the marketplace, writing *All Around the House* as an attempt to augment family income. She soldiered on, holding up her imagined experience as proof that women could and should avoid boardinghouses. More to the point, her extrapolations from "personal illustration" minimized exertion. "Remember that in living in small apartments there is less to do than if occupying a whole house," she advised her correspondent. "On Monday the washing for two cannot take more than an hour or two, and then leaves plenty of time for rest by reading, sewing, etc." Sewing ("rest") in Beecher's view was a form of leisure.[21]

Beecher reported that the young woman eagerly adopted the plan she proposed, inspired especially by "that scrap of your experience in your early married life which you gave." However, the unnamed correspondent sustained the experiment for only two months before she and her husband decided to return to their native Ireland. Whether the experience of keeping house in two rooms prompted this decision, she did not say, but clearly she believed that her sacrifice hastened their improving circumstances. "Virtue," she wrote Beecher, "is rewarded." "Here I am on the shores of old Erin, in a cozy little house, nicely furnished, and with a servant at my command." This existence was not without its trials—"the servant nearly makes my hair stand on end by her ways of doing things. I feel [housekeeping] takes no end of all the virtues, particularly that one called patience." Virtue in this tale was rewarded all too quickly. The only way Beecher could render household labor palatable was to portray it as a brief interlude that women endured before they were promoted from labor to management.[22]

Catherine Owen's more practical and more secular *Ten Dollars Enough* dwelled more extensively on the particulars of housework (especially cooking) than did Beecher's sentimental advice manuals. But the message was the same. Plucky and cheerful, Molly Bishop smoothly makes the transition from boarding to housekeeping. Once again, housekeeping meant not labor but management. The Bishops never consider doing without help; their annual budget allots twelve dollars a month for a servant. Molly faces a semblance of the servant problem. She hires a German girl fresh from Castle Garden (the predecessor to Ellis Island). Marta was not "what she had hoped to meet with." She was "thick, short, strong, but stupid-looking," but (Owen implied) at least she was not Irish. That she spoke not a word of English posed few problems, since Molly improbably spoke "fair German."

Through Molly, Owen modeled her vision of proper mistress-servant relations. Supervision required preparation. Rather than lazing about gossiping and clear-starching, Molly used her year as a boarder to best advantage, enrolling in a culinary class, practicing what she had learned at the home of a friend, and obsessively reading everything she could find about housekeeping. Thus trained, she was not one of those unprepared wives who fled to a boardinghouse at the first sign of distress. She knew better than to expect Marta to know the ins and outs of housekeeping. Well versed in them herself, she was able to show her how to do everything from making biscuits to laying the table cloth. Marta predictably had her faults. She was "stolidly attentive," but "clumsy" and prone to "lumbering movement." She ruined a cake by slamming the oven door; she made croquettes so large that they burst; her first attempt at white sauce tasted raw. But Molly remained patient, cheerful, and unruffled. Marta learned, albeit slowly, how to cook and clean so that Molly would not have to. Molly's tenure as household drudge, *Ten Dollars Enough* made clear, was temporary.[23]

Recruiting, supervising, and retaining servants were no small accomplishments in the eyes of middle-class housewives; the "servant problem" dominated late nineteenth-century discussions of domestic economy. Yet, in 1900 roughly one in ten households employed servants, and those households typically employed only one. In other words, significant numbers of housekeepers—even those who hailed from the relatively prosperous middle classes—cooked, scrubbed, swept, and laundered. Novelists and advice writers who advocated housekeeping over boarding sidestepped the problem of housework and maintained the fiction that housework was not labor. But in characterizing good wives as able managers of paid domestic servants, they acknowledged, perhaps unwittingly, the home's immersion in the world of wage labor. In shoring up one fictive barrier between home and market, they breached another.

"Flaring Exposure" and "Gossip"

Homes, so conventional nineteenth-century wisdom went, were private; boardinghouses were public. Why else would women need to dress more extravagantly in boardinghouses than they did in homes? To present-day readers, the meaning and value of privacy may seem obvious. But from the vantage point of the nineteenth century, it was—like the home itself—a recent and far from uncontested notion. In championing home life over boardinghouse life, moralists invoked an ideal of domestic privacy—indeed, isolation—that characterized few nineteenth-century residences, even those contemporaries called homes. Visitors constantly came and went; friends and relatives stopped for short and not-so-short visits. Sentimental fiction and cultural commentary might feature nuclear families, but in real life uncles, cousins, mother-in-laws—and, of course, boarders—often came to stay. Middle-class homes, moreover, ideally sheltered live-in domestics who witnessed daily life in the households they served and frequently learned their secrets. Harland's complaint that in boardinghouses one's "very bed-chambers are not secure from prying eyes and intrusive feet" glossed over an uncomfortable fact of life in middle-class homes.[24]

Novels, magazine stories, and newspaper editorials nevertheless condemned boardinghouses for their lack of privacy, contrasting home's "sacred seclusion" with the sterile "publicity" of boardinghouse life, which reduced all social interaction to mere performance. "The world, in fact, is turned literally into a stage," *Harper's Weekly* complained, "and its men and women into merely players, acting, and only *acting* their many parts." Boardinghouses offered only a "theatrical mockery of society," one in which people "converse[d]" but "never talk[ed]." The *New York Tribune* issued a similar lament: "The sense of living on the street, of grimacing and talking your best in public, is as much the atmosphere of a boarding-house as is the smell of boiled beef and soup in the halls."[25]

For women, especially, boardinghouse conversation was nothing more than "gossip." "She talks of shirred sleeves, or of the receptions and dinners of which she has read in the reports of fashionable society," a *New York Tribune* editorial complained. Of course, boardinghouse women did gossip; Catherine Thorn admitted she occasionally indulged in it.[26] But what of Thorn's earnest conversations on religion ("Quite shocked Miss Whittemore I think with my broad views")? Susan Brown Forbes's English grammar class? Elizabeth Dorr's conscientious tutoring of a young immigrant? Just as commentators reduced all interaction to acting, they reduced all women's conversation to gossip. "What does boarding do for men and women?" Parloa asked. "It makes them selfish and narrow-minded, and petty fault-finders . . . Men may not be affected to the same extent as women, because they come more in contact with the world in their business, but nobody can estimate how much the growth of a woman's character is retarded by the aimless life in a boarding-house." Parloa—herself a public figure who trained women to become professional cooks—did not suggest that otherwise aimless women seek contact with the "world" by participating in broader public life. Rather, they should retire to homes, "where all that is noble and amiable in men and women is cherished." Trapped by the terms of a debate that gave her about as much maneuvering room as the proverbial hall bedroom, the only reward she could promise to women who gave up boarding was "seclusion." Like the other participants in the *North American Review*'s forum, she saw the boardinghouse "public" as an entirely different animal than the public sphere that formed the basis of men's civic participation. Only through "seclusion" could women become broadminded. At a time when women's access to public life was hotly contested, her co-panelist Cooke conceived of home as a form of female citizenship. "If there is a sadder thing than 'a man without a country,' it is a woman without a home."[27]

The public character of boardinghouse life, various commentators agreed, posed dire threats to marriage. They feared first that communities of clear-starching and collar-working women would take the place of husbands in boardinghouse brides' hearts. They likened genteel boardinghouses during the daytime to nunneries—in Protestant cultural parlance, another form of unnatural habitation.[28] Gossiping companions turned women against their spouses and encouraged them to overspend, to embrace "tinsel show and finery." "Do not let the first years of married life be passed in a boarding-house," Beecher warned. "It is no place to learn each other's character, to become accustomed to the peculiarities that belong to every one; it is no place to accept as *home*." Hotels and boardinghouses, another observer maintained, did not provide "an atmosphere likely to encourage marital happiness." These criticisms hinted at the possibility of extramarital liaisons (against which, as Beecher's experience sadly demonstrated, home life offered little protection). Symbolically released from their matrimonial bonds and having no homes to which to retire, boarding husbands might seek their pleasures elsewhere. Denied the comforts of home, the *New York Tribune* warned, the boardinghouse husband "will have something akin to the passionate draughts of his youth, and he will go downtown to find it."[29]

Husbands were not the boardinghouse's only victims. Numerous observers lamented what they saw as the inverse relationship between boarding and childbearing. They blamed landladies for refusing to house children; indeed, in an era before legal sanctions prevented discrimination, many boardinghouses excluded them. Young Walter Hines "wrote" to his contemporary Richard Barker Jr.: "145 has been thoroughly overhauled & refurnished so an advertisement says, but adults only so you see Richard you and I couldn't go there." Other writers pointed their collective fingers at lazy wives, who reportedly chose boardinghouse residence for the very reason that it allowed them to delay or forgo childbearing. Still others emphasized the predicaments of those children who did live in boardinghouses. "They mope or romp like caged things," Harland complained. Surrounded by adults who lavished attention on dress, who "acted" rather than interacted, boardinghouse children were "pert, ill-bred, [and] noisy"—or worse. A *New York Tribune* editorialist invoked disturbing images of moral danger: "the frilled and curled little girl, hanging on the balusters to be petted and kissed and fed with bonbons by successive generations of boarders," "the young man who never has known . . . the modesties, the privacy, the hospitality, the religious teaching that belong to a home."[30]

The boardinghouses featured in nineteenth-century morality tales exposed children to physical as well as moral contagions. Fictional heroines who likened housekeeping to "slavery" and "living a dog's life" predictably received their comeuppance. Once removed to boardinghouses, they encountered ill-mannered and disreputable housemates, uninspiring cuisine, and formidable landladies. Invariably lacking the "airy rooms" that graced idealized homes, boardinghouses exposed their children to contagious disease. The heroine of Hale's *Boarding Out* pays a heavy price for renouncing her household duties; her four-year-old daughter expires but (lest the reader miss the point) not before uttering these last words: "I want to go home." The children of the Lawton family in Arthur's *Tired of Housekeeping* were luckier; they recovered from their bouts with scarlet fever and measles and the family immediately quit the boardinghouse for a "home."[31]

Fictional morality tales, while exaggerated, depicted the real consequences of living in close quarters. In an age when medical experts generally attributed disease to environmental rather than bacterial or viral sources and in a culture that sharply distinguished houses from homes, arguing that boardinghouses caused illness made perfect sense. As Cooke put it, "The halls and unventilated parlors, stuffy with the presence of crowded humanity . . . lower the vitality and charge the system with malaria." The possibility that homes might be similarly crowded escaped her. Tales of endangered children served a metaphorical function, for they not only reinforced beliefs about the "bad air" supposedly unique to boardinghouses, they hinted that women's gossip conveyed information about contraception and abortion. "How often the ranks of coming infancy have been more than decimated that the wives who evade motherhood may enjoy their languor and leisure and 'take their ease in their inn'!" These connections occasionally reached beyond the merely symbolic. Sarah Chase, a widowed physician who lectured on sexology and sold various birth-control devices—an activity that led to several arrests—kept a boardinghouse in Manhattan just a few blocks away from where the Barkers later boarded with Mrs. and Miss Brown. No doubt her lodgers and neighbors had ready access to the best contraceptives money could buy.[32]

"Spoilt for Housekeeping"

Whether they wrote "fact" or fiction, social critics who deplored the prevalence of boarding relied on cardboard characters—weak-willed, impressionable husbands; selfish, spoiled, and extravagant wives. So did the advice writers who offered handy hints for keeping house on a budget, though they stocked their literary arsenals with resourceful brides and cheerful husbands, stereotypes that lurched toward the opposite extreme. How did this cultural debate play out in people's lives? The experience of Richard Barker's wife Antoinette, or "Nettie" as her family and friends called her, provides one answer. The Barkers, we might recall, lived in a series of boardinghouses in New York and Brooklyn from the time of their marriage in 1887 until circumstances prompted Nettie's reluctant relocation to rural Kentucky four years later.

Boarding made sense for the newlywed couple, most likely, economically, and most certainly, socially. Perennially at the mercy of contingent fees, the Kentucky-born attorney, like most New Yorkers, could not afford a house. Indeed, he could not always afford room and board for two. All that ink spilled on lazy wives disguised an uncomfortable reality: couples often boarded because husbands' wages and salaries could not purchase—or even rent—homes. Advice writers like Eunice Beecher defused this potentially explosive issue by shifting responsibility onto wives' shoulders, insisting that capable domestic managers could "go to housekeeping" if only they would economize. Yet, the Barkers' story shows just how elusive "home" actually was, even for the white middle class. And as even the scornful commentary of cultural critics unwittingly revealed, boardinghouses served an important social function, especially for young brides who followed their husbands to new abodes. Boardinghouse society must have been especially attractive to twenty-year-old Nettie, who was far from her Galveston home. Several of Richard's friends, acquaintances, and relatives from Kentucky routinely visited and sometimes settled in New York, but Texas connections were scarcer, and fellow boarders offered ready companionship.

Nettie seems to have spent her days shopping, visiting "friends in and out of the house," sewing, reading, and writing letters. She hired a washerwoman to do the couple's laundry, but she mended Richard's trousers and darned his socks herself. She made many of her own clothes. She nursed Captain Phillips, an elderly boarder, when he was ill. During the summer of 1889 she assumed the guardianship of two young cousins while they waited to enroll at a female seminary in Massachusetts the coming fall. (Richard feared that this responsibility was too much for his "darling little wife.") Nettie escaped many of the burdens of housework, to be sure, but did not quite live the life of sloth and indolence that moralists imagined. And unlike the stereotypical boarding wife, she was neither adverse to childbearing nor adamantly opposed to keeping house. Ambivalence best describes Nettie's attitude. She alternately sang the praises of boarding and longed for a "home." Most of all, she wanted to be with Richard. "All I want now is to be with you," she wrote him from Galveston in May 1890, "how happy I shall be the day you hold me in your arms again. I will be *home* then."[33]

Home at that particular moment in time was Mrs. Osborne's boardinghouse on Sidney Place in Brooklyn. Like her husband, Nettie forged fond attachments to her boardinghouse friends. Anxious to preserve domestic harmony in her absence, she slipped notes that read "beware of politics" into Richard's pockets before she left for a visit to Ohio.[34] "Give my love to the two Mary's and Lena"; "Love to . . . all friends in and out of the house"; "Give Mrs. Phillips my love"; "Love to Rose and Mr. H. and children"—she instructed Richard from afar. These greetings included landladies, housemates, even servants.[35]

Sentiment did not preclude criticism. Nettie liked Mrs. Sykes, the keeper of Dellwood, the fashionable Bay Ridge boardinghouse where she, Richard, and her cousins Willie and Virginia spent the summer of 1889. She even kept up a correspondence with Mrs. Sykes. Nevertheless, we might recall, she minced few words when it came to Sykes's housekeeping. Nor did her fondness for various landladies prevent her from feeling, as many boarders did, that she was somehow being cheated. Only a few weeks after noting, "I know Mrs. Osborne will be good to you," Nettie vented her annoyance. Osborne had kept—or rather "boarded"—the Barkers' pet bird during a brief period when

Richard and Nettie were out of town. Perhaps surprised that Osborne charged at all—this was the sort of service boarders would have expected for free—Nettie found the price exorbitant. "Flip's board must have been quite an item and *I* think, entirely too much." She quickly extended a specific complaint to a general critique: "It seems to me all our land ladies have imposed on us more or less."[36]

Neither did Nettie's attachments to what she called "our boarding house friends" prevent her from fantasizing about a home of her own—especially when she visited people who *had* homes of their own. "I hope soon we can be keeping house," she wrote Richard from her sister's rented house in Batavia, Ohio, in 1888. A brief visit to Richard's brother and sister-in-law in Kentucky also inflamed her desires. "I suppose you know the place Henry & Kate are living in—it's a very lovely spot and I wish we could have one just like it—but I am too ambitious." Two years later, the Barkers were still living in boardinghouses, and Nettie's sense of relative deprivation had not diminished. Writing from her parents' house in Galveston, she insisted," I want a real home—if its [*sic*] only a little flat." She envied a local newlywed's "cosey little nest." "I can see Mamie Lee and her husband from my window—they are out in their yard planting shrubbery. I quite envy them their little home . . . I am afraid living at home is going to spoil me for boarding," she concluded.[37]

Like a real-life Molly Bishop, Nettie used her visits to relatives as opportunities to practice her housekeeping skills. She baked cakes in Galveston and learned to make biscuits and churn butter at her mother-in-law's in Crescent Hill, just outside of Louisville. "Mother says she will give us a 'beating machine' for biscuits when we start to housekeeping and cousin E. is going to give me some of her receipts for cooking your favorite dishes," she noted cheerfully. In Batavia and later Urbana, Ohio, she helped her sister Maryneal with cooking, cleaning, and childcare.[38] Yet, however much she longed for a "real home," Nettie was painfully aware of the trials of housekeeping. She could not imagine keeping house without servants; neither could she imagine keeping house without the servant problem. Her letters voiced typical complaints about incompetent and unreliable domestics. "We have been very busy all today," she wrote from Batavia, "and if we can't get a cook I don't know what we will do—Maryneal will be completely worn out." In Maryneal's situation the still childless Nettie may have glimpsed her own future. Married to a newspaper editor of somewhat doubtful prospects and burdened with two small children, her sister made her home in the relative isolation of small-town Ohio where good help was hard to find.[39]

Perhaps Nettie had Maryneal in mind when she reversed her relative assessments of boarding and housekeeping. Where she once feared that a visit "home" to her parents would "spoil me for boarding," a year and a half later, after the birth of her first child, she declared that boarding with an especially companionable landlady "has spoilt me for housekeeping."[40] Richard and Nettie's acquaintance with the Hegemans dated from the beginning of their marriage, when they, along with Richard Hegeman, a Manhattan storekeeper, and his wife, Rose, lived at a Mrs. Green's. Boarders easily became boardinghouse keepers (witness Susan Forbes's easy transformation); when the Hegemans rented a house in Flatbush, they invited Richard and Nettie to join them. It was at the Hegemans' that little Richard Barker was born. The ever-gregarious Nettie considered her friendship with the Hegemans of a special order. She frequently remembered the Hegemans in her letters and kept up an independent correspondence with Rose.[41] Even after her departure from New York, she sent gifts to the Hegeman children, Imogene and Nettie, her namesake; and nagged Richard to do the same. "Aunt Rose" in turn sent presents to young Richard, and seven-year-old "Nettie Hegeman, Artist" drew pencil portraits of the Barker family that Richard sent on to his wife.[42]

Above all, Nettie Barker loved Rose Hegeman. From the relative isolation of rural Kentucky, she dreamed of returning to Flatbush to live with Rose, who "has spoilt me for housekeeping." Nettie perceived no tensions between love and money. She recognized that Rose was the "housekeeper" to whom she paid board, an exchange that liberated her from household labor. But she also considered Rose her friend and the Hegemans part of her extended family. "I am so glad you are at Rose's . . . You will not miss us so much there as you would off by yourself," she wrote Richard in November 1891, shortly after he returned to New York without her.[43]

Nettie's affection for the Hegemans was that much more remarkable considering the social differences between them. The daughter of a bank teller, Nettie came from a more modest background than did her husband. (On the eve of the Civil War, Nettie's father owned one slave. Richard's grandfather—with whom his widowed mother then lived—forty-three.) Like many Americans, she came from a family that took in boarders. Nevertheless, she grew up in a household that owned at least one slave before the Civil War and employed servants after emancipation. Rose, on the other hand, *was* a former house servant. The Hegemans, moreover, were Catholics; Nettie, a self-described "Galveston girl," one day would become the first president of the Woman's Council of Louisville's First Christian Church.[44] If liturgical distinctions both-

ered Nettie, she never said so. Richard's opinions were another matter altogether. What he perceived as the Hegemans' utter disregard for their children's
religious instruction both "amused" and "provoked" him. Little Imogene
"had never heard of Noah, but had heard of an Ark & also a flood. Didn't know
there was even such a person as Moses," he complained to Nettie. Nettie
remained unperturbed. Just as she had advised him to avoid discussing politics,
she warned Richard, "Don't try to enlighten the children on Biblical subjects—its [*sic*] against their parents belief."[45]

All in all, Richard had less love for their landlords than did Nettie. When
the Hegemans made plans to move, they assumed that he would move with
them. So did Nettie. "Tell Rose I am in hopes she will take that big house, for
if we are in New York next year she will have to take us to board," she wrote
Richard from Kentucky in December 1891. But Richard opted for a Manhattan boardinghouse instead. He had a quintessentially modern reason: he had
tired of the commute.[46] And as he explained to Nettie, "There were some little things I didn't like." What these "things" were he did not say. They surely
included religious differences and likely the absence of a bathtub. Mr. Hegeman had the habit of helping himself to the "best part" of the stewed tripe.
Possibly the Hegemans treated him *too* much like a member of the family.
Whenever Mr. Hegeman worked late, Richard felt obliged to accompany Imogene, who was afraid of the dark, to the stables feed the horses.[47]

Not surprisingly, Richard's departure led to hurt feelings. He continued to
visit the Hegemans, mostly because Nettie insisted. "Haven't you been to Flatbush since you left there—didn't you leave there friendly?" she asked in April
1892, less than a month after Richard moved to Manhattan. In June, she wrote,
"You haven't been to see them out there yet—they must think strange of it."
Richard complied, but not frequently enough. "I expect the Hegemans think
you have treated them coldly and I am not surprised Mr. H. was not more cor-
dial," Nettie remarked some two years later. "They have always seemed very
fond of you and could not well help feeling slighted at you being so long there
without coming to see them; it would be a good plan to take the little girls a nice
box each of . . . candies when you go, as a peace offering."[48] Rose continued to
hope for a reunion. She wrote Nettie—then in Galveston—in June 1892, once
again inviting the Barkers to live with them, this time not quite as boarders, but
in an arrangement in which the Barkers would undertake "light housekeeping." "It would not suit me to keep house that way," Nettie reassured Richard.[49]

The reasons the Barkers declined the Hegemans' invitation had as much
to do with personal circumstance as with Richard's discomfort. Richard was far

from poor. But he simply could not afford to support his wife and children (Richard Jr. was born in 1891, Caroline in 1893) in New York. (That he chose to leave his family behind rather than install them in a third-rate boarding-house or a tenement apartment speaks volumes.) Love loomed as large as money (though visions of future inheritances may never have been far from the Barkers' minds). Richard's stepfather Henry J. Stites, a prominent Louisville judge, died in the fall of 1891. With his brothers, Henry and Maxwell, Richard tried to persuade his sixty-eight-year-old mother Caroline to "break up housekeeping" and move to Louisville. But Caroline Stites insisted on staying at the family plantation at White Hall, just east of the city. She also insisted on company. When Richard returned to New York after Judge Stites's funeral, he left Nettie behind in Kentucky.[50] She managed lengthy vis-its to Urbana and Galveston but would never live in New York again. Richard, for his part, visited Nettie whenever he could; it was never often enough to suit either of them. In 1892 Nettie and Richard spent only four months together. It was an especially lonely year.

Nettie viewed life at Crescent Hill as a kind of exile. She felt isolated and lonely, especially after Richard's brother Henry and his wife Kate, who "used to tide me over many a weary hour," moved to town. Nettie and her children lived a "doleful . . . existence" with only her mother-in-law and Cousin Eliza (the "cousin E." who promised her "receipts"), an elderly spinster, for com-pany. Ill and depressed, Caroline Stites often took meals alone in her room.[51] She begrudged Nettie's trips to Galveston to see her parents and to Urbana to see her sister—even when Maryneal, pregnant and dangerously ill, desper-ately needed nursing and moral support. "They seem to think here that I have no feeling for my family," Nettie complained.[52] Anxious about robbers rumored to be prowling the vicinity, Caroline even resisted Nettie's brief visits to her sister-in-law in Louisville. Sometimes Nettie rebelled. "No harm can come to them out here any sooner with baby and me away than if we are here. I want to go in for the change for one thing, and see something of the Xmas sights," she wrote in December 1892. Duty ultimately prevailed. "I wish we could stay in the city with Kate—its so lonely out there," she complained to Richard the following February. "But we will have to go of course as mother and cousin Liza are so lonely." A month later, Nettie, pregnant with her second child, had had enough: "I am very blue; you must try to make arrangements for me to be with you permanently, hereafter," she pleaded. Richard, desper-ately missing Nettie and little Richard, agreed, though it would be another year before this hope was realized.[53]

Historians tell us that middle-class fear of the city reached its zenith in the late nineteenth century. Nettie never expressed the least bit of anxiety. Traveling about New York did not daunt her. "In case something should happen to prevent you meeting me at the depot I will go right up to 161. I know the way," she assured Richard as she made plans to return from a visit to her in-laws in October 1888. "I can easily get up to the house from the depot so do not try to meet me," she insisted in a subsequent letter.[54] Life at Crescent Hill was far more frightening than life in the big city. Cousin Eliza "borrow[ed] trouble," constantly worrying about the fate of "three women . . . left alone in the house." At her insistence, Nettie borrowed her brother-in-law's pistol. Eliza armed herself with an "empty bull dog pistol," Caroline "a dull raisor." Nettie claimed "its all nonsense to be afraid," but Eliza's worries nagged at her. "I feel safer having [the gun] and will not use it carelessly." "It is just as well for the servants and Negroes to know we are protected by a good weapon and a brave woman!" Racial fears, as Nettie's reference to "servants and Negroes" makes clear, were never far from the surface; potential danger, as she saw it, loomed from within the Stites household—the (African American) "servants"—and without—"the Negroes." By "three women . . . alone," Nettie meant three *white* women.[55]

Isolation, loneliness, and daily irritations played much larger parts in shaping Nettie's attitudes toward life at Crescent Hill than did the largely hypothetical threats posed by "Negroes and servants." Domestic economy at White Hall—or more accurately, what she perceived as its absence—exasperated her. Even more exasperating was that, as a visiting daughter-in-law, she lacked authority to do anything about it. "Things get worse here every day," she wrote Richard in December 1891. "The servants waste enough to support a family twice the size of this one and it seems such a pity for mother to be so imposed on and put to such needless expense—but it doesn't do any good to talk to mother about it for she says she can't help it and doesn't want to be worried about it." The situation had only worsened two years later: "Mother is buying butter and feeding six cows—also buying eggs and feeding over a hundred chickens." "I am so glad you sent me the money you did—we have to buy all [of the] . . . butter we eat, eggs milk and cream," she wrote to Richard in April 1894, just before he left New York for good.[56]

Stranded in the rural hinterland, Nettie would have happily returned to a New York boardinghouse. By 1894, however, she was the mother of two children and had decided unequivocally that she wanted "our own home." Living for the better part of three years with a needy and sometimes critical mother-in-law, not the incessant sociability of a boardinghouse, spurred her decision. If the Barkers had divorced—and by every indication they were most happily married—boardinghouses would not have been to blame. "I think we will truly appreciate a quiet home life together in our own home with our children about us," she wrote Richard in February 1894.[57] Tired of being apart from his wife and children, Richard abandoned New York. No longer a young man—he was forty-six in 1894—he went west, deciding that Arizona was worth a try. Somehow Caroline and Cousin Eliza were persuaded to move to town. Richard, Nettie, and their children left for Phoenix in 1896, where they finally had a home of their own—a rented house. Richard must have prospered. Or, perhaps, the inheritance he received when Caroline died in 1899 helped. In any case, the couple returned to Kentucky, eventually purchasing a house lot in the desirable Louisville neighborhood of Cherokee Triangle. Richard, we have seen, was in his new home for a mere four years before his death in 1916.

The Barkers' story suggests just how elusive real and metaphorical homes could be, even for the middle classes. It also suggests the complex ways in which the boarding versus home debate resonated in real life. Nettie Barker participated in this larger cultural conversation, but her opinions fluctuated, sometimes according to whim, other times in response to changing circumstances. The Barkers rarely personified the private family of popular lore. Try as they might, they were not an autonomous duo, free to decide whether to board or keep house. To the contrary, they were enmeshed in a dense web of family relations—replete with complicated mixtures of love and money—a web that eventually stretched across much of the continental United States.

Though hardly free from the racial prejudices of her time, Nettie Barker was a likeable woman—generous, friendly, and helpful, a loving wife, a dutiful daughter-in-law, a doting mother. Despite her fleeting attachments to genteel boardinghouse life, she was also utterly conventional. Boarding neither destroyed her marriage nor in the end "spoilt her for housekeeping."

If boarding provoked the ire of social conservatives, it drew surprisingly little support from social radicals. For Melusina Fay Peirce, the nineteenth century's most prominent advocate of cooperative housekeeping, hotels and boardinghouses—"full to repletion" with refugees from "ill-regulated or extravagant households"—were symptoms of larger social problems, not solutions to them. Peirce hoped to remove production and servants from the home altogether by establishing a series of cooperative kitchens, sewing rooms, and laundries, where "lynx-eyed matrons" would supervise professionally trained domestics. No longer overworked housewives or exasperated employers of incompetent domestics, cooperative members—whom Peirce envisioned laboring as lynx-eyed supervisors for approximately three hours a day—could devote themselves to intellectual pursuits.

In Peirce's view, boardinghouses too closely resembled homes to render themselves serious candidates for alternative residential visions. They offered none of the efficiency and professionalism that she envisioned for cooperative kitchens. They were private entities, not cooperative enterprises—and they bore more than a passing resemblance to the private households that Peirce deplored. A careless reader could easily mistake Peirce's decidedly unflattering portrait of home life for a typical description of a boardinghouse: "the kitchen sink, with the greasy pots and pans that have to be continually in it . . . the kitchen floor with its greasy spots always having to be washed up; [the] dreadful smell of grease pervading the house whenever anything is fried." Unlike many of her contemporaries, Peirce saw housework for what it was: backbreaking and fatiguing labor. Like them, however, she was torn between emphasizing housewives' exhaustion and their frustrations with training and supervising inept servants. And for all her radicalism and despite her own unhappy marriage to the mathematician and philosopher Charles Sanders Peirce (which ended in divorce in 1883), she cherished conjugal privacy. Indeed, her proposals rendered the private home even more private by removing servants from their interiors.[58]

A believer in "trained professional service" rather than cooperation and a former boardinghouse keeper herself, Charlotte Perkins Gilman was more receptive to private enterprise. Considering boardinghouses a "patch-work solution" to the problem of household labor, she championed apartment hotels, especially for professional women who had neither time nor energy to keep house. Each family, according to Gilman's scheme, would have its own kitchenless flat, cleaned by hotel staff. Each could eat in the common dining room or choose to have meals delivered to private quarters. Gilman envisioned thoroughly professional operations, beset by none of the pitfalls and uncertainties that marred home or boardinghouse life. And to a certain extent, her dream temporarily came true. Apartment hotels catering to the well-to-do proliferated in late nineteenth-century cities. But because they exempted women from housework, they triggered many of the same criticisms that commentators leveled at genteel boardinghouses.[59]

Yet the concerns that boarding couples provoked did help to expand prevailing definitions of *home* beyond the single-family detached house. Increasingly, journalists and advice writers recognized that what passed for suburbia in nineteenth-century America was out of reach of all but relative elites. As early as 1857 *Harper's* suggested that if house rents were beyond the reach of families of moderate means, "why not build tenements with *flats* as in Edinburgh, or a multiplicity of *étages* as in Paris?" Dwellings like these, the editorial explained, offered "the occupant of each story all the completeness of a separate house, with the seclusion and privacy of an individual home." "Any thing would be better than the publicity and indolence of boarding-house life," its author concluded. By the 1880s and 1890s, a veritable chorus seconded *Harper's* call.[60] Most who championed apartments did so reluctantly, endorsing them only as a last resort for those who could not afford single-family houses. It is also worth noting that most who championed apartments saw them not just as remedies for high house rents but as antidotes to boarding-house life, especially the "indolence" it visited on boarding women. *If* apartments could successfully distinguish themselves from boardinghouses—if dining, housekeeping, and food preparation could be rendered "private," then perhaps apartments might become homes.

CHAPTER SEVEN

Charity Begins at Home

> *home:* An institution providing refuge or rest for the destitute,
> the afflicted, the infirm, etc., or for those who either have no
> home of their own, or are obliged by their vocation to live at a
> distance from the home of their family.
>
> *Oxford English Dictionary*

Homes dominated the nineteenth-century American landscape. Most secure in meriting this nomenclature were the single-family, increasingly suburban, domiciles of the new middle classes. Residents of tenements, boardinghouses, and modest cottages might also invoke the term, but, as many cultural arbiters saw it, their claims—if not entirely invalid—rested on the shakiest of foundations. Curiously, in light of this proprietary definition, benevolent institutions appropriated the language of bourgeois domesticity, styling themselves as homes. Their choice was anything but arbitrary. State-sponsored institutions such as mental hospitals, poorhouses, and orphan asylums typically adopted familial models, but *Home* usually signified a private endeavor—the result of private benevolence—not a publicly funded *house* of refuge, alms*house*, or poor*house*.

If the supporters of Homes insisted on distinguishing them from state-sponsored houses, they also expended considerable energy distinguishing them from boardinghouses—in some cases deliberately advertising their creations as alternatives to boardinghouses. That early nineteenth-century prisons and almshouses dubbed their inmates *boarders* partly explains this denial. But as boarding came more and more to mean the "private" act of paying for room, meals, and housekeeping services, the founders and managers of Homes— with varying degrees of success—sought to distance themselves from the transience, immorality, and marketplace calculations that boardinghouses seemingly embodied. Only properly managed Homes, they maintained, could provide religious and moral guidance. Only Homes could suitably shelter the deserving poor. Only Homes could produce permanent ties of affection instead of fleeting associations, protect newcomers from the evils of the city, and transform motley assemblages of strangers into "families."[1]

The stories of four benevolent institutions—each of which catered to age- and sex-specific clienteles—reveal a common set of values and a landscape of semantic confusion. Their originators grappled with many of the same problems that bedeviled nineteenth-century Americans in general—defining the meaning of home, establishing the proper scope of the market, drawing the boundaries between public and private, determining the obligations family members owed each other. If it proved difficult to differentiate boardinghouses from "private" homes, it proved even more difficult to distinguish benevolent Homes from boardinghouses—or, for that matter, from "public" institutions. Ironically, the typical boardinghouse bore a much closer resemblance to home than did the typical Home. Indeed, the history of Homes shows just how insistently the home versus boardinghouse distinction resonated throughout American culture and ultimately how elastic and meaningless that distinction could become. More to the point, by the mid-nineteenth century, Homes had become places to which many people did not want to go.

A Home for the "Tempest-Tost"

Sailors' boardinghouses were an especially notorious variant of an often-notorious institution. Located along urban waterfronts, they served as first and last resorts for mariners who came ashore. They offered food, lodging, and drink in abundance. They provided women as well, situating themselves in close proximity to houses of prostitution or doubling as brothels. They were, one reformer declared, "dens of infamy . . . among the sons of daughters of shame." Their keepers, in rare cases "honest men," more often turned out to be "land sharks" who fleeced their hapless customers. They charged seamen inflated prices for liquor and board, kept them continually inebriated, and stole from them as they lay in drunken stupors, leaving them unable to pay what they owed. In league with unscrupulous captains, they created a system akin to peonage, requiring mariners to work off their debts by signing on to a particular vessel, robbing sailors of their "manhood." The vicious cycle of drunkenness and debt only repeated itself at the next port. Temperance advocate John Gough grimly noted the unintentional accuracy of the sign that graced a New York boardinghouse: "Sailors taken in, and done for."[2]

The Boston Seaman's Friend Society, founded in 1827, was one of many similar associations that materialized along the eastern seaboard in the early nineteenth century. An outgrowth of the Boston Society for the Religious and Moral Instruction of the Poor, it affiliated with the American Seaman's Friend Society, a national organization established in New York a year earlier. (The Boston Society would later declare its independence in the wake of disputes over money and turf.) Like its sister societies, it tried to combat the pernicious influences of seafaring life in general and sailors' boardinghouses in particular. It initially hoped to effect "a thorough reform in the system of boardinghouses for sailors." It settled, however, for attempting to replace sailors' boardinghouses with a Sailor's Home.[3]

The Home complemented the society's wide-ranging missionary efforts, which included a Mariner's Church ("open to Evangelical Christians [that is, Protestants] of all denominations"), a Savings Bank for Seamen, lending libraries that could be taken aboard ships, and missions in foreign ports. The society's founders, most of them merchants associated with the maritime trade, acted partly out of a sense of social responsibility. Sailors "have been suffered to lodge here unregarded, in dens of infamy huddled in between *your* [emphasis added] massive granite warehouses, and the sons and daughters of shame," the Rev. F. D. Huntington thundered to an audience of society members.[4] But the society offered practical benefits to its sponsors as well. Pleased with the sober and industrious crew he had recruited from the Sailor's Home, a captain explained, "if the merchants would patronize these houses *only*, and even give extra wages, there could be an immense saving of property and lives."[5] In this sense the members of the society differed little from the numerous businessmen who tried to inculcate habits of temperance, industry, and thrift among those they employed. The difference was that the Seamen's Friend Society believed that these transformations could be accomplished only with the help of a Home.

The society began modestly enough, assuming the management of first one, and eventually three, sailors' boardinghouses along the city's waterfront. It delegated fundraising and furnishing to its women's auxiliary. If home was woman's sphere in this as in other endeavors, the gentlemen of the society put the wheels in motion. Men, too, might be social housekeepers, even if they left the details to women. The society's boardinghouses quickly proved inadequate. For one thing, there was not enough space to shelter ever increasing numbers of applicants. For another, "decent places" though they were, they were still boardinghouses. If the society meant to provide a true alternative to the countless "dens of infamy" that tempted its clientele, it needed a Home. In 1836 it acquired a dwelling at the corner of Purchase and Belmont Streets in the vicinity of its existing boardinghouses in the city's Fort Hill neighborhood. It was not a home in the later suburban sense of the word; distinctions between residential and commercial space mattered little in 1830s Boston, and any such abode needed to be accessible to disembarking sailors. Thus, the new Sailor's Home positioned itself on the waterfront but in relatively respectable territory, sufficiently distant from the most notorious sailor's dives on Ann Street in the North End. Once again, the Female Seaman's Friend Society assumed responsibility for interior decoration. "These ladies are co-workers with us," an annual report explained. "They are angels of mercy to the tempest-tost mariner."[6]

The new establishment provided "a peaceful and quiet home" to "400 sons of the ocean" during its first year of operation alone. It deftly combined two emerging definitions of *home*, housing destitute ("shipwrecked") sailors for free and the upwardly mobile for a modest cost. Like ideal homes everywhere it taught its inhabitants bourgeois habits of sobriety, thrift, and upward striving. If annual reports can be believed (and there is reason for skepticism), the Sailor's Home transformed drunken spendthrifts into model citizens. Here they "learned . . . lesson[s] of providence." They "learned to respect themselves and to look forward to places of profit and usefulness." They also learned temperance, for the Home allowed alcohol only if ordered by a physician for medicinal purposes. Here they learned to renounce "profane swearing" and even "loud talking."[7] Virtue was hardly its own reward. The Home, its supporters maintained, made common sailors into officers, "elevated to their present situations after they became residents." Not even a decade after its founding, the society claimed that a staggering five to six hundred sailors had achieved officer status as a result of the Home's good influences.[8]

The Home's history followed what would become a common institutional trajectory. Beginning in makeshift quarters, it commissioned its own specialized and increasingly commodious structures as demand for its services increased. In less than a decade it outgrew the house it had purchased, erecting a five-story building on the same lot in 1845 with funds raised by its women's auxiliary. The new Home included seventy-four rooms quaintly called "dormitories" but which held only two beds each, offering a degree of privacy that only captains and officers experienced at sea. This Home proved short-lived, for it burned down in 1853. Not easily deterred, the society built a new, even larger establishment (still called the Sailor's Home) a few blocks away, intended to accommodate 150 residents. Twenty years later it moved again, ostensibly to be nearer the city's deepwater harbor but also to escape the influences of the "foreign papists" who increasingly populated the neighborhood. This time it erected a massive building that combined with residential quarters a Mariner's Church capable of accommodating five hundred worshippers.[9]

Structures of this size and capacity might reasonably have been dubbed very large boardinghouses or sailors' hotels. But the Seamen's Friend Society insisted that its purpose remained the same even as its patronage grew: "To provide a moral, religious, and temperate [*sic*] home for seamen." What made these successive institutions Homes? Certainly not their waterfront locations. The society believed, however, that moral geography trumped physical space. Like model homes elsewhere, the Sailor's Home distanced itself from the market metaphorically if not geographically—especially the traffic in rum and women in which sailor's boardinghouses specialized. At the same time the Home, or so its sponsors liked to believe, trained residents for success in the legitimate maritime marketplace, helping to spread "Protestant thrift and enterprise" across the globe. Even as its inmates multiplied into the hundreds and thousands, the Home continued to embrace a familial model of management. Two sets of fathers and mothers presided. A male Board of Managers from the Seamen's Friend Society, in whose hands rested final authority, and the Ladies' Seamen's Friend Society jointly administered its workings. A succession of retired sea captains and their wives, serving as heads of the Home's constantly changing family, oversaw daily activities.[10]

More than anything else, the daily rituals of pious family life—as society members saw it—ensured that the Sailor's Home was indeed a home. "We endeavor to make a *Christian household*," the Female Society declared. "For this end, we would by all lawful means persuade seamen, as they enter this port, to make it their home." Residents worshipped at a "family altar." They "gather[ed] around . . . [a] table spread with the bounties of divine providence." Sailors' stays at home were necessarily fleeting, but the society hoped "to throw about them influences which will restrain them from vice, and lead them when away from this Home, to think of it, its comforts,—to return to it and be blessed by it."[11]

How successfully the Home accomplished these purposes is anyone's guess. Annual reports published glowing testimonials. "There is no place to which I feel so much attached for it was there I found a Saviour precious to my soul," wrote one resident; "the Home in Boston is all that is professes to be, a *Sailor's*

Home," wrote another. Still another suggested that if sailors' boardinghouses robbed their inmates of their masculinity, the Sailor's Home and the proprietary privacy that it offered restored it: "This Home is a great and blessed institution, because it makes the sailor feel not only that he is a man, but that he is regarded as a man by others, and can have his *room* like other men." Annual reports predictably left much unsaid. The Home was the scene of at least one drunken "affray," and at least one critic accused it of "land sharking." Nevertheless, one sailor considered the place his true home, even though its lessons evidently failed to endow him with the material success they promised. He bequeathed his sole possessions ("$134, a silver watch, and a chest of clothes") to "the only place that had ever befriended him."[12]

"Not a Mere Boarding House"

We think of "convalescent" or "old age" "homes" as convenient euphemisms. We know that their residents rarely convalesce in any literal sense, and we know that such institutions are really nothing like "homes." But their nineteenth-century originators took the concept of home seriously. Self-consciously and deliberately, they named the institutions they created Homes. The benevolent bluebloods ("the Appletons, the Sturgises, the Lawrences, the Shaws, the Tappins, the Bradlees, the Brookses, the Phillipses," an annual report fondly recalled) who founded the Boston Home for Aged and Indigent Females (later the Boston Home for Aged Women) wished to provide residents "with a comfortable Home" and "to surround them with some of the associations which attach to that sacred name." "Our house," founding president Henry Rogers explained in 1850, "is designed to be a permanent place of refuge for those who seek its shelter, and not a mere boarding house."[13]

With that bold declaration, the Association for the Relief of Aged and Indigent Females embarked on a remarkably long-lived career (the Home, now called Goddard House, continues to operate to this day). From the start, however, its motives and purposes were contradictory. From the start, the association navigated treacherous terrain between heartlessness and indulgence, deference and duty. Struggling to define itself against a variety of unsavory foils—boardinghouses, public almshouses, and tenements—the Home emerged as a curious amalgam of middle-class domesticity, boardinghouse culture, and institutional discipline.

The "sacred name" of home meant many things to the association's membership. First and foremost, as the "no mere boarding house" statement implied, *Home* connoted permanence, not transience; the association expected residents to remain for the duration of their "natural li[ves]."[14] *Home* also signified a private institution, distinct in purpose, clientele, and sponsorship from publicly funded alms*houses* and *houses* of refuge. Most important, the association envisioned an institution that mirrored idealized homes in all their facets, offering residents material comfort and emotional support. Deserving inmates enjoyed the accouterments of bourgeois life, removed from "comfortless and ill-furnished apartment[s]" in the city's worst neighborhoods, surrounded by "filth and disorder," "to a spacious and comfortable Home."[15] Ideally, they developed lasting attachments to "my own little room" and the institution itself. "I am so glad to get home," the association imagined grateful newcomers exclaiming.[16] Modeling itself on similar efforts in New York and Philadelphia, it designed the Home's "government" to replicate "as nearly as possible" that of "a well-ordered domestic home." Upon entering the Home, residents abandoned the solitary isolation of their rooms in "dilapidated tenements" to join "one contented family."[17] Annual reports used *inmate* and *family*, *home* and *institution* interchangeably, betraying little awareness of any tension between the terms.

The Home's raison d'etre showed just how restrictive a definition of family it employed, revealing how class-and culture-bound its ideal was. Certainly, the Home, like its kindred institutions, never considered housing the promiscuous assortments of men and women who typically inhabited boardinghouses and bourgeois homes. And only certain sorts of elderly women were eligible for admission to its thoroughly feminine family. Rogers, who remained president of the association until his death in 1887, defined the Home's purpose thus: "an INSTITUTION for the relief and succor of 'Respectable, Aged, and Indigent American Females.'" He conjured up an appealing set of stock characters: "the aged nurse, who has spent the strength of her days in watching by the bedside of the sick and dying . . . the needle woman,—whose patient industry, from early dawn to late night, has scarcely sufficed for the necessities of the passing day . . . the widow of fourscore years, who has seen better days," all of them "respectable" and American born. "Bone of our bone, and flesh of our flesh," they deserved a home. The "foreign poor"—lacking "our habits of industry and thrift"—could safely be consigned to the city's poorhouse. (Nevertheless, Rogers felt compelled to reassure potential donors who might question the industry and thrift of the Home's inmates: "Our beneficiaries have passed the age of active effort, and we may freely lavish upon them our bounty without any fear of injurious consequences.") Embellishing his statements with Dickensian scenarios, Rogers emphasized the plight of the respectable poor, who feared "dropping to the level of alms-house inmates and paupers." The city almshouse offered "no adequate provision" for the "poor of our own people," who possessed a "natural repugnance which we cannot but respect . . . a repugnance to be herded with paupers of every character, condition, and clime."[18] "Our own people" excluded the foreign born and the non-white (although the latter assumption remained unspoken; a Home for Aged Colored Women would be established in 1864). "Our own people" also excluded the truly indigent. "Tranquil faces and grateful hearts"—the rewards of admission—came at a price: a one-hundred-dollar fee (to be paid by the applicant or a benevolent society who sponsored her), "a good bedstead (iron one preferred), bed, bedding, and furniture for a room." In addition, residents had to sign over their remaining property and future inheritances to the association.[19]

In keeping with the rewards deserving women merited, it was no mere poorhouse. From the Home's beginnings in a small rented house on Charles Street, its plan was self-consciously residential. Deserving applicants soon outpaced available space; nevertheless, the association, with inmates' enthusiastic approval, spurned a grant of land from the city because of the lot's dreary aspect, an impression enhanced by its location in the vicinity of public charitable institutions.[20] Instead, it purchased two additional existing houses, connecting all three to create additional space. By 1862 it had raised the funds to construct "a large and imposing brick structure of its own." Its builders intended it to resemble a large house, not an institution. Promotional literature stressed its suburban ambience: "both the building and locality, secluded as they are, and must always be, from dust and noises, open to light and air on every side, commanding at all times an unobstructed view of the Charles River, of the varied and picturesque country beyond, and of what to declining years is more than all, the setting sun." Single rooms far outnumbered doubles, offering privacy of which "public" inmates who huddled in the city's miserably overcrowded poorhouse could only dream. Indeed, "my own little room" was a necessary perquisite for the deserving poor. "Often the better the character of persons, the more they wish for the privacy of their own apartment," an annual report explained. The association took pride in state-of-the-art steam heating (which alas, failed to live up to its billing), ample ventilation, bathing rooms, and "necessary conveniences" (indoor privies), features that distinguished the Home from overcrowded almshouses and tenements—and, indeed, from many single-family homes.[21]

Yet, its careful symmetry and functional design resembled nothing so much as the "well-ordered" institutions that dotted the nineteenth-century landscape—prisons, insane asylums, and even almshouses. Equipped to house up to 134 residents, the Home stretched the definitions of home and family to their breaking points. Like Sailors' Homes and similar institutions elsewhere, the Boston Home modeled itself on the family, long after the utility of the model had faded. Promoters and administrators continued to evoke the language of family, and no doubt residents fashioned ties of intimacy and affection. But the goal of "one family" must have seemed increasingly elusive.[22]

From its beginnings, the association had envisioned a peculiarly authoritarian family, one whose relations reversed the "respect and reverence" it claimed to accord to age. Supervision, "eminently maternal," fell to the institution's matron. Home rules prohibited "find[ing] fault" with her, one of many measures intended "to preserve order and harmony in the family." The Home's administrators interpreted maternal government literally; they imagined the matron as a mother to women in the throes of their "second childhoods." Respectable and deserving though they might be, residents of the Home were childlike and poor—a powerful recipe for dependency. They were not quite bone of *our* bone and flesh of *our* flesh, after all. To the contrary, their status as children and dependents justified a draconian set of rules and regulations. These changed little over time. Whether housed in the first small thirty-person residence on Charles Street or in the new building that held more than a hundred, inmates were to appear "punctually" at "family prayers" and at the "general table." Regulations forbade "intoxicating drinks" and "strong stimulants" ("except by order of the physicians; and, in such case, they must be administered by the Matron"). Friends could visit only at particular times and only after the matron had approved their admittance. Inmates who desired to venture beyond the Home's four walls had to obtain "leaves of absence" issued by the matron. Because the association took pride in its accomplishments—and depended on charitable contributions—it sacrificed the "sacred seclusion" that supposedly characterized private bourgeois homes and opened its Home to the public, in much the same way that prisons and asylums hosted visitors from near and far.[23]

But if the association unwittingly replicated the example of the institutions it claimed to deplore, it preserved one of the private home's most notable features: housework. To be sure, promotional literature described the "object" of the Home as "not activity, but repose." The text of annual reports imagined elderly inmates "relieved of toil" whiling away "vacant hours" engaged in reading, religious observance, or mere "contemplation." The list of rules printed at the end of each volume told a different story. Able-bodied residents were to "make their own beds and sweep their own rooms every morning, and to assist those who are unable to do the same." The association insisted that they "sew, knit, assist in domestic duties, and generally, to render all the services they can for the benefit of the Institution and the comfort of those who are still more helpless than themselves." It required residents to do their own laundry, according to time-honored housekeeping schedules: washing on Mondays, ironing on Tuesdays. Prominent architect Nathaniel J. Bradlee, designer of the new building, made sure to include a "private laundry for the old ladies" in his plans.[24]

Residents' household labor lowered employment costs, but perhaps more importantly underscored residents' dependent status by reducing them to servants. Requiring residents to work recalled the daily routines of mental hospitals, public almshouses, and poor farms—a resemblance of which inmates undoubtedly were aware. If such comparisons troubled members of the association, they never publicly said so. Besides, the very idea of home offered them a useful rubric. The Home's Board of Managers did not define "services" such as sweeping, sewing, and washing, as work; work, in their parlance, meant leaving the institution to undertake paid labor and was expressly forbidden. Indeed, the spectacle of elderly women past "the age of active effort" (the Home seldom admitted residents under sixty) forced to sweep and launder suggests just how powerfully domestic ideology masked the fact that housework was indeed labor. This Home was indeed no mere boardinghouse, for boardinghouses typically exempted all but landladies and their servants from household labor.[25]

It would be easy to interpret the association's familial language as so much empty rhetoric, useful for fundraising purposes and little more. But the association took home and family seriously, insisting on portraying as family quarrels even the inevitable conflicts that arose within its walls. Only once did it falter; in a particularly revealing passage, its 1870 annual report compared the working of the Home to a "parallel case": "Was it ever known in any hotel or boardinghouse, large or small, that the inmates were wholly satisfied, never finding fault with the cooking, or service, or general management, nor insisting that the food was not what it should be in quantity or quality?" Perhaps in response to this apparent gaffe, the report for the year that followed made a point of reiterating—with only slight variation—Henry Rogers's founding statement: "As our worthy President has well said: 'Our house is designed to be a permanent place of refuge for those who seek its shelter, and not a mere boarding-place.' "[26]

The Home's beneficiaries did not always share these sentiments. Even public pronouncements obliquely alluded to residents' contrariness, but inmates' voices surface most distinctly in the records of the association's Executive Committee, the mixed-sex group of proper Bostonians who oversaw the institution's workings in minute detail. The very embodiment of micromanagement, the committee met weekly at the Home, appointing subcommittees to investigate issues such as whether the inmates should be allowed to carry candles or open their windows. It allotted much of its time, however, to addressing instances of insubordination. Offenses included "improper language," "prowl[ing] about the house" at night, "grumbling constantly," and "behaving disrespectfully" toward the matron. Residents might also refuse to attend religious services or appear at "family meals"; their responses tell us a good deal about the tensions between the privacy inmates believed their due and the enforced sociability family life required.[27]

Meals provoked considerable tension. Much of the "grumbling," as the annual report implied, concerned the quality of the food; indeed, the same volume publicly denied an "idle rumor" that "our inmates are kept upon poor and scanty diet."[28] Sometimes residents took matters into their own hands, demanding special diets or supplementing the offering themselves. In 1863 the committee reprimanded two residents, Mrs. Quigley and Mrs. Bennett, for bringing tea—a prohibited "strong stimulant" evidently supplied them by friends on the outside—to the dinner table. Quigley claimed the right to consume what she pleased because "she had paid her money" to the Home. Like her partner in crime, Bennett was not the least cowed in the presence of Boston's upper crust. "Mrs. Shaw," she informed the widow of the chief justice of the Massachusetts Supreme Court, "you have told me once, twice, thrice [about the ban on tea], and you have no need to speak to me about it again." Other sorts of stimulants created trouble; the committee found it necessary to instruct the matron to keep medicinal liquors under lock and key. Much to members' and matrons' dismay, many residents came and went as they pleased, sometimes to buy snuff and gin, often neglecting to inform the matron of their plans. They acted, in fact, as if they were lodgers in a boardinghouse instead of residents of a Home. As one inmate boldly proclaimed to the committee, "She will do just as she pleases."[29]

Work proved the most potent source of conflict. All too often, inmates simply refused to undertake required labor, as did Miss Hanes, who "when requested by the Matron to assist by 'washing the plate,' refused in a Very Saucy manner . . . declar[ing] that she would prefer to leave the Home rather than do the work desired." Equally recalcitrant was Eleanor Young, a sixty-five-year-old semiretired nurse, whom the matron described as "quarrelsome" and "ungovernable." Young flagrantly violated the rules, refusing to nurse her infirm roommate and explicitly rejecting the servile status Home residence sought to impose. "She did not come into the Home to wait upon others, but to be waited upon." This was insubordination and "impertinence" at its worst, a glaring absence of the "quiet, gentle and lady-like deportment" the rules required. Young, it turned out, *was* willing to wait upon others—but for a price. In an era when nurses resided with their patients until they recovered or succumbed, she left the Home when paying opportunities arose—ignoring the rule against paid employment—and returned between jobs. Other inmates, like Martha Davis, disguised remunerative labor as friendly visiting, claiming, when confronted by the committee, "that she does not go out to nurse, but only visits friends who do not feel very well."[30]

The ladies and gentlemen of the Executive Committee dealt harshly with insubordination, threatening disobedient "children" with expulsion and sometimes making good on the threat. They turned at least one inmate over to the administrators of the dreaded city almshouse.[31] Certainly, the mere fact of defiance riled committee members, who expected gratitude not insolence. Gainfully employed inmates were a special embarrassment, for they implied that the Home—already fending off rumors that it nearly starved its inmates—did not adequately support them. Women who publicly pursued wages, more so than those who labored invisibly and unpaid within the Home's walls, belied pretensions to "repose." In insisting on pursuing their previous professions, women like Davis and Young refused the dependent image their benefactors had constructed for them. They saw their relation to the Home as governed by contract, not sentiment. Having "paid their money," they transformed relations of benevolence into market transactions. They cast their lots not with the sentimental model of the idealized home but with the contractual freedoms of the marketplace—even if that marketplace had once failed them. In doing so they did their best to turn their Home into a mere boardinghouse.

Boarding "Homes"

"What is your first impression of the life in the Warrenton St. Home?" a newcomer was asked. "More than anything else it is a home." This bit of dialogue, recorded in an unpublished "Account of the Origin of the Boston Young Women's Christian Association," neatly summed up the goals of the YWCA and kindred agencies. Like the organizations responsible for sailors' and old age homes, associations that provided refuge to young workingwomen insisted that the residences they sponsored were "boarding *homes*," not boardinghouses.[32]

Boarding homes for young women proliferated in American cities from the 1850s onward. Organizations like the YWCA, the Ladies Christian Union (for Protestants), and the Young Woman's Catholic Association identified a distinctive clientele: "friendless" young women new to the city. To the "young, the inexperienced, the morally weak, the stranger within our city doors, the discouraged, and perhaps the tempted," boarding homes offered "protection and prevention." Annual reports, institutional histories, testimonials, and government documents repeated melodramatic tales of rescue. These stories, fast becoming clichés, invariably pitted rural innocence against urban vice and corruption. "Ignorant of the dangers and snares in which our cities abound," young women found safety, spiritual guidance, and moral supervision at boarding homes. There they were "carefully shielded from the evils and dangers that surround them." As a grateful mother explained, residence at one of the YWCA's boarding homes saved her daughter "from impending ruin."[33]

The YWCA and kindred organizations adopted this nomenclature partly in self-defense. Given the widespread association between boarding and moral danger, Christian associations could hardly claim that they ran boardinghouses for young women. As for conventional sorts of homes, boardinghouses provided convenient foils. "The main point of difference between boarding-houses and boarding-homes," explained the *Seventeenth Annual Report of the Boston Young Women's Christian Association,* "is in the primary object of each; that of boarding and lodging-houses being to make money, or otherwise to further self-interest, while boarding-homes seek solely the benefit of those they entertain." Motivated by benevolence, boarding homes offered "protection and watchful care." Motivated by profit, boardinghouses did not. "Some of those who come to us say 'that their life in boarding houses is one unbroken series of temptations, and that those who are kept from evil almost wonder at their own escape,'" the Boston YWCA solemnly declared. Travelers' aid societies, organized by the YWCA and the Young Travelers' Aid Society met at docks and train stations "friendless" women, who might otherwise fall into the clutches of boardinghouse runners, who promised desirable accommodations but who planned to convey their unsuspecting victims to houses of prostitution. Even legitimate boardinghouses, as the YWCA saw it, offered temptations. "Their room-mates are not of the right kind, and exert an influence unfavorable to what is elevating and refined." Echoing familiar complaints, the YWCA reasoned that boardinghouses, in contrast to boarding homes, revolved around "harmful gossip." "Spiritual life" was absent. Boardinghouse residents, "thrown together by chance," could only compose an "ill-assorted group." Young women who lived in boardinghouses, the author of "Boarding Homes and Clubs for Working Women" explained, "may even cherish the idea of home, but what a home! Cold and cheerless rooms, insanitary [*sic*] conditions, poorly cooked and poorly served food, uncultured and even uncouth associates, unattractive and filthy streets, and perhaps other social surroundings that tend to take the blush of modesty from the cheek and the sense of shame from the heart—these are the characteristics of such a home." This, then, was the mission of organizations like the YWCA and the Ladies Christian Union: to save young women from assorted evils by making sure they lived in boarding homes, not boardinghouses.[34]

"The central object of the Young Women's Christian Association is its HOME," the fifth annual report of the organization's Boston branch asserted in 1871. Its rhetoric changed little over the next two decades. "It is a pleasant sound to ears that are often weary with the discord of daily life, to hear the ring of a merry laughter, and the bouncing step of our girls returning 'home' as they call it," the association noted in 1896. "We love to hear them say: 'I haven't had a homesick minute since I came.'" Familial metaphors abounded. "We would reaffirm the statement that our homes are not boarding-houses merely, but embrace families," explained one annual report. In 1889 the YWCA proudly claimed that it "shelter[ed] three hundred daughters." A former resident signed her letter, "One of the Children." Another emphasized her "earnest desire to express to you my affectionate and grateful appreciation of the Home,—for, indeed, it has been such to me for the past three years." Most important of all was the "maternal love"—"pre-eminent in the idea of home"—that YWCA families provided. Even as it invoked home, the YWCA redefined the term, for the homes it created were exclusively the domain of mothers and daughters, not "ill-assorted groups" that included both sexes. Maternity, appropriately enough, fell to the matron, who (as in the Home for Aged Women) shouldered enormous administrative and psychic responsibilities. "On her depend the existence and power of the home-feeling, which we are so desirous should be enjoyed by every member of the family."[35]

"*Christian* love"—in the YWCA's case, exclusively Protestant—in addition to maternal affection, provided a necessary ingredient for home life.

YWCA residents went "to their daily employment in the morning, and return[ed] at evening to a home of refinement, Christian influence, and rest," and, of course to "family devotions."[36] Even institutional rules ("founded on liberal principles . . . without being too arbitrary or too strict") worked in the service of home, for they were "regulations established for the government of the family." Boarding homes, the Boston YWCA claimed, offered "all the freedom and all the protection of a family roof."[37]

As might be expected, considerable distance separated rhetoric and reality. What sort of home—or what sort of boardinghouse for that matter—sheltered "three hundred daughters"? Daughters, for their part, expressed ambivalence, even animosity, toward the homes that protected them. They often found their surroundings less than cheerful, their food less than appealing, and their rules less than "liberal."

Dorothy Richardson's semifictional "story of a New York working girl," *The Long Day* (1905), painted a grim portrait of a boarding home. Homeless and nearly penniless after a fire destroys her lodging house, Richardson's heroine seeks shelter at a working-girls home, quite possibly the Margaret Louisa Home of the New York YWCA.[38] The Home was anything but welcoming. Located in a "shabby, respectable, unfriendly-looking building of red brick," its black door with its silver nameplate reminded Richardson of "a coffin set on end." An attendant ushered her into a cheerless reception room decorated with "a series of framed scriptural texts, all of which served to remind one in no ambiguous terms of the wrath of God toward the forward-hearted and of the eternal punishment that awaits unrepentant sinners." "Gloomy hallways" and "unpainted oaken stairs scoured white as a bone" awaited her as she passed beyond the reception room. The sitting room, "an empty, ugly place, with bare floors and whitewashed walls," offered none of the accouterments that would have graced the parlor of a late-Victorian home or even a third-rate boardinghouse. No overstuffed furniture, no florid wallpaper, no carpets, pianos, houseplants, or mirrors, no decorations, save a second sampling of "framed scriptural texts." Nothing but "whitewashed purity." Richardson's message was clear: this Home was no home.[39]

Richardson depicts an unappealing cast of characters: a greedy and dishonest matron named Mrs. Pitbladder and her assistant, nicknamed "Old Gum Heels" by the residents. Either could have come from the pages of Gunn's *Physiology*. Old Gum Heels, named for her rubber capped shoes ("What her real name was I never found out")—was a "flat-figured, elderly spinster" as spare as the Home itself. Mrs. Pitbladder, on the other hand, was "very fat." She possessed a "round, red face—the very sort of face in which one would have expected good nature to repose." Alas, her "huge, beaked nose" and "furtive eyes" suggested otherwise. Here Richardson resorted to the peculiar anti-Semitism of boardinghouse lore, the Gentile boardinghouse keeper with a "Jewish" demeanor and behavior. Like a "cheap" boarding-house keeper, Mrs. Pitbladder literally swallowed her boarders' meager resources. She routinely cheated "girls" as they paid their rent, refusing to give them their change. She overcharged them for inadequate meals. She masqueraded as the matron of a working-girls' home, but she was a boardinghouse keeper in all but name. The Home's overseers, guilty of pious neglect, offered little relief. "There was a board of managers,—ladies who sometimes came to look at the dormitories, and the bath-rooms and then went away again in their carriages."[40]

Someone associated with the Boston YWCA clipped an undated newspaper story for its files. Authored by Evelyn Malcolm, a prolific producer of romantic fiction, and written in the investigative style popular at the turn of the twentieth century, it, too, offered a less than complimentary portrait of a boarding home. "In a Working-Girls Home" did not name the institution it described, but knowledgeable readers would have quickly identified it as the Young Women's Home run by the Ladies' Christian Union, located in the once-fashionable New York neighborhood of Washington Square.[41] Posing as a working girl in search of lodging and echoing Richardson's funereal themes, Malcolm first encountered the establishment's parlor, "a marvel of funereal severity. Sofas and chairs of black horsehair were arranged in prim rows, a few faded steel engravings in dingy gilt frames hung on the walls, hymn-books were arranged in stiff piles upon a well-worn piano, and on the center-table was a huge family Bible." The forbidding matron, "one of those sternly good women to whom self-denial appears a paramount virtue," bore little resemblance to the motherly figures that populated annual reports. Her first task was to ensure that Malcolm was a Protestant, a requirement for admission. In keeping with themes echoed in the YWCA's promotional literature, she assured Malcolm that the establishment's purpose was to protect young women "from the dangers which beset them in this great city." The "danger" in Malcolm's partly tongue-in-cheek account turned out to be the theater. The 10:30 curfew, deliberately set before the theaters closed, allowed "the residents to enjoy a concert occasionally" but not the theater. As the matron made explained, "We prefer not to take boarders who are fond of worldly amusements."

Malcolm found the Home's routines petty and restrictive. The "rising bell, as noisy as a train of cars," awakened residents at six. "You must be down to breakfast at 7 o'clock or go without any." Young women who had completed a grueling week's labor had the choice of rising for an eight o'clock breakfast on Sunday, their one day of rest, or going hungry. Going hungry might have been preferable, for Malcolm's description of the food easily could have passed for boardinghouse satire: a piece of steak for breakfast "about as large as a visiting card," "dried herring and weak tea" for lunch, mutton soup, a "thin, watery fluid, in color like a mixture of chalk and water" for supper.

Malcolm also found fault with the close quarters—six to seven women to a room, the thin walls through which snoring "sound[ed] like a bugle call to duty." A "caste" system substituted for family feeling. "The $5 per week aristocrats who luxuriated two and four in a room" snubbed "$3 per week plebians." Both the size of the establishment and its unrelenting femininity made for a most unnatural family. "Grace was said, bean soup was served and eighty-five unmarried, honest, Protestant working women attacked their dinner. Think of it. I looked at this startling array of petticoats and sighed. There was no variety, no little children, no men—women everywhere!" Malcolm articulated what most observers failed to say: the sex and age-specific population of places like the Young Women's Home unmasked any pretension to replicate home.

Nor did this Home succeed in extracting itself from the market. Malcolm ended on a gloomy note, quoting one of the residents thus: "We are supposed in a Home of this kind to get good board at very low rates, but what we live on isn't worth a penny more than $3 per week."[42] A Home whose worth could readily be calculated in dollars and cents was no home at all.

It isn't clear why Malcolm's piece made it into the Boston YWCA's files. Perhaps it was cause for smug self-congratulation, the Boston organization concluding that its boarding homes were nothing like the New York establishment Malcolm described. More likely, it supported an exercise in self-criticism. Officers of the association were puzzled when the new home on Warrenton Street, which opened in 1874, did not immediately fill. Perhaps, they acknowledged, "the boarders are placed under too many regulations, and young women cannot give up their independence." Still, they remained perplexed, for the regulations were no more than what "any reasonable father or mother" would impose. The problem, which YWCA officials only dimly seemed to grasp, was partly generational. Young women new to the city more often hoped to escape home than to recreate it. As successive generations adapted to urban life—

as they increasingly perceived the city as offering adventure rather than danger—they bypassed Homes altogether, opting for boarding, lodging, and rooming houses—and eventually, apartments—instead. Against this newly cosmopolitan backdrop, the YWCA's warnings sounded increasingly shrill, its rules and regulations outmoded.[43]

"Independence" also meant avoiding dependence of the sort that inmates in other Homes experienced; the YWCA worried that young women had "the impression . . . that the Home of the Boston Young Women's Christian Association is a charitable institution." Or, as Mary Fergusson, the author of a national study of boarding homes commissioned by the U.S. Department of Labor, admitted, "The objection often urged to the name of 'Home,' [is] that it is suggestive of an institution and has about it the odor of charity."[44] Highly aware of these associations, at least one organization tried to create an institution that was not a home at all.

"The House Is Not a Home"

Describing yet another New York landmark in his mammoth *Great Metropolis*, *Tribune* reporter Junius Browne noted, "The house is not a home, as many suppose. It is the special design of the directors that it should not be." This was a curious "design" for a nineteenth-century charitable institution, especially one whose client population consisted of young boys. But the administrators of the Newsboys' Lodging House deliberately termed their establishment a lodging house, *not* a home. "If it were," Browne explained, "the lodgers would lose their self-reliance and ambition."[45] The etymology of the Newsboys' Lodging House, founded in 1854, suggests just how quickly Homes had become associated with charity and dependence, qualities that disparaged and symbolically feminized their inhabitants. The Newsboys' Lodging House, then, attempted to solve a key social problem: preserving its residents' independence, ambition, and incipient masculinity by creating a house that was not a home.

The Lodging-House and its parent organization, the Children's Aid Society (CAS), were the creations of child saver Charles Loring Brace, who had first come to New York to study at the Union Theological Seminary. Jolted by the death of his beloved sister and confronted with the rampant crime, vice, and poverty of the metropolis, social problems he quickly realized that religion alone could not solve, Brace abandoned his plans for a ministerial career. A year of working for the Five Points Mission convinced him that the adult inhabitants of the notorious slum were long past redemption. Children, not yet hardened by their debauched environments, might still be saved.[46]

Brace was every bit as enamored with home as other nineteenth-century reformers, perhaps even more so. Homes were central to Brace and the organization he founded. But he distinguished between actual homes and institutional homes, finding the latter wanting. Brace, a fawning admirer recalled, "solved the problem which had baffled the philanthropists of preceding centuries. He saw that home life, and not institution life, was needed for children, and so he set himself to finding homes for homeless children."[47] Best known for its controversial practice of placing street children in rural homes (a goal it termed "Emigration"), the CAS rejected orphanages and asylums in favor of the "individual influence" private homes could provide. Crowding homeless and delinquent children together in institutions, Brace believed, only increased their tendencies toward vice. Equally important, asylum children absorbed lessons of dependency. Institutions, Brace explained, "breed a species of character which is monastic, indolent, unused to struggle; subordinate, indeed, but with little independence and manly vigor." Asylum residence "weaken[ed] . . . true masculine vigor." Brace's particular concern, his gendered language suggests, was with maintaining self-reliance among boys, whom he imagined as future masters of their own modest households, a role for which he believed asylum life offered little preparation. A boy "ought to learn to draw his own water, and to split his wood, kindle his fires, and light his candle," Brace insisted. "As an 'institutional child,' he is lighted, warmed, and watered by machinery." Institutional homes bred dependency; "real" homes, self-reliance. Far better than confining children to orphanages was to remove them from the urban "wilderness of vice and degradation" to wholesome rural environments, where they would learn "honest, healthy labor."[48]

"Emigration" was Brace's ideal solution, but it was only one of the society's interlocking strategies. The CAS constructed a remarkable network of children's social services within New York City itself. It opened offices in "every miserable neighborhood," dispensing moral and material assistance to poor children and their families. It held "boy's meetings" intended to bring the gospel to impoverished waifs. It sponsored "industrial schools," which taught "habits of industry" and trade skills of dubious value to impoverished young girls and eventually to young boys as well. It set up lodging houses for homeless boys and, eventually, separate establishments for homeless girls. The first of these was the Newsboys' Lodging House.

Brace considered newsboys (a generic term that included boot blacks, match sellers, and "independent little dealers" of all sorts as well as boys who hawked newspapers) "a distinct class." He believed they merited inclusion among those he famously termed the "dangerous classes," for they "bore to the busy, wealthy world about them something of the same relation which Indians bear to the civilized Western settler." Like the Indians of Brace's imagination, "they had no settled homes, and lived on the outskirts of society . . . their wits sharpened like those of a savage, and their principles often no better."[49] Yet Brace was drawn to these homeless youngsters (as was the pulp writer Horatio Alger, who made the Newsboys' Lodging House his informal headquarters and modeled many of his boy heroes on its inmates). Indeed, as one historian notes, Brace was an "instinctive Darwinist" who believed that those who survived the fierce struggles of slum life constituted a superior breed of humanity. The trick, of course, was to set these hardy individuals on the right path before their environments got the best of them.[50]

Brace treated the readers of his magnum opus, *The Dangerous Classes*, to a romantic newsboy culture. The newsboy possessed a "light-hearted nature" and was "always ready to make fun of his own suffering." Brace admired his pluck, his generosity ("he . . . will always divide his last sixpence with a poorer boy"), and his "code." ("He will not get drunk; he pays his debts to other boys, and thinks it dishonorable to sell papers on their beat.") Most of all, Brace admired his "sturdy independence."[51]

Brace wished to help newsboys without weakening this independence, the "best quality of this class." Help they certainly needed. Some were orphans; some had fled abusive parents; others had reluctantly left homes that could not or would not support them. Brace found them sleeping under stairwells, atop steam gratings, and inside boxes, burnt-out safes, even "in the iron tube of the bridge at Harlem." He conceived of the Lodging House, which provided a bed for six cents a night and supper for an additional three, as a "hotel for boys." In keeping with his antipathy toward dependence, Brace determined "to treat the lads as independent little dealers, and give them nothing without payment, but at the same time to offer them much more for their money than they could get anywhere else."[52]

The Lodging House debuted in the spring of 1854, staking its claim in the heart of newsboy territory in an upper story of the *New York Sun* building at the corner of Nassau and Fulton Streets. Occupying commercial rather than residential space, it was not to be mistaken for a home. It was, as its name implied, properly termed a *lodging house*. It was not even a boardinghouse, for it offered one, not three, meals a day, and boys had to pay extra for their supper. Brace rejected the familial language and internal practices associated with institutional homes. Indeed, he publicly ridiculed their familial pretensions: "We hear, in these Reports from the Institutions, of one person presiding over five hundred children, and it is asserted that he manages this family on the purest parental principles." The Lodging House refused admission to applicants its supervisors deemed "too old or too vicious." Otherwise, its policies, in contrast to most Homes, were remarkably ecumenical. It took in boys of all ethnicities and religions, serving Protestants, Catholics, and Jews (religious education at the Lodging House, however, was predictably Protestant), occasionally crossing the color line. Boys were not confined to the establishment, as they would have been in an orphanage or house of refuge, but came and went as they pleased. Transience was expected and desired. "It is not our wish that the lodgers should remain long," an early annual report declared.[53]

But if the Newsboys' Lodging House was not a home, it was not a run-of-the-mill "cheap" lodging house either, as two contrasting illustrations reproduced in *The Dangerous Classes* made clear. The first, titled "Lodging Houses Prior to 1854," depicted a ragged assemblage of all ages and both sexes, some sitting, some reclining, on a bare, and presumably dirty, floor. They have come, literally, to occupy a "spot" for the night. Cleanliness, light, and order prevail in the second image, "The Newsboys' Lodging House." Boys prepare to retire under the watchful eyes of kindly superintendents, some of them kneeling in prayer before climbing into one of the bunks that line the walls. These portraits, embellished though they must have been, were not entirely fictional. Divided into two large rooms—one a combination schoolroom, reading room, playroom, and meeting room, and the other a dormitory fitted up for ninety boys—the Newsboys' Lodging House offered little privacy, a quality few street children experienced or expected. But it promised considerable comfort, especially compared to the available alternatives. Years later, one early resident still remembered his "nice little bed with warm comforters and clean sheets."[54]

The story of the Lodging House's first night, repeated in Brace's *Dangerous Classes* and Children's Aid Society histories, quickly assumed the status of founding myth. Potential lodgers, so the story goes, eyed the establishment with suspicion but decided to try it for "a lark," some plotting to create chaos by starting "a general scrimmage in the school room—first cutting off the gas," which would have plunged the rooms into darkness, and then creating "a row in the bedroom." The superintendent, a former carpenter named Christian Tracy, learned of the scheme, and "in a bland and benevolent way, nipped their plans in the bud." He stood guard over the gas valves, and the lights remained on. He "politely dismissed . . . the rough ring-leaders." The first boy to throw his boots—the signal to start the planned bedroom brawl—was quickly evicted. The remaining lodgers consequently "thought it better to nestle in their warm beds." Few of them actually slept. Instead, they spent the night marveling at their new surroundings. Brace recorded their "ejaculations" in his rendition of newsboy dialect: "I say, Jim, this is rather better 'an bummin'. My eyes! What soft beds these is!' 'Tom, it's 'most as good as a steamgratin', and there ain't no M.P.'s to poke, neither. I'm glad I ain't a bummer to-night.' "[55]

Soft beds were merely means to a larger end: transforming street boys—independent little dealers who already possessed the necessary raw materials—into "honest and industrious citizens." The society's religious, educational, and moral goals had to be introduced gradually, Brace explained. Newsboys not only had a "peculiar dread of Sunday schools," they feared such institutions were "pious dodges" intended to lure them to houses of refuge. (He failed to mention that one of the dodges poor children feared was the Children's Aid Society itself, which eagerly transported "orphans" westward, often without bothering to confirm the absence or approval of parents or relatives.) Apart from a bath (a requirement of admission), persuasion, not coercion, prevailed. When Mr. Tracy reported that a potential employer had visited, promising the sizeable sum of three dollars a week to any boy "who could write a good hand" (a skill few "newsies" possessed), lodgers reacted enthusiastically to his proposition: "Well, now, suppose we have a night-school, and learn to write—what do you say, boys?" Sunday meetings, which quickly become a Lodging House "institution," as Brace put it, arose "in a similarly discreet manner." When a public funeral "impressed" the boys, "Mr. Tracy suggested they listen to a little reading from the Bible." Hoping to curb newsboys' "especial vice of money-wasting," Tracy opened a savings bank, "allowing the boys to vote how long it should be closed." "The small daily deposits accumulated to such a degree that the opening gave them a great surprise at the amounts which they possessed," Brace recalled. No longer savages, "they began to feel thus the 'sense of property,' and the desire of accumulation, which, economists tell us, is the base of all civilization."[56]

Brace offered an appealing account of self-reformation that required little encouragement, save a bit of well-intentioned prodding. Newsboys themselves reportedly participated in this moral suasion, urging their comrades to abandon extravagance and vice. A reporter for the *New York Times* recorded a colorful speech by "Paddy" (reprinted in the CAS's 1861 annual report and again in *The Dangerous Classes*), who adopted the confessional idiom popularized by Washingtonian temperance men in the 1840s: "I say, bummers—for you're *all* bummers—*I was a bummer once*—I hate to see you spendin' your money on penny ice creams. Why don't you save your money? You feller without no boots, how would you like a new pair, eh?" The Newsboys' Lodging House, in Brace's view, stood in stark and agreeable contrast to conventional asylums and houses of refuge. The latter promoted "an increase of apparent virtues, and a hidden growth of secret and contagious vices," while the boys' Lodging House inspired the development of genuine virtues—piety, cleanliness, ambition, and thrift—nipping vice in the bud just as surely as Tracy had thwarted plans for a first-night riot.[57]

Yet, in several respects Brace's Newsboys' Lodging House bore more than a passing resemblance to institutions he deplored. Certainly, it resorted to not entirely dissimilar methods of coercion. Boys who arrived early got a free supper but could not leave until morning—a means of preventing theater attendance—which contradicted assertions that boys "could come and go as they pleased." The kindly Mr. Tracy deviated from his supervisor's intentions, describing himself as "father" to the boys. But he was not above threatening absent boys he encountered on the streets with arrest and confinement to the House of Refuge if they failed to return to the Lodging House. Even Brace got a bit carried away, praising Tracy's successors, the O'Connors, for "their discipline, order, good management, and excellent housekeeping." Without a trace of misgiving, he noted Charles O'Connor's "very good preliminary experience for this work" in the British army during the Crimean War and his resulting "excellent" discipline. (Mixing his military metaphors, Brace claimed the floors of the Lodging House were "as clean as a man-of-war's deck.") "The Sunday-evening meetings are as attentive and orderly as a church, the week-evening school quiet and studious," Brace reported approvingly. "All that mass of wild young humanity is kept in perfect order, and brought under a thousand good influences." Lapsing uncharacteristically into language more appropriate to institutional homes, he noted that Mrs. O'Connor "has been almost like a mother to the boys."[58]

Yet, Brace insisted, the Newsboys' Lodging House was not a Home. It did not offer mere charity; boys had to pay for the privilege of a night's lodging. They worked at their street trades by day, returning to the "Lodge" at night for supper, evening school, and religious meetings. Brace emphasized, even overemphasized, the transient nature of the Lodging House's population. He reported the number of lodgings first, lodgers second. "In the course of a year the population of a town passes through the Lodging-house—in 1869 and '70, *eight thousand eight hundred and thirty-five* different boys."[59] In an era in which homes implied permanence and boardinghouses transience, the Newsboys' Lodging House fell safely in the latter category.

Brace's celebration of transience raised as many questions as it answered. How did the Lodging House impart "economy, good order, cleanliness, . . . morality" and "Religion" to a constantly shifting population? How did successive generations of newsboys learn these lessons without the kinds of external restraints for which asylums were famous? (Brace's glowing portrait of the O'Connors' discipline suggests they did not.) How long did a boy have to reside at the Lodging House in order for Brace's lessons to "take"? How could one be certain that it didn't operate just like an asylum, ensuring only "an increase of apparent virtues," instead of genuine transformation?[60]

For many boys the Lodging House's goals succeeded all too well. Complaints that "it is exceedingly difficult to get them in here and induce them to stay" suggested that newsies could be *too* transient, leaving before the institution had effected any meaningful reformation. Some left because the Lodging House (serving as "intelligence office" as well as "school, church, . . . and hotel") found them better paying jobs as clerks-in-training. In the society's eyes, it succeeded best when it persuaded newsboys to "emigrate," departing with Mr. Tracy (who took over the position of escort in 1857) for "homes" in the "west." Emigration demanded that little adults turn back into children; it is difficult to imagine Brace's idealized newsboy—self-supporting, self-reliant, imbued with a "sense of property"—adjusting easily to a farmer's paternal authority. And as several scholars have noted, the happy endings described in CAS reports materialized all too rarely. All too often, children placed by the CAS in rural homes endured physical and sexual abuse; all too often farmers saw them not as sons and daughters but as cheap labor. Demonstrating that "homes" could be just as fleeting as lodging-houses, many abandoned their new "families." Even Brace admitted "the larger boys" sent west left "their places frequently."[61]

The majority of Lodging House residents seem neither to have "emigrated" nor to have acquired more respectable employment or habits. Rather, they used the House when it served their needs, "snoozing" (sleeping outdoors) when it did not, especially in warm weather.[62] And a small number confounded the Lodging House's purposes altogether by staying not "for days, weeks, or months, but for years"—turning the Lodging House into a home.

The Newsboys' Lodging House survived well into the twentieth century, moving to ever-larger quarters, serving ever-larger numbers of boys, who no doubt continued to use the institution for their own purposes. Its legacy, like that of the other institutions profiled here, is to demonstrate the difficulty of distinguishing between transience and permanence, homes and market-places, boardinghouses and homes—indeed, between different types of "homes." Since boardinghouses served in part to define the very meaning of *home,* the founders of benevolent Homes predictably enlisted them as convenient foils. In some cases, like that of the Home for Aged Women, the contrast was largely metaphorical. (Though surely some of the "dilapidated and cheerless rooms" in which future residents huddled were in boarding-houses.)[63] In others, like the Seaman's Home and boarding homes for working girls, benevolent men and women self-consciously advocated Homes as alternatives to actual boardinghouses. Thwarted by the growing size and "unnatural" homogeneity of the "families" they housed, the rules and regulations their management necessitated, and the often-conflicting desires of their inmates, Homes rarely lived up to their names. Charles Loring Brace's caustic critique of institutions, public and private, unmasked their domestic pretensions. Yet, the rural homes to which his clients ideally "emigrated" just as rarely resembled the bourgeois ideal.

In short, the language of domesticity was both rich and impoverished, the influence of home both powerful and fragile. Brace, however, was correct to tout the modernity of his creation. Increasingly, adults of modest means—like boys who had few options—would choose to live in lodging houses, in part because boardinghouses had become too much like homes.

"Decay of the Boarding-House"

The boardinghouse, the *New York Times* declared in 1878, "represents the sinking industry of Manhattan, and . . . in its sinking evokes few tears even from them whose lachrymose glands are most easily and needlessly disturbed." In claiming that boarding was a "sinking industry," the *Times* reporter exaggerated, for boardinghouses would remain important institutions for decades to come. Yet, he did pinpoint the very beginnings of a trend. As the nineteenth century waned and the twentieth century beckoned, American urbanites increasingly abandoned boardinghouses for greener pastures. As the *Times* put it, "boarders have simply ceased to be boarders; they have decided to live more wholesomely and satisfactorily."[1]

Not surprisingly, given nearly half a century of antiboardinghouse discourse, living more wholesomely in the *Times*' view meant relocating to a "home" or its equivalent by removing to "suburban places" or "set[ting] up house-keeping in a small way." Improvements in public transportation made suburban residence practical and affordable for increasing numbers of white-collar employees; apartments would emerge as the domiciles of choice for middle-class families who could not or would not escape the city. For the *Times* reporter and numerous other Americans, keeping house, even "in a small way," was key to wholesomeness, for the apartments the *Times* championed were not the cooperative endeavors or kitchenless apartment hotels envisioned by feminist housing reformers. Apart from residences constructed specifically for bachelors, the apartments that eventually triumphed were the sorts with which we are familiar today, each with its own kitchen. Only dwellings that ensured that women performed their wifely duties by allowing them to keep house "in a small way"—in other words, those that resembled miniature versions of middle-class homes—achieved widespread social approval.[2]

Working-class families had always lived in "apartments"; indeed, one of the key challenges early apartment builders faced was to distinguish them from the crowded tenements that packed urban slums. Single people of moderate means, what housing reformer Albert Wolfe called "the great middle class of clerks, salesmen, skilled mechanics, and miscellaneous industrial workers," might also room together in apartments or, if uncommonly prosperous, live alone. More often, they opted for lodging houses (also called rooming houses and furnished-room houses), which provided a place to sleep but no meals. Wolfe found that the number of boarders in Boston had decreased from 15,938 to 9,496 between 1885 and 1895; at the same time the number of lodgers increased from 24,280 to 44,926 (though in the state's smaller cities the change was far less pronounced and boarders in many cases continued to outnumber lodgers).[3]

Like the boardinghouses they slowly replaced, the quality and clientele of rooming and lodging houses varied. In some cities, for example, Boston and San Francisco, the term *lodging house* described all sorts of establishments. More often, *rooming house* or *furnished room house* connoted fairly comfortable quarters that housed skilled and clerical workers, *lodging house* a flophouse that charged transients a few cents a night for a tiny cubicle or a spot on the floor. Both *tenement* and *apartment* families might take in a lodger or two, offering him a room or a portion of a room, expecting him to take his meals elsewhere. At the other end of the scale were the purpose-built structures that sheltered twenty to thirty souls. Most commonly, however, lodging houses were either former "homes" or former boardinghouses. Even more so than boardinghouses, they clustered in particular places. Usually located within walking distance of their inhabitants' workplaces and dependent on the presence of nearby restaurants, saloons, and laundries, lodging-house districts emerged in neighborhoods like Boston's South End (a neighborhood Wolfe described as having been invaded by "an army of lodgers and lodging-house keepers"), San Francisco's Western Addition, and Chicago's Near North Side.[4]

Like the apartments that sheltered their wealthier counterparts, lodging houses offered their residents greater privacy and freedom. Lodgers, especially those who chose not to live with "private families," could lock their doors and theoretically live safe from the prying eyes of inquisitive landladies and curious housemates. (In reality, lodging-house keepers, ever alert to the coming and goings of residents and their guests, could be every bit as nosy as their predecessors.) They could eat their meals whenever they wished and, depending on the size of their respective pocketbooks and the quality of the available "cuisine," they could eat *whatever* they wished instead of having to subsist on what penny-pinching landladies might lay before them.[5]

Such arrangements, however imperfect, appealed to landladies as well. Keeping lodgers instead of boarders vastly decreased their workloads and allowed them to do without the trouble and expense of hiring servants. Lodging houses, moreover, provided landladies and their lodgers with greater psychological if not physical space, freeing them from some—although by no means all—of the emotional intimacies that led to misunderstanding.[6]

Yet boardinghouses lived on—in fact and in the popular imagination. A glance at any city newspaper—the *Indianapolis News*, the *Louisville Courier-Journal*, the *San Francisco Chronicle*, the *Boston Globe*, the *New York Times*—shows that some people continued to take in boarders and others continued to search for places that offered board—continuing as well to specify their preferences for "private families"—well into the 1920s, 1930s, and 1940s, even the 1950s. "BOARD AND ROOM—HOME COOKING," a 1949 ad in the *Chicago Tribune* promised.[7]

Boardinghouse lore and boardinghouses themselves remained alive and well in twentieth-century popular culture. During World War I–era speaking tours that promoted "thoroughgoing 100 per cent Americanism," former president Theodore Roosevelt warned that "divided loyalty" and the "politico-racial hyphen" would transform "the republic founded by Washington and saved by Lincoln . . . into a mere polyglot boarding house." In the winter and spring of 1920, the *Chicago Tribune* invited readers to submit their "human interest stories" to "Boarding House Tales," promising to pay one dollar for each entry it published. The tales trod familiar territory. They featured the usual cast of characters—stingy landladies, star boarders, nosy lodgers—and inevitably focused on food—weak coffee, watered-down cream, biscuits so heavy that boarders dubbed them "sinkers," and butter "old enough to speak for itself." Long after the *Tribune* moved on to other subjects, mothers continued to admonish their children for using the boardinghouse reach at the dinner table. As late as the 1940s, an advice columnist for *Calling All Boys* reminded "Frank," a teenage reader who complained about chores, of the folly of thinking of "home" as "a place where a fellow is the star boarder, where he can get a lot of free service from people who love him." In Frank Capra's iconic masterpiece, *It's a Wonderful Life* (1946), the angel Clarence shows the suicidal George Bailey what would have happened if he'd never been born. Bedford Falls becomes Pottersville (named after the town's misanthropic millionaire), its downtown a maze of neon lights advertising tawdry entertainments. At the climax of this dystopian scene, Bailey knocks on his mother's door and finds that his childhood home has been transformed into "Ma Bailey's Boardinghouse," his loving mother into a suspicious landlady who doesn't recognize him: "I don't take in strangers unless they're sent here by somebody I know."[8]

Even in this gloomy scenario, the widowed "Ma Bailey," driven to boardinghouse keeping because she has no sons to support her, does not aid and abet vice; rather, she stands as a bulwark against it, adamantly refusing to admit "strangers." TR's bombastic nationalism aside, what's striking about twentieth-century representations of boardinghouses—as opposed to their nineteenth-century predecessors—is that they seem to have been uniformly benign. They drew on longstanding traditions of boardinghouse humor, poking gentle fun at boarding places and their inhabitants, but rarely portrayed either as physical or moral threats. Cartoonist Rube Goldberg—known for his fantastical creations—sketched a "special meatball passer for boarding houses . . . a little device [that] does away with the boarding house reach." *The Boarding House Reach* also served as the title of a 1948 comic play in which Wilbur Maxwell, an enterprising youngster who wants money to buy a bicycle, turns his family's home into "Maxwell's Boardinghouse" in his parents' absence. Predictably, he attracts a series of seedy and eccentric characters: Limpy McGuire and his wife, Nora; Ninety-Volt Jones, a boxer, and his wife, Roughhouse Ruby, a wrestler; Lucy Burns ("the typical old maid school teacher type"), and Mrs. Mott ("a little old lady who never says a word"). Comic mischief ensues; it turns out that McGuire is a bank robber. Despite a close call, all ends well. McGuire gets his just deserts, Wilbur gets his bicycle, and "home" is restored.[9]

It was in a long-running comic strip that boardinghouses perhaps made their most enduring twentieth-century mark. A nineteenth-century reader would have found *Our Boarding House* (1921–81) utterly familiar. Thomas Butler Gunn could have created it. Mrs. Hoople, the landlady, fends off misbehaving lodgers and suspicious interlopers with mops and brooms; she insists that boarders pay their "feed and stall bills." Major Hoople, her deadbeat husband, is a "boardinghouse betty." He continually dreams up get-rich-quick schemes that come to naught, managing to avoid honest labor and physical effort. He plans a "gypsy exit" when Mrs. Hoople enlists his aid in "general housecleaning"; a "fat, fireplace porpoise," he even refuses to shovel the front sidewalk. The boarders, too, are characters that nineteenth-century Americans would have recognized: luckless spinsters, nervous bachelors, and peculiar "Professors." All compete in the "Saturday night marathon," hoping to avoid the long line that forms outside the single bathroom as boarders wait to take their weekly baths.[10]

Increasingly, then, producers and consumers of popular culture viewed boardinghouses not as an unfortunate fact of life but as old-fashioned, inevitably shabby institutions, run by married women with worthless husbands or widows down on their luck, and inhabited by spinsters, failures, leeches, and cheapskates. If the nineteenth-century folklore pioneered by Gunn, Q. Philander Doesticks, and countless lesser-known and anonymous humorists survived in *Our Boarding House*, fears of moral and physical danger did not. By the mid-twentieth century, boardinghouses had become quaint reminders of a bygone age and, by and large, harmless.

Battered by such developments as the 1920s "revolution in manners and morals," the sexual revolution of the 1960s, feminist critiques, and rising divorce rates that have nothing to do with boardinghouses, the home has lost some of its luster. Yet, in its physical and its metaphorical forms, its appeal endures, although what makes for a "good" home and who makes for a "good" or even a "real" family are questions that remain hotly contested. While participants in these debates may enlist nostalgic images of "traditional" homes to bolster their arguments, the history of boarding shows us that earlier living arrangements were no less varied than our own. Indeed, the very volatility of nineteenth-century society defies nostalgia. Home—for all its rhetorical dominance—remained elusive and domesticity fleeting. Sociability mattered as much as privacy (itself a fluid concept), mobility as much as stability. Americans moved constantly, not only (most famously) from East to West but from West to East, North to South, state to state, country to city, city to city, town to town, boardinghouse to boardinghouse, home to home. They continually crossed both cultural and geographic borders, changing their identities—if ever so subtly—as they changed residences, mingling with friends and strangers whose political, religious, class, and ethnic affinities might—or might not—match their own. In the process, they constantly renegotiated the imaginary but still very meaningful boundaries that separated home from market, love from money, boardinghouse from home. Americans continue to grapple with tensions between love and money, home and marketplace; witness, for example, contemporary discussions surrounding childcare, adoption, and surrogacy. But their battles have shifted to different terrain.[11]

As they gradually vanished from urban landscapes, boardinghouses underwent a symbolic transformation, even rehabilitation. Concerned with what they termed the "lodger evil," early twentieth-century housing reformers looked back fondly on the "old-time boardinghouse." "There usually was in it something of the home element," Wolfe noted in *The Lodging House Problem in Boston* (1906), and boarders "often found themselves becoming a part of the family even against their wills." No longer creatures of a corrupt marketplace, the boardinghouses of Wolfe's imagined past provided their inmates with the comforts of home.[12] Wolfe recognized what Susan Brown and countless other boarders instinctively understood. Boardinghouses could be homes.

Abbreviations

AAS	American Antiquarian Society, Worcester, Massachusetts
AHB	Antoinette Hutches Barker
Barker Letters	Richard Henry Barker and Antoinette Hutches Barker Letters (in possession of Moseley Putney, Louisville, Kentucky)
BL	Baker Library, Harvard Business School, Boston, Massachusetts
BYWCA	Young Women's Christian Association of Boston, Records, Arthur and Elizabeth Schlesinger Library, Radcliffe Institute of Advanced Study, Harvard University, Cambridge, Massachusetts
FMPC	Federal Manuscript Population Census, National Archives Microfilm Publications
Forbes Diary	Susan Parsons Brown Forbes, Diary, October 24, 1861–March 1866 (original at American Antiquarian Society, Worcester, Mass.), *American Women's Diaries (New England)* [microfilm] (New York, [1983?])
HAW	Home for Aged Women, Boston, records, Arthur and Elizabeth Schlesinger Library, Radcliffe Institute of Advanced Study, Harvard University, Cambridge, Massachusetts
HML	Hagley Museum and Library, Wilmington, Delaware
MHS	Massachusetts Historical Society, Boston
RGD	R. G. Dun & Co. Collection, Baker Library, Harvard Business School, Boston, Massachusetts
RHB	Richard Henry Barker
SL	Arthur and Elizabeth Schlesinger Library, Radcliffe Institute of Advanced Study, Harvard University, Cambridge, Massachusetts
Thorn Diary	Catherine Thorn, Diaries, 1881, 1887, Arthur and Elizabeth Schlesinger Library, Radcliffe Institute for Advanced Study, Harvard University, Cambridge, Massachusetts
WL	Joseph Downs Collection of Manuscripts and Printed Ephemera, Winterthur Library, Winterthur, Delaware
WRHS	The Western Reserve Historical Society, Cleveland, Ohio

Introduction • Houses and Homes

1. Judith Martin, "Miss Manners: Adult Children Living at Home Can be Desirable Experience," *Bloomington Herald-Times*, March 22, 1998; Martin, "Miss Manners: Multigenerational Households Find Compromise Difficult," *Bloomington Herald-Times*, August 16, 1998.

2. See, e.g., Nancy F. Cott, *The Bonds of Womanhood: "Woman's Sphere" in New England, 1780–1835* (New Haven, CT: Yale University Press, 1977), 63–100; Mary P. Ryan, *Cradle of the Middle Class: The Family in Oneida County, New York, 1790–1865* (Cambridge: Cambridge University Press, 1981), 186–229; Gwendolyn Wright, *Moralism and the Modern Home: Domestic Architecture and Cultural Conflict in Chicago, 1873–1913* (Chicago: University of Chicago Press, 1980), and *Building the Dream: A Social History of Housing in America* (New York: Pantheon, 1981); Clifford Edward Clark Jr., *The American Family Home, 1800–1960* (Chapel Hill: University of North Carolina Press, 1986); and Elizabeth Blackmar, *Manhattan for Rent, 1785–1850* (Ithaca, NY: Cornell University Press, 1989).

3. Richard Crawford, *America's Musical Life: A History* (New York: W. W. Norton, 2001), 178–80; Alaric A. Watts, "My Own Fireside," in *Home Life Made Beautiful*, ed. Margaret Sangster (New York: Christian Herald, 1897), 33–34; Alice Fahs, [on Elizabeth Stuart Phelps's *The Gates Ajar* (1868)] *The Imagined Civil War: Popular Literature of the North and South, 1861–1865* (Chapel Hill: University of North Carolina Press, 2001), 147–48.

4. "Home Influences," *Christian Recorder*, May 1, 1869; "The Pleasures of Home," *Boston Pilot*, June 9, 1838, 158.

5. Clark, *The American Family Home*, 11–12; Blackmar, *Manhattan for Rent*, 55, 57–60; Laurel Thatcher Ulrich, *A Midwife's Tale: The Life of Martha Ballard, Based on Her Diary* (New York: Vintage, 1991), 21, 80–82, 161, 223–26.

6. Sean Wilentz, "Society, Politics, and the Market Revolution, 1815–1848," in *The New American History*, ed. Eric Foner (Philadelphia: Temple University Press, 1990), 51–71; Charles Sellers, *The Market Revolution: Jacksonian America, 1815–1846* (New York: Oxford University Press, 1991); Melwyn Stokes and Stephen Conway, eds., *The Market Revolution in America: Social, Political, and Religious Expressions, 1800–1880* (Charlottesville: University Press of Virginia, 1996); Karen Haltunnen, *Confidence Men and Painted Women: A Study of Middle-Class Culture in America, 1830–1870* (New Haven, CT: Yale University Press, 1982), 35. For the best and most sustained scholarly treatments of boardinghouses, see Paul Groth, *Living Downtown: The History of Residential Hotels in the United States* (Berkeley and Los Angeles: University of California Press, 1994); Rachel Amelia Bernstein, "Boarding-House Keepers and Brothel Keepers in New York City, 1880–1910" (Ph.D. diss., Rutgers University, 1984); Mark Peel, "On the Margins: Lodgers and Boarders in Boston, 1860–1900," *Journal of American History* 72 (March 1986): 813–34; Blackmar, *Manhattan for Rent*, 60, 63–67, 88, 134–38; and Kenneth A. Scherzer, *The Unbounded Community: Neighborhood Life and Social Structure in New York City, 1830–1875* (Durham: Duke University Press, 1992). Boardinghouses receive brief attention in Christine Stansell, *City of Women: Sex and Class in New York, 1789–1860* (New York: Knopf, 1986), 9, 13, 53, 85, 185–86; Richard B. Stott, *Workers in the Metropolis: Class, Ethnicity, and Youth in Antebellum New York City* (Ithaca, NY: Cornell University Press, 1990), 169–71, 179–80, 204–9, 241–43; Gwendolyn Wright, *Building the Dream: A Social History of Housing in America* (New York: Pantheon, 1981), 37–38, 125; Susan Strasser, *Never Done: A History of American Housework* (New York: Pantheon, 1982), 145–61; Ruth Schwartz Cowan, *More Work for Mother: The Ironies of Household Technology from the Open Hearth to the Microwave* (New York: Basic Books, 1983), 108–9; Elizabeth Collins Cromley, *Alone Together: A History of New York's Early Apartments* (Ithaca, NY: Cornell University Press,

1990), 16, 21–27; Timothy J. Gilfoyle, *City of Eros: New York City, Prostitution, and the Commercialization of Sex, 1790–1920* (New York: W. W. Norton, 1992), 73, 78, 165–72; and Joanne J. Meyerowitz, *Women Adrift: Independent Wage Earners in Chicago, 1880–1930* (Chicago: University of Chicago Press, 1988), 24, 70–76.

7. John Modell and Tamara K. Hareven, "Urbanization and the Malleable Household: An Examination of Boarding and Lodging in American Families," *Journal of Marriage and the Family* 35 (1973): 467–79; Michael B. Katz, *The People of Hamilton, Canada West: Family and Class in a Mid-Nineteenth-Century City* (Cambridge, MA: Harvard University Press, 1975), 36, 222–36, 264–70; Peel, "On the Margins," 816–17; and Groth, *Living Downtown*, 92.

8. Thomas Butler Gunn, *The Physiology of New York Boarding-Houses* (New York: Mason Brothers, 1857), 12; Emory Holloway and Ralph Adimari, eds., *New York Dissected by Walt Whitman: A Sheaf of Recently Discovered Newspaper Articles by the Author of Leaves of Grass* (New York: Rufus Rockwell Wilson, 1936), 96–97; "Boarding Out," *Harper's Weekly* (March 7, 1857), 146; Helen A. Hawley, "Concerning an American Institution," *Chautauquan* 13 (1891): 230. Neither boardinghouses nor complaints about them were unique to the United States. See Sharon Marcus, *Apartment Stories: City and Home in Nineteenth-Century Paris and London* (Berkeley and Los Angeles: University of California Press, 1999), 104–8.

9. On the history of housework, see Strasser, *Never Done;* Cowan, *More Work for Mother;* and Jeanne Boydston, *Home and Work: Housework, Wages, and the Ideology of Labor in the Early Republic* (New York: Oxford University Press, 1990). Sarah Josepha Hale, *Keeping House and House Keeping: A Story of Domestic Life* (New York: Harper and Brothers, 1845), 132. *Pastoralization* is Boydston's term; see esp. 142–63.

10. On this point, see esp. Blackmar, *Manhattan for Rent*, 112.

11. T. S. Arthur, "Blessings in Disguise," *Godey's Lady's Book* 21 (July 1840): 15–20; Elizabeth White Nelson, *Market Sentiments: Middle-Class Market Culture in Nineteenth-Century America* (Washington, DC: Smithsonian Books, 2004); Nan Enstad, *Ladies of Labor, Girls of Adventure: Working Women, Popular Culture, and Labor Politics at the Turn of the Twentieth Century* (New York: Columbia University Press, 1999), 23–29.

12. See, e.g., Matthew Hale Smith, *Sunshine and Shadow in New York* (Hartford, CT: J. B. Burr and Co., 1869); Wright, *Building the Dream*, 98; Blackmar, *Manhattan for Rent*, 109–48.

13. George Thompson, *Venus in Boston: A Romance of City Life*, ed. Davis S. Reynolds and Kimberly R. Gladman (1849; reprint, Amherst: University of Massachusetts Press, 2002), 5; Carlin T. Kindilien, "Sangster, Margaret Elizabeth Munson," in *Notable American Women, 1607–1950: A Biographical Dictionary*, ed. Edward T. James, Janet Wilson James, and Paul S. Boyer (Cambridge, MA, Harvard University Press, 1974), 234–35; Margaret Sangster, "Home Life Made Beautiful. Home Life and Heart Life. The New Home," in Sangster, *Home Life Made Beautiful*, 17–18; Katz, *People of Hamilton*, 77–78; Blackmar, *Manhattan for Rent*, 121; Cromley, *Alone Together*, 12–14; Sam B. Warner Jr., *Streetcar Suburbs: The Process of Growth in Boston, 1870–1900* (1962; reprint, New York: Atheneum, 1973), 26, 120; Robert G. Barrows, "Beyond the Tenement: Patterns of American Urban Housing, 1870–1930," *Journal of Urban History* 9 (August 1983): 415–18.

14. See, e.g., *Boston Courier*, December 28, 1849. Jeanne Boydston, *Home and Work: Housework, Wages, and the Ideology of Labor in the Early Republic* (New York: Oxford University Press, 1990), esp. 142–63. Sentimental ideology was vulnerable to other contradictions. It coexisted with thriving markets in human flesh (though sentimental ideology provided abolitionists with powerful arguments). Men might turn to the language of sentiment to describe their adventures—and especially their failures—in the marketplace; women and men profited by selling the artifacts of sentimental culture. On these issues, see Walter Johnson, *Soul by Soul:*

Life Inside the Antebellum Slave Market (Cambridge, MA: Harvard University Press, 1999); Amy Dru Stanley, "Home Life and the Morality of the Market," in *The Market Revolution in America: Social, Political, and Religious Expressions, 1800–1880,* ed. Melwyn Stokes and Stephen Conway (Charlottesville: University of Virginia Press, 1996), 74–96; Amy Dru Stanley, *From Bondage to Contract: Wage Labor, Marriage, and the Market in the Age of Slave Emancipation* (Cambridge: Cambridge University Press, 1998), 17–35; Scott A. Sandage, "The Gaze of Success: Failed Men and the Sentimental Marketplace, 1873–1893," in *Sentimental Men: Masculinity and the Politics of Affect in American Culture,* ed. Mary Chapman and Glenn Hendler (Berkeley and Los Angeles: University of California Press, 1999), 181–201; and Elizabeth White Nelson, *Market Sentiments: Middle-Class Market Culture in Nineteenth-Century America* (Washington, DC: Smithsonian Books, 2004).

15. See Peel, "On the Margins," 813–15; Groth, *Living Downtown,* 5–7; and Elisabeth Anthony Dexter, *Career Women of America, 1776–1840* (1950; reprint, Clifton, NJ: Augustus M. Kelley, 1972), 123, for discussions of these distinctions.

16. Gunn, *Physiology of New York Boarding-Houses;* John C. Gunn, *Gunn's Domestic Medicine; or, Poor Man's Friend, in the Hours of Affliction, Pain, and Sickness,* 5th rev. ed. (New York: Saxton and Miles, 1845). Both Thomas Butler Gunn's use of physiology as his organizing device and his description of the medical students' boardinghouse suggest some familiarity with medical practice. *Frank Leslie's Illustrated Newspaper,* July 11, 1858, 95. On occupational and ethnic identities, see Scherzer, *Unbounded Community,* 104–5; and Peel, "On the Margins," 824–27. A Mrs. McCollick advertised her boardinghouse as being run "on Temperance principles"; *New York Tribune,* May 13, 1841. See also the advertisement placed in an unidentified newspaper by Miss A. A. Burr, who, "being herself of the New Church," hoped to attract fellow worshippers to her New York boardinghouse by offering them "very reasonable terms" (enclosed in letter from Margaretta Lammot du Pont to Alfred V. du Pont, March 6, 1853, folder 2, box 2, Du Pont Family Papers, HML); Stephen Nissenbaum, *Sex, Diet, and Debility in Jacksonian America: Sylvester Graham and Health Reform* (Westport, CT: Greenwood Press, 1980). On boardinghouses that reflected political and regional, albeit not necessarily partisan, identities, see James Sterling Young, *The Washington Community, 1800–1828* (New York: Columbia University Press, 1966), 98–109, 123–42.

17. Lawrence J. Friedman, *Inventors of the Promised Land* (New York: Alfred A. Knopf, 1975), 168; George G. Foster, *New York by Gas-Light: With Here and There a Streak of Sunshine* (New York: Dewitt and Davenport, 1850), 10; Gunn, *Physiology,* 34, 36. Britons who condemned boardinghouses in their own country were similarly vague about the characteristics of homes. See Marcus, *Apartment Stories,* 107–8.

One • Away from Home

1. John G. Locke, Reminiscences, 1820–1831 [1831?], MHS; FMPC, Boston, Ward 9, 1850, roll M432–337, p. 271; *The Directory of the City of Boston . . . From July 1850, to July 1851* (Boston: George Adams, 1850), 220.

2. By *middle class,* I mean people who inhabited a particular occupational niche, white-collar men and women: clerks, small businesspeople, professionals, teachers. Being middle class also meant having particular attitudes and outlooks, foremost among them the maintenance of respectability. Class in nineteenth-century America was both fluid and at least partly socially constructed. See Mary P. Ryan, *Cradle of the Middle Class: The Family in Oneida County, New York, 1790–1865* (Cambridge: Cambridge University Press, 1981); Stuart M. Blumin, *The Emergence of the Middle Class: Social Experience in the American City, 1760–1900*

(Cambridge: Cambridge University Press, 1989); Debby Applegate, "Henry Ward Beecher and the 'Great Middle Class': Mass-Marketed Intimacy and Middle-Class Identity," in *The Middling Sorts: Explorations in the History of the American Middle Class,* ed. Barton J. Bledstein and Robert D. Johnston (New York: Routledge, 2001), 107–24; and Andrea Volpe, "Cartes de Visite Portrait Photographs and the Culture of Class Formation," in Bledstein and Johnston, *Middling Sorts,* 157–69.

3. George G. Foster, *New York by Gas-Light: With Here and There a Streak of Sunshine* (New York: Dewitt and Davenport, 1850), 10.

4. Forbes Diary, March 31, 1856.

5. Ibid., April 29 and June 2, 1856.

6. *Boston Directory* (Boston: George Adams, 1855–57); *Boston Directory* (Boston: Adams, Sampson, and Co., 1858–60).

7. Forbes Diary, August 8, 15, 16, 19, 1856.

8. Ibid., August 1, 1859; November 14, 1856; May 3, 1858.

9. Ibid., February 2, 1859.

10. Ibid., May 12, 1857; January 11, 1859.

11. Ibid., January 1, 1859.

12. Ibid., 1857–60; for social activities and grammar class, see December 23, 1857; March 22, April 28, May 7, June 10, August 20, October 19, November 2, and December 31, 1858; January 1, 10, and 17, 1859; September 21, 1856; Elizabeth Dorr Diary, June 21, 1854, MHS.

13. Forbes Diary, November 4, 1856; March 2, 1857.

14. Ibid., June 18, 1856.

15. Ibid., July 16, 1856.

16. Ibid., June 23, 1857.

17. Ibid., December 26, 1857.

18. Ibid., December 30, 1857.

19. Ibid., August 7, 13, and 16, September 6, and November 11, 1859.

20. Ibid., November 8, 1856.

21. When Brown began keeping boarders herself a few years later, she posted vacancies in the YMCA's reading rooms; see Forbes Diary, July 1, 1865. Given the frequency with which the residents of 34 attended YMCA activities, it is likely that Haskell had done so as well.

22. Forbes Diary, April 22, 1858. No text of Chapin's "Woman and Her Work" seems to have survived. Very likely the sentiments it expressed resembled those of his *Duties of Young Women,* which was reprinted several times. Chapin's views on the home were utterly unoriginal. See *Duties of Young Women* (Boston: George W. Briggs, 1848), 161–76.

23. Thomas Dublin, *Transforming Women's Work: New England Lives in the Industrial Revolution* (Ithaca, NY: Cornell University Press, 1994), 99–100.

24. See, e.g., Forbes Diary, October 10, 1857.

25. Ibid., February 5, May 11 and 22, 1859.

26. Ibid., January 15 and 16, 1860.

27. This is how Brown would advertise her own boardinghouse after her marriage; see chapter 2.

28. Forbes Diary, October 2 and 25, 1861.

29. "Mrs. Catherine Thorn," *Troy Daily Times,* August 23, 1890; Thorn Diary, June 15, 1881; *The Troy Directory* (Troy, NY: Sampson, Murdock, and Co. , 1882); "Mrs. Helen M. Price," *Troy Daily Times,* January 8, 1890.

30. *The Troy Directory* (Troy, NY: Sampson, Murdock, and Co., 1871–89); *The Directory of Troy and Lansingburgh* (Troy, NY: Sampson, Murdock, and Co., 1890).

31. Thorn Diary, November 19 and February 10, 1881.

32. Ibid., September 22, October 1 and 11, February 28, March 3 and 4, 1881; February 2, 1887.

33. Ibid., October 12, 1881.

34. *The Troy Directory* (Troy, NY: Sampson, Murdock, and Co., 1880–82); FMPC, 1880, Troy, New York, enumeration district 132, roll T9–920, p. 112A. See, e.g., Thorn Diary, May 6, July 5, September 17 and 25, and October 19, 1881. Whittemore disappears from the Troy city directory after 1882. By 1887, quite possibly earlier, she had moved to Washington, D.C.; she and Thorn continued to correspond regularly. Thorn Diary, January 2, 9, and 28; September 14, 1887.

35. Thorn Diary, October 21 and 22, 1881.

36. FMPC, 1880, Troy, New York, enumeration district 132, roll T9–920, p. 112A; *The Troy Directory* (Troy, NY: Sampson, Murdock, and Co., 1871–89); *The Directory of Troy and Lansingburgh* (Troy, NY: Sampson, Murdock, and Co., 1890).

37. Thorn Diary, May 14, September 18, and October 13, 1881; January 14 and 30, April 14, and June 11, 1881.

38. Ibid., November 1 and 2, December 23, 1881.

39. Ibid., October 29, June 24, and July 11, 1881; "Boarders for a Living: White Hair and a Face Worn by Anxiety. Why the Experienced Housekeeper Advised her Friend Not to Keep Boarders," *New York Times,* November 10, 1889.

40. Thorn Diary, April 2, 1881; January 27, July 21, and May 7, 1887.

41. "The Last Rites," *Troy Daily Times,* August 23, 1890.

42. "R. H. Barker is Heart Victim," *Louisville Courier-Journal,* February 13, 1916.

43. One surviving letter places Barker in New York City in 1875; see John Stites to Richard Henry Barker (RHB), March 13, 1875; for references to Washington Place, see RHB to Antoinette Hutches Barker (AHB), January 16, 1892; and RHB to AHB, March 8, 1894, Barker Letters. RHB to AHB, August 19, September 2 and 15, 1888, Barker Letters.

44. See Howard P. Chudacoff, *The Age of the Bachelor: Creating an American Subculture* (Princeton: Princeton University Press, 1999); Peter Laipson, "'I Have No Genius for Marriage': Bachelorhood in Urban America, 1870–1930" (Ph.D. diss., University of Michigan, 2000); and, for an earlier period, Lisa Wilson, *Ye Heart of a Man* (New Haven, CT: Yale University Press, 1999).

45. See, e.g., Richard's comment to Nettie that "your [sewing] machine is in Miss Thompson's room"; RHB to AHB, September 11, 1888; AHB to RHB, October 8 and 13, 1888, Barker Letters.

46. RHB to AHB, May 2, 1892; December 3, 1893, Barker Letters.

47. See esp. Barker's account of marching in the lawyers' contingent of a Democratic Party parade, RHB to AHB, October 27, 1888, Barker Letters.

48. RHB to AHB, May 21, June 7 and 11, 1890; March 29 and January 9, 1894, Barker Letters.

49. See, e.g., RHB to AHB, January 28, February 24 and 27, March 1, 1892; March 17, 1894, Barker Letters.

50. RHB to AHB, November 24, 1891; January 22 and December 10, 1893, Barker Letters.

51. RHB to AHB, March 3 and 24, 1894, Barker Letters.

52. RHB to AHB, February 12, 1893; March 3, 1894, Barker Letters.

53. RHB to AHB, March 9, 1893, Barker Letters.

54. RHB to AHB, February 20, 1894; January 31 and March 28, 1893, Barker Letters.

55. RHB to AHB, November 28 and December 21, 1893; AHB to RHB, February 4, 1894; Walter Palmer Hines to Master Richard Barker, [n.d., postmark July 21, 1893], Barker Letters.

56. AHB to RHB, September 10, 1888; RHB to AHB, September 19, 1888; AHB to RHB, September 21, 1888, Barker Letters.

57. RHB to AHB, November 17, 1892, Barker Letters.

58. "R. H. Barker is Heart Victim."

59. Biography and description, T. C. O'Donovan Papers; George R. Fuller to T. C. O'Donovan, July 2 and 12, and August 4, 1879; receipt of payment to George R. Fuller, n.d.; T. C. O'Donovan to J. M. Montgomery, February 17, 1883; T. C. O'Donovan, Diary, March 7, 1883. Possibly O'Donovan lost his leg earlier than the archival biography implies, for he was training to be a telegrapher as early as 1876; see T. C. O'Donovan to G. L Lang, October 21 [n.d., 1876?]; and G. L Lang to T. O'Donovan, December 27, 1876, T. C. O'Donovan Papers, WL.

60. O'Donovan, Diary, January 24, August 10, 11, and 14, 1883.

61. Ibid., August [n.d.], 1883; September 10, 1883.

62. FMPC, 1880, Collier, Allegheny County, Pennsylvania, Enumeration District 53, roll T9–1089, pp. 172D, 174D.

63. FMPC, 1870, Robinson, Allegheny, Pennsylvania, roll M593–1299, p. 316.

64. O'Donovan, Diary, June 25 and March 20, 1883. Loose papers interspersed between the pages of O'Donovan's diary include a list of books and their prices, including his estimated expenditures on books for 1886, $15.00; for patent application, see August 24, September 1, and November 1, 1883. According to the 1860 manuscript census, which listed O'Donovan's father Michael as a laborer, neither of his Irish-born parents could read or write (FMPC, 1860, Robinson, Allegheny County, Pennsylvania, roll M653–1064, p. 602).

65. O'Donovan, Diary, September 10, 1883.

66. Ibid., September 12 and 13, 1883.

67. Ibid., September 18 and 29, 1883.

68. Ellen D. Larned, *History of Windham County, Connecticut*, vol. 2 (Worcester, MA: published by the author, 1880), 557–60; Richard M. Bayles, *History of Windham County, Connecticut* (New York: W. W. Preston and Co., 1889), 310–12, 315–17, 340–48; A. B. Cunningham, "The History of Willimantic," in *A Modern History of Windham County Connecticut: A Windham County Treasure Book*, vol. 1, ed. Allen B. Lincoln (Chicago: S. J. Clarke Publishing Co., 1920), 105–7; Rev. Dwight A. Jordan, "Willimantic as a Factory Village," in Lincoln, *Modern History of Windham County*, 107–12; A. C. Andrews, "Outline Sketch of Willimantic," in Lincoln, *Modern History of Windham County*, 116–19; Bruce M. Stave and Michele Palmer, *Mills and Meadows: A Pictorial History of Northeast Connecticut* (Virginia Beach, VA: The Donning Co., 1991), 8–9, 36–38, 77; Thomas R. Beardley, *Willimantic Industry and Community: The Rise and Decline of a Connecticut Textile City* (Willimantic, CT: Windham Textile and History Museum, 1994), ix–x, 2–12, 15–26; O'Donovan, Diary, October 24–25 and November 1, 1883; Charles Dickens, *Bleak House* (1853; reprint, New York: New American Library, 1980), esp. 366–72, 653; FMPC, 1880, Windham, Windham County, Connecticut, Enumeration District 124, roll T9–109, p. 264.

69. Beardley, *Willimantic Industry and Community*, 27, 30; O'Donovan, Diary, November 1, 1883; May 19, 1884.

70. Ibid., May 19–21, and May 27, 1884. Here and probably in other places as well, O'Donovan departed from a strictly diary format, noting at the end of the May 19 entry, "(Wrote this June 10th . . .)."

71. Ibid., June 4, 1884; FMPC, 1900, Crescent Township, Allegheny County, Pennsylvania, roll T623–1366, p. 123A; FMPC, 1910, Coraopolis, Allegheny County, Pennsylvania, Ward 3, roll T624–1293, part 2, p. 167A; FMPC, 1920, Coraopolis, Allegheny County, Pennsylvania,

Ward 3, roll T625–1510, p. 3B; FMPC, 1930, Coraopolis, Allegheny County, Pennsylvania, Enumeration District 556, roll 1962, p. 5B.

72. Matthew Hale Smith, *Sunshine and Shadow in New York* (Hartford, CT, 1869), 431.

73. *New York Tribune,* March 28, 1878.

74. In 1880, three years before O'Donovan's arrival, a never-married dressmaker named Clara L. Page boarded in the house next door to the Tafts. FMPC, 1880, Windham, Windham County, Connecticut, Enumeration District 124, roll T9–109, p. 264.

75. Peter Baskerville, "Familiar Strangers: Urban Families with Boarders, Canada, 1901," *Social Science History* 25 (Fall 2001): 321–46; Noel Ignatiev, *How the Irish Became White* (New York: Routledge, 1995); for O'Donovan's attitudes toward African Americans, see his diary, May 20, 1884.

76. Joanne J. Meyerowitz, *Women Adrift: Independent Wage Earners in Chicago, 1880–1930* (Chicago, 1988), 69–91.

Two • Keeping House

1. Paul Groth, *Living Downtown: The History of Residential Hotels in the United States* (Berkeley, CA: University of California Press, 1994), 92.

2. Forbes, Diary, October 24, 1861–March 1866; Susan L. Porter and Laura B. Driemeyer, "Like a Large Family: Genteel Boarding Houses in Nineteenth Century Boston," unpublished paper, 2002; FMPC, 1860, Boston, Ward 5, roll M653–521, pp. 382–83.

3. Morrill evidently arrived in Boston in 1864; see *The Boston Directory . . . For the Year Commencing July 1, 1864* (Boston: Sampson, Davenport, and Co., 1864), 397. FMPC, 1870, Boston, Ward 4, roll M593–642, p. 244; Massachusetts, vol. 72, p. 472, RGD. She was still in business in 1880; FMPC, 1880, Boston, Enumeration District 654, roll T9–555, p. 510C.

4. FMPC, 1860, Boston, Ward 7, roll M653–522, p. 209–10; Oscar Handlin, *Boston's Immigrants, 1790–1880: A Study in Acculturation,* rev. and enlarged ed. (New York: Atheneum, 1969), 254.

5. FMPC, 1850, Boston, Ward 6, roll M432–336, p. 402. Although the Haydens did not appear in the 1860 census, they still resided in Boston at that time; James Oliver Horton and Lois E. Horton, *Black Bostonians: Family Life and Community Struggle in the Antebellum North,* rev. ed. (New York: Holmes and Meier, 1999), 2–4, 134; *Frederick Douglass Newspaper,* August 26, 1853, Accessible Archives, African American Newspapers: The 19th Century, item #47075 available at www.accessible.com (accessed June 20, 2004).

6. " 'Our Boarding-House.' From First-class Houses Down to Free Lunches. What Boarders Pay in Boston. The Peculiarities of Boarding-house Life in Town," *Boston Globe,* May 12, 1878; Fannie Benedict, "Boarding-house Experience in New York," *Packard's Monthly* (April 1869), 101.

7. *New York Tribune,* April 17, May 8, June 15, and May 5, 1841; see also *New York Times,* January 11, 17, and 28, 1875; *Boston Globe,* May 14, 1878.

8. See, e.g., *New York Tribune,* May 8, June 2, 12, 15, and 18, 1841. "Boarding and Lodging," *New York Times,* February 15, 1888; "Boarders Wanted," *New York Times,* April 17, 1915.

9. *New York Times,* April 17, 1915; *New York Times,* May 3, 1888.

10. FMPC, 1860, Boston, Ward 8, roll M653–522, pp. 493–94; *The Boston Directory . . . for the Year Commencing July 1, 1860* (Boston: Adams, Sampson and Co., 1860), 308, 413.

11. *New York Times,* January 4 and 3, 1875; May 13, 1888.

12. See, e.g., *New York Tribune,* June 8, 1841; *New York Sun,* February 23, March 16, September 3 and 23, and November 23, 1835. For "no boarding house keepers need apply," see

New York Sun, September 26, 1835. For examples of ads placed by boardinghouse keepers, see *New York Sun,* January 28 and 31, and September 2, 1835; *New York Tribune,* May 25 and 27, June 1 and 15, 1841.

13. "My Boarding-House," *Harper's Weekly* (January 9, 1858), 21.

14. *Boston Evening Transcript,* June 13, 1863. On the English grammar class, see Forbes Diary, January 20, February 10, March 3, 6, 19, and 31, 1862. Forbes made no further mention of it after March 31, 1862. On socializing with boarders, see January 20, 1862; March 14 and May 7, 1863; and September 29, 1865. On Forbes's use of *household* and *boarders,* see January 28 and November 15, 1863; and July 3, 1865.

15. Massachusetts vol. 74, p. 390, RGD; Rutherford Hayner, *Troy and Rensselaer County, New York: A History,* vol. 1 (New York: Lewis Historical Pub. Co., Inc., 1925), 148; Thorn Diary, February 26, 1881; "Decay of the Boarding-House," *New York Times,* March 28, 1878.

16. Elizabeth Collins Cromley, *Alone Together: A History of New York's Early Apartments* (Ithaca, NY: Cornell University Press, 1990), 16–17, 26–27; *Insurance Map of Boston,* vol. 1 (New York: D. A. Sanborn, 1867), 20; *Boston Massachusetts,* vol. 1 (New York: Sanborn Map and Publishing Co., 1885), 22.

17. *Boston Globe,* May 5, 1878; *Colored American,* February 23, 1839.

18. "Real Estate," *Boston Courier,* November 15, 1849; *Boston Globe,* May 14, 1878.

19. "Boarders for a Living: White Hair and a Face Worn by Anxiety," *New York Times,* November 10, 1889. See, e.g., "To Let," *Boston Courier,* November 7 and 13, 1849; "20 WEST 48th-ST" and "122 WEST 12th-ST," *New York Times,* April 1, 1888.

20. Thomas Butler Gunn, *The Physiology of New York Boarding-Houses* (New York: Mason Brothers, 1857), 25; Forbes Diary, July 13, 1865.

21. "A Sample Boarding House," *Brooklyn Eagle,* March 18, 1900; Guy W. Moore, *The Case of Mrs. Surratt: Her Controversial Trial and Execution for Conspiracy in the Lincoln Assassination* (Norman: University of Oklahoma Press, 1954), 7–8.

22. Albert Benedict Wolfe, *The Lodging House Problem in Boston* (Boston: Houghton Mifflin, 1906), 46–47; Forbes Diary, January 28, 1863; Thorn Diary, January 9, 1887.

23. Henry Pierce, Diary, December 10 and 31, 1843; October 27, 1844; and July 13, 1845, folder 1840–49, Henry Pierce Family Papers, MHS; *New York Tribune,* June 5, 1841; [James Boardman], *America, and the Americans* (1833; reprint, New York: Arno Press, 1974), 27.

24. Gunn, *Physiology,* 18, 95; Sarah Josepha Hale, *Boarding Out: A Tale of Domestic Life* (New York: Harper and Brothers, 1855), 32; Philip Farley, *Criminals of America; Or, Tales of the Lives of Thieves, Enabling Every One to Be His Own Detective. With Portraits, Making a Complete Rogues' Gallery* (New York: Author's Edition, 1876), 425–26.

25. Gunn, *Physiology,* 17–18; Boardman, *America, and the Americans,* 27; see also Blanche Murphy, "American Boarding-house Sketches," *Catholic World* 41 (1885): 456–57.

26. "Boarders for a Living," 14.

27. See, e.g., Junius Henri Browne, *The Great Metropolis: A Mirror of New York: A Complete History of Metropolitan Life and Society, with Sketches of Prominent Places, Persons and Things in the City, As They Actually Exist* (1869; reprint, New York: Arno Press, 1975), 207–8.

28. Mrs. Felton, *American Life: A Narrative of Two Years' City and Country Residence in the United States* (Bolton Percy: Printed for the authoress, 1843), 31, 70; Stuart Blumin, *The Emergence of the Middle Class: Social Experience in the American City, 1760–1900* (Cambridge: Cambridge University Press, 1989), 109–10.

29. "Boarders for a Living," 14; Forbes Diary, December 2, 1863.

30. "Empty is the House Now," *New York Times,* December 9, 1887.

31. New York, vol. 374, p. 176; Massachusetts, vol. A 85, p. 23, RGD.

32. AHB to RHB, October 29, 1888, Barker Letters.

33. "Mr. White's Predicament," *New York Times*, December 9, 1889.

34. Editorial, *New York Times*, September 10, 1879; Forbes Diary, July 24 and June 6, 1863.

35. Forbes Diary, October 21–22, 25–26, 30–31, 1865.

36. Andrew Sandoval-Strausz, *Hotel: An American History* (New Haven, CT: Yale University Press, 2007); L. A. Jones, "Innkeeper's and Boarding-House Keeper's Lien," *American Law Review* 21 (1887): 679; "Innkeepers—Hotels and Boarding Houses," *American Law Review* 48 (1914): 622–23; *Report of the Women's Educational and Industrial Union . . . for the Year Ending May 7, 1889* (Boston: Geo. E. Crosby and Co., Printers, 1889), 39; *Report of the Women's Educational and Industrial Union . . . for the Year Ending May 6, 1890* (Boston: George E. Crosby and Co., Printers, 1890), 40; Minutes, January 20, 1890, Women's Educational and Industrial Union Protective Department, folder 106, carton 6, SL; "Zella and Ruhman, Again," *New York Times*, March 10, 1894.

37. John S. Farmer, *Americanisms—Old and New: A Dictionary of Words, Phrases and Colloquialism Peculiar to the United States, British America, the West Indies, etc.* (London: Thomas Poulter and Sons, 1889), 70; "A Baby Held as Collateral," *New York Times*, August 22, 1893; "Willie Clung to His Father," *New York Times*, August 23, 1893; "Mother Against Father," *New York Times*, August 26, 1893; and "Willie Finneran Goes to His Father," *New York Times*, August 27, 1893.

38. *Directory of New York City, 1890* (Orem, UT: Ancestry, Inc., 1999).

39. Dorothy Richardson, *The Long Day: The Story of a New York Working Girl*, ed. Cindy Sondik Aron (1905; reprint, Charlottesville: University Press of Virginia, 1990), 8–11.

40. Roger Angell, "Hard Lines Life in Rerun, Now Playing Near You," *New Yorker* (June 7, 2004), 52.

41. RHB to AHB, December 3, 1893, Barker Letters.

42. *The Troy Directory, For the Year Commencing July 1st 1887* (Troy: Sampson, Murdock and Co., 1887), 192, 213, 231, listed Price as Clark House's proprietor and Morrison, a bank clerk, and David Thatcher, a hatter, as boarders. The 1888 directory listed Morrison as proprietor; by 1890, Morrison had "removed to Cohoes" and Thatcher had taken over Clark House, though most likely his wife managed it. *The Troy Directory, For the Year Commencing July 1st, 1888* (Troy: Sampson, Murdock and Co., 1888), 192; *The Directory of Troy and Lansingburgh . . . For the Year Commencing June 15, 1890* (Troy: Sampson, Murdock, and Co., 1890), 199, 255; *The Directory of Troy and Lansingburgh . . . For the Year Commencing June 15, 1891* (Troy: Sampson, Murdock, and Co., 1891), 255.

43. "Personal," *Troy Daily Times*, January 7, 1890; "Died," *Troy Daily Times*, January 9, 1890; "Obituary: Mrs. Helen M. Price," *Troy Daily Times*, January 8, 1890; "Victims of La Grippe," *Troy Daily Times*, January 11, 1890; FMPC, 1900, Waukegan, Illinois, Enumeration District 143, roll T623–314, p. 33A.

44. Collection description, Diary of Susan E. Parsons Brown Forbes, American Antiquarian Society; Mrs. Susan E. P. Forbes, "Eben Parson and Fatherland Farm," *New England Historical and Genealogical Register* 50 (1896): 59–64.

45. Forbes Diary, 1857–60, April 5 and 14, 1860. Haskell briefly returned to boardinghouse keeping, but after less than six months turned her establishment over to another landlady. See Forbes Diary, October 4, 1860; February 25, March 2, 11, and 12, 1861. FMPC, 1860, Boston, Ward 8, roll M653–522, pp. 518–19; FMPC, 1880, Chelsea, Massachusetts, Enumeration District 797, roll T9–562, p. 486A.

46. Karen V. Hansen, *A Very Social Time: Crafting Community in Antebellum New England* (Berkeley and Los Angeles: University of California Press, 1994), 79–113. Haskell was a

frequent visitor to the Forbes household. Some calls may have been purely social; during others she worked and visited; see Forbes Diary, January 15 and 18, March 1, 1862, April 11, 1865.

47. Lynn M. Hudson, *The Making of Mammy Pleasant: A Black Entrepreneur in Nineteenth-Century San Francisco* (Urbana: University of Illinois Press, 2002), 55–60; AHB to RHB, December 2 and 29, 1891; June 12, 1892, Barker Letters; Porter and Driemeyer, "Like a Large Family"; "Empty is the House Now," *New York Times,* December 9, 1887.

48. New York, vol. 374, p. 176; Massachusetts, vol. 74, p. 390, and vol. 89, p. 294, RGD.

49. "J. A. M.," "American Boarding-Houses," *Dublin University Magazine* 75 (1870): 471.

50. "Mr. White's Predicament," *New York Times,* December 9, 1889.

51. Gunn, *Physiology,* 60, 77.

52. *Report of the Women's Educational and Industrial Union . . . for the Year Ending May 6, 1890* (Boston: George E. Crosby and Co., Printers, 1890), 44; WEIU annual report, 1880–81 (front cover missing; no publication information), 34; *Report of the Women's Education and Industrial Union for the Year Ending May 3, 1881* (Boston: No. 157 Tremont Street, 1881), 41; *Report of the Women's Education and Industrial Union for the Year Ending May 2, 1882* (Boston: No. 157 Tremont Street, 1882), 48; *WEIU for Year Ending April 1899* (Cambridge: Cooperative Press, 1899), 51.

53. Minutes, November 8, 1880, Women's Educational and Industrial Union Protective Department, folder 106, carton 6, SL.

54. Gunn, *Physiology,* 66, 79–82; "A Gilt-Edged Boarding-House," *New York Daily Tribune,* February 16, 1881.

55. See, e.g., *Boston Globe,* evening ed., May 16, 1878; and *New York Times,* May 13, 1888.

56. *Provincial Freeman,* July 19, 1856; Frederick Douglass, *Narrative of the Life of Frederick Douglass: An American Slave Written by Himself,* ed. David W. Blight, 1st ed. (Boston: Bedford/St. Martin's, 1993), 99; FMPC, 1850, Boston, Ward 6, roll M432–336, p. 402; [William Craft], *Running a Thousand Miles for Freedom; Or, the Escape of William and Ellen Craft* (London: William Tweedie, 1860); Horton and Horton, *Black Bostonians,* 110.

57. Catharine E. Beecher, *A Treatise on Domestic Economy, for the Use of Young Ladies at Home and at School* (Boston: Marsh, Capen, Lyon, and Webb, 1841), 177; Catharine E. Beecher and Harriet Beecher Stowe, *The American Woman's Home; or, Principles of Domestic Science,* ed. Nicole Tonkovich (1869; reprint, Hartford, CT: Harriet Beecher Stowe Center and New Brunswick, NJ: Rutgers University Press, 2002), 185–90.

Three • *"The Most Cruel and Thankless Way a Woman Can Earn Her Living"*

1. "Boarders for a Living: White Hair and a Face Worn by Anxiety. Why the Experienced Housekeeper Advised Her Friend Not to Keep Boarders," *New York Times,* November 10, 1889.

2. See, e.g., Forbes Diary, March 23, April 20, May 9, 14, and 15, 1863; September 10–13 and October 7, 1864; September 30 and October 2, 1865.

3. Ibid., January 1 and May 11, 1863; December 1–2, 1864.

4. Ibid., March 10, 1865; October 24, 1861; October 3, 1862; March 5 and May 7, 1865.

5. Forbes Diary, April 6, 1865. On servants' reluctance to work in boardinghouses, see "Boarders for a Living." On Forbes's antislavery views, see her diary, January 27 and February 2, 1865. On domestic service, see Faye E. Dudden, *Serving Women: Household Service in Nineteenth-Century America* (Middletown, CT: Wesleyan University Press, 1983); David M. Katzman, *Seven Days a Week: Women and Domestic Service in Industrializing America* (University of Illinois Press, 1981); and Thomas Dublin, *Transforming Women's Work: New England Lives in the Industrial Revolution* (Ithaca, NY: Cornell University Press, 1994), 195–98. On hierarchies within domestic service, see Dublin, *Transforming Women's Work,* 162.

6. Forbes Diary, January 26, 1864.

7. Susan Strasser, *Never Done: A History of American Housework* (1982; reprint, New York: Henry Holt, 2000), 53–57; Catharine E. Beecher, *A Treatise on Domestic Economy, for the Use of Young Ladies at Home and at School* (Boston: Marsh, Capen, Lyon, and Webb, 1841), 367–69. Forbes listed the composition of her "household" on January 1, 1866; in various entries throughout the previous year, she noted which rooms were occupied by which boarders. For their occupations, see *The Boston Directory . . . for the Year Commencing July 1, 1865* (Boston: Adams, Sampson, and Co., 1865), 158, 375, 432; *The Boston Directory . . . for the Year Commencing July 1, 1866* (Boston: Sampson, Davenport, and Co., 1866), 198, 209, 261. For entries discussing Drury's illness and hospitalization, see January 1–5, 1866.

8. The genteel boardinghouse run by the Williams sisters in Boston's Bowdoin Square did not have indoor toilet facilities; see Susan L. Porter and Laura B. Driemeyer, "Like a Large Family: Genteel Boarding Houses in Nineteenth Century Boston," unpublished paper, 2002; and Susan L. Porter, "Making 'A Home for Some of the Finest People': The Politics of the Genteel Boarding House in Nineteenth-Century Boston," paper presented at Organization of American Historians annual meeting, Boston, March 2004. On the other hand, several ads for new and recently built houses in the 1840s promised indoor bathrooms and hot and cold running water. See, e.g., "Real Estate. To Let," *Boston Courier*, November 15, 1849; "Large House on Washington Street," *Boston Courier*, November 16, 1849; and "Real Estate. To Let," *Boston Courier*, December 20, 1849; Beecher, *Treatise on Domestic Economy*, 362, 345; Forbes Diary, 1861–66.

9. Edward H. Dixon, M.D., *Scenes in the Practice of a New York Surgeon* (New York: De Witt and Davenport, 1855), 210–11.

10. Fannie Benedict, "Boarding-house Experience in New York," *Packard's Monthly* (April 1869), 102.

11. Forbes Diary, January 21 and December 16, 1865.

12. Ibid., January 10, 1866.

13. Thomas Butler Gunn, *The Physiology of New York Boarding-Houses* (New York: Mason Brothers, 1857), 54.

14. Beecher, *Treatise on Domestic Economy*, 351–52.

15. Forbes Diary, May 23 and 30, 1863; January 9, 1866; April 15, 1864.

16. Beecher, *Treatise on Domestic Economy*, 144–45, 149.

17. Forbes Diary, January 4, 1864.

18. Ibid., May 19, 1863; August 19, 1864.

19. Beecher, *Treatise on Domestic Economy*, 148.

20. Ibid., 145; Forbes Diary, January 2, 1866.

21. Louisa May Alcott, *Little Women*, ed. Valerie Alderson (1869; reprint, New York: Oxford University Press, 1998), 262–70; "Boarders for a Living."

22. Benedict, "Boarding-house Experience in New York," 102; Blanche Murphy, "American Boarding-House Sketches," *Catholic World* 41 (1885): 457–58; Q. K. Philander Doesticks [Mortimer Neal Thomson], *Doesticks: What He Says* (1855; reprint, Delmar, N.Y.: Scholars' Facsimiles and Reprints, 1986), 52.

23. Julia du Pont Shubrick to Gabrielle Shubrick Crofton, March 9 [n.d.], Julia du Pont Shubrick Correspondence, folder 2, HML; AHB to RHB, June 1, 1890; RHB to AHB, April 29, 1892, Barker Letters.

24. Alice Flagg Simons to Elise Simons du Pont, April 9, 1889, Francis Guerney du Pont Papers, HML.

25. Gunn, *Physiology*, 226–27.

26. Ibid., 54.

27. Jeanne Boydston, *Home and Work: Housework, Wages, and the Ideology of Labor in the Early Republic* (New York, 1990), 142–63.

28. Benedict, "Boarding-house Experience in New York," 101.

29. Gunn, *Physiology*, 52.

30. Ibid., 50, 254; Benedict, "Boarding-house Experience in New York," 101.

31. See, e.g., Eliza Leslie, *Leonilla Lynmore and Mr. and Mrs. Woodbridge; or, A Lesson for Young Wives* (Philadelphia: Carey and Hart, 1847); and T. S. Arthur, "Blessings in Disguise," *Godey's Lady's Book* 21 (July 1840): 15–20.

32. Sarah Josepha Hale, *Boarding Out: A Tale of Domestic Life* (New York: Harper and Brothers, 1855), 13, 27–32, 38–40, 53–61.

33. Beecher, *Treatise on Domestic Economy*, 103, 374–76; Catharine E. Beecher and Harriet Beecher Stowe, *The American Woman's Home; or, Principles of Domestic Science*, ed. Nicole Tonkovich (1869; reprint, Hartford, CT: Harriet Beecher Stowe Center and New Brunswick, NJ: Rutgers University Press, 2002), 116–21, 276–77; Suellen Hoy, *Chasing Dirt: The American Pursuit of Cleanliness* (New York: Oxford University Press, 1995), 22.

34. Una Pope-Hennessy, *The Aristocratic Journey: Being the Outspoken Letters of Mrs. Basil Hall Written during a Fourteen Months' Sojourn in America, 1827–1828* (New York: G. P. Putnam's Sons, 1931), 293; RHB to AHB, January 28, 1894; November 28, 1891, Barker Letters; Hoy, *Chasing Dirt*, 3, 10–19, 65.

35. Gabrielle Shubrick Crofton to Julia du Pont Shubrick, January 2, 1866, Julia du Pont Shubrick Correspondence, folder 4, HML.

36. Gunn, *Physiology*, iii, 183, 282.

37. Alice Flagg Simons to Elise Simons du Pont, April 30, 1877; December 18, 1889, Francis Guerney du Pont Papers, HML.

38. Forbes, July 12, 1865; for "old mattress," see January 2, 1863; Philip Farley, *Criminals of America; Or, Tales of the Lives of Thieves, Enabling Every One to be His Own Detective. With Portraits, Making a Complete Rogues' Gallery* (New York: Author's Edition, 1876), 426.

39. "Boarding House Account Book," William Peck of Providence, November 15, 1800, BL; Forbes Diary, May 14, 1865; T. S. Arthur, "Taking Boarders," *Godey's Lady's Book* 42 (February 1851): 84.

40. "Boarders for a Living."

41. Julia du Pont Shubrick to Gabrielle Crofton [n.d.], Julia du Pont Shubrick Correspondence, folder 2, HML.

42. "Boarders for a Living."

43. Ibid.; Forbes Diary, March 25 and 29, 1864.

44. Forbes Diary, February 1–4, 7–9, 11, 17, and 25, 1865.

45. Metta Victoria Victor, *Miss Slimmens' Boarding House* (New York: J. S. Ogilvie and Co., 1882), 43; Alice Flagg Simons to Elise Simons du Pont, May 19, [1890], Francis Guerney du Pont Papers, HML; "Boarders for a Living."

Four • Boarders' Beefs

Epigraphs: "Godey's Arm-Chair," *Godey's Lady's Book* 86 (April 1873): 382; Marcia and Jon Pankake, eds., *Joe's Got a Head Like a Ping-Pong Ball: A Prairie Home Companion Folk Song Book* (New York: Penguin, 1990), 114. Several versions of this song exist. See "The Traditional Ballad Index: An Annotated Bibliography of the Folk Songs of the English-Speaking World," www.csufresno.edu/folklore/ballads/RJ19194.html (accessed November 20, 2005).

Vance Randolph's *Ozark Folksongs*, vol. 3 (Columbia: State Historical Society of Missouri, 1949), 242, dated one version to 1895; Douglas Gilbert's *Lost Chords: The Diverting Story of American Popular Songs* (New York: Doubleday, 1942), 191–92, dated another, "The All Go Hungry Hash House," to the 1880s.

1. Thomas Butler Gunn, *The Physiology of New York Boarding-Houses* (New York: Mason Brothers, 1857), 32, 49–57, 127; "Wanted—A Boarding-House," (October 10, 1857), 652; Sarah Josepha Hale, *Boarding Out: A Tale of Domestic Life* (New York, 1855), 39; Edward H. Dixon, *Scenes in the Practice of a New York Surgeon* (New York, 1855), 210–11; Q. K. Philander Doesticks [Mortimer Neal Thomson], *Doesticks: What He Says* (1855; reprint, Delmar, NY: Scholars' Facsimiles and Reprints, 1986), 52; Julia du Pont Shubrick to Gabrielle Shubrick Crofton, March 9 [n.d.], Julia du Pont Shubrick Correspondence, folder 2, HML.

2. Gunn, *Physiology*, 36; "Picture of a New York Boarding-house," quoted in [James Boardman], *America, and the Americans* (1833; reprint, New York: Arno Press, 1974), 29, 31; "Wanted—A Boarding-House," 652; Hale, *Boarding Out*, 74; Doesticks [Thomson], *Doesticks*, 51–54. "Sorrows of the Boarder: How the Census Might Touch on Burning Issues of the Day," *New York Times*, June 8, 1890, 9.

3. Gunn, *Physiology*, 36. *The Oxford English Dictionary*, 2d ed. (http://dictionary.oed .com/) lists the first reference for *home cooked* in 1923, but a quotation search yielded a reference from 1860. Harvey Levenstein, *Revolution at the Table: The Transformation of the American Diet* (New York: Oxford University Press, 1988), 8–9; Richard Osborn Cummings, *The American and His Food*, 2d ed. (1941; reprint, New York: Arno Press, 1970), 10–30.

4. Gunn, *Physiology*, 230; "Sorrows of the Boarder"; "Old Mr. Rottle: A Boarding House Episode," *New York Tribune*, April 17, 1887.

5. "'Our Boarding-House.' From First-Class Houses Down to Free Lunches. What Boarders Pay in Boston. The Peculiarities of Boarding-house Life in Town," *Boston Globe*, May 12, 1878; "J. A. M," "American Boarding-Houses," *Dublin University Magazine* 75 (1870): 470; Cummings, *The American and His Food*, 10–30; Levenstein, *Revolution at the Table*, 4–5, 14–22.

6. "Picture of a New York Boarding-house," 29; Alice Flagg Simons to Elise Simons du Pont, November 16, 1881, Francis Guerney du Pont Papers, HML.

7. British traveler James Boardman reprinted the comic "Picture of a New York Boarding-house"; see above. "Extra Supper Soup," appeared originally in the *Philadelphia Mercury* but was reprinted in the *Provincial Freeman* (Toronto), an African American expatriate newspaper, July 1, 1854; item #26792, available at www.accessible.com (accessed May 15, 2003); on Irish boardinghouse humor, see Thomas E. Powers, "McCarthy's Boarding House" (New York: Mrs. Pauline Lieder, 1878), Historic American Sheet Music, http://scriptorium.lib.duke .edu/sheetmusic (accessed May 15, 2003); and C. Frank Horn, "Murphy's Boarding House" (Boston: W. F. Shaw, 1887), Lester S. Levy Sheet Music Collection, http://levysheetmusic.mse .jhu.edu (accessed May 15, 2003).

8. Junius Henri Browne, *The Great Metropolis: A Complete History of Metropolitan Life and Society, With Sketches of Prominent Places, Persons and Things in the City, as They Actually Exist* (1869; reprint, New York: Arno Press, 1975), 206.

9. "The Cost of the Table," *New York Times*, September 20, 1872; "Our Boarding-House"; "American Boarding-Houses," 473; Levenstein, *Revolution at the Table*, 4–5, 14–22; Cummings, *The American and His Food*, 10–30.

10. Browne, *Great Metropolis*, 209.

11. Timothy C. O'Donovan, Diary, September 12, 1883, Timothy C. O'Donovan Papers, WL; "Declines Boarding Diet," *New York Times*, February 8, 1921; "Boarding-House Ameni-

ties: Stray Bits of Conversation from the Table and in the Store," *New York Tribune*, August 24, 1890; Levenstein, *Revolution at the Table.*

12. Susan Strasser, *Never Done: A History of American Housework*, 2d ed. (New York: Henry Holt, 2000), 14–22; Forbes Diary, October 21, 1865.

13. Strasser, *Never Done*, 29; Helen Green, *The Maison de Shine: More Stories of the Actors' Boarding House* (New York: B. W. Dodge and Co., 1908), 15.

14. "Picture of a New York Boarding-house," 29; Gunn, *Physiology*, 230.

15. Ruth Schwartz Cowan, *More Work for Mother: The Ironies of Household Technology from the Open Hearth to the Microwave* (New York: Basic Books, 1983), 62; Strasser, *Never Done*, 32–49.

16. Forbes Diary, August 23, 1864.

17. Cowan, *More Work for Mother*, 51–52, 55–57, 61–62; Mary Douglas, "Deciphering a Meal," *Daedalus* 101 (Winter 1972): 68; Peter Farb and George Armelagos, *Consuming Passions: The Anthropology of Eating* (Boston: Houghton Mifflin, 1980); Amy Bentley, *Eating for Victory: Food Rationing and the Politics of Domesticity* (Urbana: University of Illinois Press, 1998), 64–66.

18. Forbes Diary, July 12, 1865; November 26, 1861; November 5, 1862; February 9, 1864; March 27, 1865.

19. Catharine E. Beecher and Harriet Beecher Stowe, *The American Woman's Home*, ed. Nicole Tonkovich (1869; reprint, Hartford, CT: Harriet Beecher Stowe Center and New Brunswick, NJ: Rutgers University Press, 2002), 138.

20. "American Boarding-Houses," 469–70; Jane C. Nylander, *Our Own Snug Fireside: Images of the New England Home, 1760–1860* (New Haven, CT: Yale University Press, 1994), 198–99; Forbes Diary, January 28 and July 13–14, 1863.

21. "Our Boarding-House."

22. Gunn, *Physiology*, 157; "Boarding-House Amenities," *New York Tribune*, August 24, 1890; "Boarding House Amenities: Exchanging the Compliments of the Season with the Landlady," *New York Tribune*, September 21, 1890; *Oxford English Dictionary*, 2d ed. (http://dictionary.oed.com/); John Russell Bartlett, *Dictionary of Americanisms* (New York: Bartlett and Welford, 1848), 179.

23. Boardman, *America, and the Americans*, 32; J. A. M., "American Boarding-Houses," 470; Gunn, *Physiology*, 95, 113, 119, 158.

24. "Picture of a New York Boarding-house," 29; "Sorrows of the Boarder"; "Boarding House Amenities," *New York Tribune*, September 21, 1890.

25. Browne, *Great Metropolis*, 411; "Fish in the Markets," *New York Times*, July 17, 1854; "Our Green Bag, Number Five," *New York Times*, March 11, 1853; Metta Victoria Victor, *Miss Slimmens' Boarding House* (New York: J. S. Ogilvie and Co., 1882), 91. *Miss Slimmens' Boarding House* originally appeared in serial form in *Godey's* in 1860.

26. Forbes Diary, November 20, 1862.

27. "Extra Supper Soup," *Provincial Freeman*, July 1, 1854; Green, *The Maison de Shine*, 1–15.

28. Doesticks [Thomson], *Doesticks*, 53.

29. The *Oxford English Dictionary*, 2d ed. (http://dictionary.oed.com/), dates *leftovers* to 1891; Catharine E. Beecher, *A Treatise on Domestic Economy, For the Use of Young Ladies at Home, and at School* (Boston: Marsh, Capen, Lyon, and Webb, 1841), 70, 79, 82–84. Beecher had a much higher opinion of soup twenty-eight years later, although she reserved her admiration for French soups; see Beecher and Stowe, *American Woman's Home*, 138, 140–41. Joyce G. Williams, J. Eric Smithburn, and M. Jeanne Peterson, ed., *Lizzie Borden: A Case Book of Family and Crime in the 1890s* (Bloomington, IN: T. I. S. Publication Division, 1980), 13–14;

Farb and Armelagos, *Consuming Passions*, 102; on the concept of the "ordered meal," see Bentley, *Eating for Victory,* 59–84, esp. 60–61.

30. Jacob Deterly, Diary, August 28, 1823, WRHS; see also September 2, 1822; Alice Flagg Simons to Elise Simons du Pont, August 28, 1877; July 2, 1878, Francis Guerney du Pont Papers, HML.

31. Alice Flagg Simons to Elise Simons du Pont, April 9, 1889, Francis Guerney du Pont Papers, HML.

32. Browne, *Great Metropolis,* 207.

33. Gunn, *Physiology,* 156 (illustration); "Boarding-house Amenities," *New York Tribune,* August 24, 1890.

34. See, e.g., Eliza Leslie, *Leonilla Lynmore, and Mr. and Mrs. Woodbridge; or, A Lesson for Young Wives* (Philadelphia: Carey and Hart, 1847).

35. Frances Trollope, *Domestic Manners of the Americans* (1832; reprint, London: The Folio Society, 1974), 210; "Picture of a New York Boarding-house," 32–33; Gunn, *Physiology,* 160–61; "Our Green Bag, Number Five."

36. Victor, *Miss Slimmens' Boarding House,* 39–40.

37. Gunn, *Physiology,* 127–28, 288–90; Green, *Maison de Shine,* 24, 45–46, 51, 101–5, 121; RHB to AHB, December 10, 1893; April 7, 1894, Barker Letters.

38. Gunn, *Physiology,* iii (dedication page).

39. "Our Boarding-House"; J. A. M., "American Boarding Houses," 469–70.

40. J. A. M., "American Boarding Houses," 468, 470.

41. Forbes Diary, March 16, 1857; Alice Flagg Simons to Elise Simons du Pont, March 8, 1890, Francis Guerney du Pont Papers, HML.

42. RHB to AHB, November 30, 1893; February 22 and April 7, 1894, Barker Letters.

43. *The Boston Directory . . . for the Year Commencing July 1, 1862* (Boston: Adams, Sampson and Co., 1862), 147, 153, 375; Forbes Diary, February 5 and 8, 1863; March 12 and December 3, 1864.

44. "Our Green Bag, Number Five."

45. For early references see "A Line-'O-Type or Two: On Mars," *Chicago Tribune,* February 2, 1901; "A Municipal Ownership Joke," *Los Angeles Times,* January 7, 1908; Edwin L. Sabin, "What did Duncan Do?" *Lippincott's Monthly Magazine* 84 (December 1909): 726; Elizabeth Van Rensselaer, "Etiquette: In a Boarding House," *Chicago Tribune,* October 12, 1919; "The Boarding-House Reach," *Washington Post,* May 24, 1925; and December 6, 1925; [Eliza Leslie], *Miss Leslie's Behaviour Book: A Guide and Manual for Ladies* (1859; reprint, New York: Arno Press, 1972), 134.

46. Thomas E. Hill, *Hill's Manual of Social and Business Forms* (1885; reprint, Chicago: Quadrangle Books, 1971), 147, 148; Kenneth L. Ames, *Death in the Dining Room and Other Tales of Victorian Culture* (Philadelphia: Temple University Press, 1992), 209–13. *Hill's Manual,* first published in 1873, went through several editions. Ames cites the 1882 edition; both it and the 1885 edition featured the two illustrations.

47. Leslie, *Miss Leslie's Behaviour Book,* 101, 120.

48. See, e.g., "Boarding and Lodging," *New York Times,* August 22, 1882, 11; "Boarders Wanted," *New York Times,* April 4, 1893; June 4, 1895; and November 5, 1899.

49. Charlotte Perkins Gilman, *The Home: Its Work and Influence,* ed. Michael S. Kimmel (1903; reprint, Walnut Creek, CA: Altamira Press, 2002), 124–42; Dolores Hayden, *The Grand Domestic Revolution: A History of Feminist Designs for American Homes, Neighborhoods, and Cities* (Cambridge, MA: MIT Press, 1981), 183–205.

50. Joan Jacobs Brumberg, "Beyond Meat and Potatoes: A Review Essay," *Food and Foodways* 3 (1989): 278.

Five • Nests of Crime and Dens of Vice

1. Laurie Verge, "Mary Elizabeth Surratt," in *The Trial: The Assassination of President Lincoln and the Trial of the Conspirators*, ed. Edward Steers Jr. (Lexington: University Press of Kentucky, 2003), 52–53; Elizabeth Steger Trindal, *Mary Surratt: An American Tragedy* (Gretna, LA: Pelican Publishing Co.), 88–89, 99; John W. Clampitt, "The Trial of Mrs. Surratt," *North American Review* 131 (September 1880): 225; Guy W. Moore, *The Case of Mrs. Surratt: Her Controversial Trial and Execution for Conspiracy in the Lincoln Assassination* (Norman: University of Oklahoma Press, 1954), 3–17, 36–38. On Surratt's appearance, see "Trial of the Conspirators," *Harper's Weekly* (June 3, 1865), 341; "Trial of the Assassins," *New York Times*, May 15, 1865; and Clampitt, "Trial of Mrs. Surratt," 225.

2. Janet Coryall, review of *Mary Surratt: An American Tragedy*, *Journal of Southern History* 63 (August 1997): 673–74.

3. Johnson, quoted in Moore, *Case of Mrs. Surratt*, 38.

4. Karen Halttunen, *Confidence Men and Painted Women: A Study of Middle-Class Culture in America, 1830–1870* (New Haven, CT: Yale University Press, 1982).

5. *National Police Gazette*, 1845–48; see esp. March 7, 1846, 232; March 14, 1846, 234; June 6, 1847, 307; October 28, 1848, 3.

6. Ibid., March 4, 1846, 234; "A Boarding-House Thief," *New York Times*, April 1, 1883; "Boarding-House Thieves," *New York Times*, January 2, 1880; "A Bad Gray 'Professor,' " *New York Times*, July 15, 1887; "Look out for Mrs. King," *New York Times*, December 19, 1878; "A Boarding-house Thief," *New York Tribune*, November 28, 1879.

7. See, e.g., "Arrest of a Boarding House Thief," *National Police Gazette*, October 28, 1848; "Caution to Boarding House Keepers," *National Police Gazette*, March 7, 1846; "Boarding-House Thieves," "Catching a Clever Thief," *New York Tribune*, March 25, 1886; "Not a Desirable Boarder," *New York Times*, August 27, 1879; "Mrs. Casselman Arraigned," *New York Times*, November 25, 1876; and "A Female Swindler," *New York Times*, November 18, 1876; Thomas Byrnes, *Professional Criminals of America* (New York: Cassell and Co., 1886), 21.

8. "Young Klein Again Arrested," *New York Times*, May 24, 1895.

9. Byrnes, *Professional Criminals of America*, 21.

10. Philip Farley, *Criminals of America; or, Tales of the Lives of Thieves, Enabling Every One to be His Own Detective. With Portraits, Making a Complete Rogues' Gallery* (New York: Author's Edition, 1876), 429, 433.

11. Edward Winslow Martin, *The Secrets of the Great City: A Work Descriptive of the Virtues and the Vices, the Mysteries, Miseries and Crimes of New York City* (Philadelphia: National Publishing Co., 1868), 216–19.

12. Byrnes, *Professional Criminals of America*, 374.

13. Forbes Diary, October 21, 1865.

14. Matthew Hale Smith, *Sunshine and Shadow in New York* (Hartford, CT: J. B. Burr and Co., 1869), 378, 381, 431; George G. Foster, *New York by Gas-Light: With Here and There a Streak of Sunshine* (New York, 1850), 30; Timothy J. Gilfoyle, *City of Eros: New York City, Prostitution, and the Commercialization of Sex, 1790–1920* (New York: Norton, 1992), 73, 166–69; Ned Buntline, *The B'Hoys of New York: A Sequel to the Mysteries and Miseries of New York* (Halifax: Milner and Sowerby, 1866), 17–19, 121.

15. Smith, *Sunshine and Shadow*, 375–76.

16. Martin, *Secrets of the Great City*, 301.

17. "A Boarding House for Actresses: The Haul Made by the Police of the First Precinct Last Night," *Brooklyn Eagle*, July 26, 1887.

18. Martin, *Secrets of the Great City*, 254.

19. Smith, *Sunshine and Shadow,* 385; Reverend Henry Morgan, *Boston Inside Out! Sins of a Great City! A Story of Real Life* (Boston: Shawmut Publishing Co., 1880), 344–45.

20. George Ellington, *The Women of New York: Or the Under-World of the Great City* (1869; reprint, New York: Arno Press, 1972), 438.

21. Smith, *Sunshine and Shadow,* 129; Thomas Butler Gunn, *The Physiology of New York Boarding-Houses* (New York: Mason Brothers, 1857), 140, 143.

22. Only one advertisement placed in the *New York Sun* in 1835 (November 20) advertised boarding for "young ladies." Not a single boarding advertisement placed in the *New York Tribune* in 1841 asked for women lodgers. Junius Browne, *The Great Metropolis,* quoted in Gilfoyle, *City of Eros,* 166; Virginia Penny, *The Employments of Women: A Cyclopedia of Women's Work* (Boston: Walker, Wise, and Co., 1863), 416.

23. "A Boarding House Episode," *New York Times,* August 10, 1884; "Will Be Aired: Revelations Succeeding a Boarding House Scandal," *Brooklyn Eagle,* May 16, 1889; "The Perkins and the Pipers. 'Oh, this is Too Low!' Exclaimed the Landlady. A Row in a Fashionable Boarding House," *Brooklyn Eagle,* March 29, 1894.

24. T. S. Arthur, "Taking Boarders," *Godey's Lady's Book* 42 (January 1851): 14, 19; *Godey's Lady's Book* 42 (February 1851): 85; *Godey's Lady's Book* 42 (March 1851): 161, 164; Emory Holloway and Ralph Adimari, ed., *New York Dissected, by Walt Whitman: A Sheaf of Recently Discovered Newspaper Articles by the Author of Leaves of Grass* (New York: R. Wilson, 1936), 92–96, quotation on 96; Patricia Cline Cohen, *The Murder of Helen Jewett: The Life and Death of a Prostitute in Nineteenth-Century New York* (New York: Alfred A. Knopf, 1999), 10–11, 201–4.

25. Henry Pierce, Diary, inside front cover; and December 31, 1843, folder 1840–49, Henry Pierce Family Papers, MHS; Stuart M. Blumin, *The Emergence of the Middle Class: Social Experience in the American City, 1760–1900* (Cambridge: Cambridge University Press, 1989), 212–13.

26. Gunn, *Physiology,* 103–10; quotations on 104, 110.

27. Arthur, "Taking Boarders," *Godey's Lady's Book* 42 (February 1851): 85–87; *Godey's Lady's Book* 42 (March 1851): 160–62, 166–67.

28. Arthur, "Taking Boarders," *Godey's Lady's Book* 42 (March 1851): 167.

29. Frank Harris, *My Life and Loves,* ed. John F. Gallagher (1925; reprint, London: W. H. Allen, 1964), 118–67; Gunn, *Physiology,* 104, 108; Amy Gilman Srebnick, *The Mysterious Death of Mary Rogers: Sex and Culture in Nineteenth-Century New York* (New York: Oxford University Press, 1995).

30. *Whip,* April 9, 1842, AAS.

31. Testimony of Louis J. Weichmann, in Steers, *The Trial,* 116.

32. Louisa May Alcott, *Little Women* (1868; reprint, New York: Oxford University Press, 1994), 321–31, 337–46; Jonathan Messerli, *Horace Mann: A Biography* (New York: Alfred A. Knopf, 1972), 165–80, 194, 382–85, quotation at 382; Clifford H. Scott, *Lester Frank Ward* (Boston: Twayne Publishers, 1976), 39–41.

33. *Harper's Weekly* (March 21, 1857), 179.

34. Metta Victoria Victor, *Miss Slimmens' Boarding House* (New York: J. S. Ogilvie and Co., 1882), 127–34.

35. Ibid., 9, 11–12, 77, 19.

36. Ibid., 39, 84–88.

37. Farley, *Criminals of America,* 425–26, 429.

38. Gunn, *Physiology,* 33.

39. *Lawrence Daily Journal,* February 13, 1885 (reprinted from *Chicago Tribune*).

40. Elizabeth Blackmar, *Manhattan for Rent, 1785–1850* (Ithaca, NY: Cornell University Press, 1989), 128; Rachel Amelia Bernstein, "Boarding-House Keepers and Brothel Keepers in New York City, 1880–1910," (Ph.D. dissertation, Rutgers University, 1984).

41. Gunn, *Physiology*, 40, 47–48, 138; "Our Boarding-House. From First-class Houses Down to Free Lunches. What Boarders Pay in Boston. The Peculiarities of Boarding-house Life in Town," *Boston Globe*, May 12, 1878.

42. "Boarding Out," *Harper's Weekly* (March 7, 1857), 146.

43. "Horrible Murder in Bond Street," *Harper's Weekly* (February 7, 1857), 86; "The Bond Street Tragedy," *Frank Leslie's Illustrated Newspaper*, February 14, 1857.

44. "How the Murder May Have Been Committed," *Frank Leslie's Illustrated Newspaper*, February 21, 1857; Byrnes, *Professional Criminals of America*, 347–49; "Another Terrible Act in the Burdell Tragedy," *Frank Leslie's Illustrated Newspaper*, August 15, 1857; "Horrible Murder in Bond Street," *Harper's Weekly* (February 7, 1857), 86.

45. "Wanted—A Boarding-House," *Harper's Weekly* (October 10, 1857), 652.

46. Arlie Russell Hochschild, *The Managed Heart: Commercialization of Human Feeling* (Berkeley and Los Angeles: University of California Press, 1983), esp. 7–23; Penny, *Employments of Women*, 416.

47. Gunn, *Physiology*, 103, 126, 147.

48. RHB to AHB, September 5 and 8, 1888, Barker Letters.

49. "Mrs. Cunningham in the Tombs," *Frank Leslie's Illustrated Newspaper*, August 22, 1857; "The False Heir to the Burdell Estate," *Frank Leslie's Illustrated Newspaper*, August 15, 1857.

50. Clampitt, "Trial of Mrs. Surratt," 226; testimony of Anna E. Surratt and Honora Fitzpatrick, in Steers, *The Trial*, 130, 132.

Six • *"Will They Board, or Keep House?"*

1. Mrs. H. W. Beecher [Eunice Beecher], *Motherly Talks with Young Housekeepers* (New York: J. B. Ford and Co., 1873), 146; Judge John A. Jameson, "Divorce," *North American Review* 136 (April 1883): 320.

2. Francis J. Grund, *The Americans, in their Moral, Social, and Political Relations* (Boston: Marsh, Capen and Lyon, 1837), 328.

3. On boardinghouse sociability, see Anne C. Rose, *Victorian America and the Civil War* (Cambridge: Cambridge University Press, 1992), 175; and Susan L. Porter and Laura B. Driemeyer, "Like a Large Family: Genteel Boarding Houses in Nineteenth Century Boston," unpublished paper.

4. Eric Rauchway, "The High Cost of Living in the Progressives' Economy," *Journal of American History* 88 (December 2001): 898–924.

5. Arthur Calhoun, *A Social History of the American Family*, vol. 2, *From Independence through the Civil War* (1918; reprint, New York: Barnes and Noble, 1960), 238–41; and vol. 3, *From 1865 to 1919* (1919; reprint, New York: Barnes and Noble, 1960), 179–84.

6. "Boarding Out," *Harper's Weekly* (March 7, 1857), 146; Edward H. Dixon, M.D., *Scenes in the Practice of a New York Surgeon* (New York: De Witt and Davenport, 1855), 213–14; Paul Groth, *Living Downtown: The History of Residential Hotels in the United States* (Berkeley and Los Angeles: University of California Press, 1994), 208–10.

7. Shirley Dare, Rose Terry Cooke, Marion Harland, Catherine Owen, and Maria Parloa each wrote untitled statements grouped under the title "Is Housekeeping a Failure?" (*North American Review* 148 [February 1889]: 243–61). Parloa, in Dare et al., "Is Housekeeping a

Failure?" 257; Laura Shapiro, *Perfection Salad: Women and Cooking at the Turn of the Century* (New York: Farrar, Straus and Giroux, 1986), 41, 44, 48, 52–59, 64–65, 106–7, 194.

8. Cooke, in Dare et al., "Is Housekeeping a Failure?" 247.

9. Ibid.; Harland, in Dare et al., "Is Housekeeping a Failure?" 252.

10. Dare, in Dare et al., "Is Housekeeping a Failure?" 243–44; Owen, in Dare et al., "Is Housekeeping a Failure?" 254–55.

11. Beecher, *Motherly Talks with Young Housekeepers,* 193, 195.

12. Mrs. H. W. Beecher [Eunice Beecher], *All Around the House; or, How to Make Homes Happy* (New York: D. Appleton and Co., 1879), 228; Jane Shaffer Elsmere, *Henry Ward Beecher: The Indiana Years, 1837–1847* (Indianapolis: Indiana Historical Society, 1973), 63, 67, 73, 115–16, 159; Minnie Myrtle, "The Two Homes," *National Era,* May 22, 1856; Dare, in Dare et al., "Is Housekeeping a Failure?" 246.

13. Anonymous, *Six Hundred Dollars a Year: A Wife's Effort at Low Living under High Prices* (Boston: Ticknor and Fields, 1867) was reprinted several times, at least until 1888; Emma Churchman Hewitt, *How to Live on a Small Income* (Philadelphia: G. W. Jacobs, 1909); Solon Robinson, *How to Live, Saving and Wasting; or, Domestic Economy Illustrated by the Life of Two Families of Opposite Character, Habits, and Practices* (New York: Fowler and Wells, 1860); Catherine Owen [Helen Alice Nitsch], *Ten Dollars Enough: Keeping House Well on Ten Dollars a Week; How it Has Been Done: How it May be Done Again* (Boston: Houghton Mifflin, 1893), 1–6, 52, 234, 77, 67.

14. Ibid., iii–iv; Susan L. Porter, "Making 'A Home for Some of the Finest People': The Politics of the Genteel Boarding House in Nineteenth-Century Boston," paper presented at annual meeting, Organization of American Historians, Boston, Massachusetts, March 2004.

15. Harland, "Is House Keeping a Failure?" 253; Sara L. Zeigler, "Wifely Duties: Marriage, Labor, and the Common Law in Nineteenth-Century America," *Social Science History* 20 (Spring 1996): 63–96, esp. 64–69.

16. Harland, "Is House Keeping a Failure?" 248; Frances Trollope, *Domestic Manners of the Americans* (1832; reprint, London: The Folio Society, 1974), 209, 210; T. S. Arthur, *Tired of Housekeeping* (New York: D. Appleton, 1842), 58; Sarah Josepha Hale, *Boarding Out: A Tale of Domestic Life* (New York: Harper, 1855); and Dixon, *Scenes in the Practice of a New York Surgeon,* 206–14.

17. Mark Twain, quoted in Pamela Walker Laird, "Mark Twain and the Beautiful House: The Virtues of Domestic Decoration," unpublished paper, 12; Walter Palmer Hines to Master Richard Barker [n.d., postmark July 21, 1893], Barker Letters; Helen A. Hawley, "Concerning an American Institution," *Chautauquan* 13 (1891): 230; Elizabeth Blackmar, *Manhattan for Rent, 1785–1850* (Ithaca, NY: Cornell University Press, 1989), 117.

18. Arthur, *Tired of Housekeeping,* 32, 40; Mary W. Janvrin, "Mrs. Deming's Troubles," *Godey's Lady's Book* 72 (April 1866): 347.

19. Beecher, *Monthly Talks with Young Housekeepers,* 150.

20. Ibid., 148; Beecher, *All Around the House,* 228–33.

21. Altina L. Waller, *Reverend Beecher and Mrs. Tilton: Sex and Class in Victorian America* (Amherst: University of Massachusetts Press, 1982); Richard Wightman Fox, *Trials of Intimacy: Love and Loss in the Beecher-Tilton Scandal* (Chicago: University of Chicago Press, 1999); Beecher, *All Around the House,* 233–34.

22. Beecher, *All Around the House,* 248–49.

23. Owen [Nitsch], *Ten Dollars Enough,* iv, 4, 7–11, 14, 22–23, 40–41.

24. Harland, in Dare et al., "Is Housekeeping a Failure?" 252.

25. Parloa, in Dare et al., "Is Housekeeping a Failure?" 250; "Boarding Out"; "Boarding-House Influences," *New York Tribune,* April 10, 1881.

26. "The Stand-point of the Boarding-House," *Atlantic Monthly* 19 (February 1867): 250–51; "Boarding-House Influences"; Blanche Murphy, "American Boarding-house Sketches," *Catholic World* 41 (1885): 458; Thorn Diary, February 27, June 8, July 26, November 27, and December 31, 1881.

27. Thorn Diary, September 25, 1881; Elizabeth Dorr, Diary, June 21, 1854, MHS; Parloa, in Dare et al., "Is Housekeeping a Failure?" 257; Cooke, in Dare et al., "Is Housekeeping a Failure?" 249; Shapiro, *Perfection Salad*, 64–65; Sarah Stage, "Ellen Richards and the Social Significance of the Home Economics Movement," in Sarah Stage and Virginia B. Vincenti, eds., *Rethinking Home Economics: Women and the History of a Profession* (Ithaca, NY: Cornell University Press, 1997), 17–33.

28. Murphy, "American Boarding-house Sketches," 458; Daniel A. Cohen, "Miss Reed and the Superiors: The Contradictions of Convent Life in Antebellum America," *Journal of Social History* 30 (Fall 1996): 149–84; Tracy Fessenden, "The Convent, the Brothel, and the Protestant Woman's Sphere," *Signs* 25 (Winter 2000): 451–78.

29. Dixon, *Scenes in the Practice of a New York Surgeon*, 213; Beecher, *Motherly Talks with Young Housekeepers*, 148.

30. Groth, *Living Downtown*, 211–12. Ads like these were typical: "151 WEST 43D-ST.—PRIVATE FAMILY; (adults;) back parlor, room second floor, and hall room, with or without board; references exchanged. 206 WEST 44TH.—SECOND AND THIRD story rooms; adults only; parlor floor, dining room," *New York Times*, May 1, 1888; Walter Palmer Hines to Master Richard Barker, [n.d., postmark July 21, 1893], Barker Letters; Harland, "Is Housekeeping a Failure?" 252; "Boarding-House Influences," 6.

31. Trollope, *Domestic Manners*, 209; Arthur, *Tired of Housekeeping*, 33, 82, 130–55; Hale, *Boarding Out*, 8–15, 78–86, 111.

32. Cooke, in Dare et al., "Is Housekeeping a Failure?" 249; Andrea Tone, *Devices and Desires: A History of Contraceptives in America* (New York: Hill and Wang, 2001), 32–35, 41; FMPC, 1880, New York City, Enumeration District 406, roll T9–886, p. 615C.

33. RHB to AHB, May 23, 1890; RHB to AHB, February 6, 1892; AHB to RHB, May 18, 1890, Barker Letters.

34. RHB to AHB, August 29, 1888, Barker Letters.

35. AHB to RHB, August 23, September 14, 1888; May 13, 1890; November 22, 1891, Barker Letters.

36. AHB to RHB, April 4 and 27, 1890, Barker Letters.

37. AHB to RHB, September 18 and 30, 1888; March 21, 1890, Barker Letters.

38. AHB to RHB, August 24–25, September 30, 1888; March 21, April 16 and 30, June 1, 1890, Barker Letters.

39. AHB to RHB, August 24, September 19–20, 1888; September 11, 1890, Barker Letters.

40. AHB to RHB, December 2, 1891, Barker Letters.

41. AHB to RHB, September 27, 1888; December 4, 1892, Barker Letters.

42. AHB to RHB, November 28, December 9, 16, and 23, 1891, Barker Letters.

43. AHB to RHB, November 25, 1891, Barker Letters.

44. "Mrs. Antoinette Barker," *Louisville Courier-Journal*, May 5, 1957.

45. RHB to AHB, February 9, 1892; AHB to RHB, February 11, 1892, Barker Letters.

46. AHB to RHB, December 2, 1891; RHB to AHB, March 26 and April 2, 1892, Barker Letters.

47. RHB to AHB, December 23, 1891, Barker Letters.

48. AHB to RHB, April 24, June 6 and 12, 1892; March 6, 1894, Barker Letters.

49. AHB to RHB, June 12, 1892, Barker Letters.

50. "Deaths," *Louisville Courier-Journal,* May 10 and 11, 1899.

51. AHB to RHB, December 16, 1891; December 11, 1892, Barker Letters.

52. AHB to RHB, December 29–30, 1891; March 16, 1892, Barker Letters.

53. AHB to RHB, December 15, 1892; February 6 and March 1, 1893, Barker Letters.

54. AHB to RHB, October 31, 1888, Barker Letters.

55. AHB to RHB, November 22 and December 9, 1891, Barker Letters.

56. AHB to RHB, December 30, 1891; March 6 and April 22, 1894, Barker Letters.

57. AHB to RHB, February 4, 1894, Barker Letters.

58. Melusina Fay Peirce, quoted in "Cooperative Housekeeping," *Revolution* 4 (July 29, 1869): 57; see also Melusina Fay Peirce, *Cooperative Housekeeping: How Not to Do It and How to Do It, a Study in Sociology* (Boston: James R. Osgood, 1884), 125–26; Dolores Hayden, *The Grand Domestic Revolution: A History of Feminist Designs for American Homes, Neighborhoods, and Cities* (Cambridge, MA: MIT Press, 1981), 68–69, 84.

59. Charlotte Perkins Gilman, *Women and Economics: A Study of the Economic Relation Between Men and Woman as a Factor in Social Evolution* (1898; reprint, Berkeley and Los Angeles: University of California Press, 1998), 240–41; Gwendolyn Wright, *Building the Dream: A Social History of Housing in America* (Cambridge, MA: MIT Press, 1981), 135–51.

60. "Boarding Out," 146; Elizabeth Collins Cromley, *Alone Together: A History of New York's Early Apartments* (Ithaca, NY: Cornell University Press, 1990).

Seven • Charity Begins at Home

1. Ellen Dwyer, *Homes for the Mad: Life Inside Two Nineteenth-Century Asylums* (New Brunswick, NJ: Rutgers University Press, 1987), esp. 1–5, 57–75; Peggy Pascoe, *Relations of Rescue: The Search for Female Moral Authority in the American West, 1874–1939* (New York: Oxford University Press, 1990); Anne M. Boylan, *The Origins of Women's Activism: New York and Boston, 1797–1840* (Chapel Hill: University of North Carolina Press, 2002); *Miscellaneous Remarks on the Police of Boston; As Respects Paupers; Alms and Work House: Classes of Poor and Beggars; Laws Respecting Them . . .* (Boston: Cummings and Hilliard, 1814), 6; John S. Farmer, *Americanisms—Old and New: A Dictionary of Words, Phrases and Colloquialism Peculiar to the United States, British America, the West Indies, etc.* (London: Thomas Poulter and Sons, 1889), 70.

2. *First Annual Report of the Boston Seamen's Friend Society* (n.p.: n.p, 1829), 6–7; *Fiftieth Annual Report of the Board of Managers of the Boston Seaman's Friend Society* (Boston: J. H. Barnard, 1878), 12; Rev. F. D. Huntington, *Our Duty, as Christian Citizens, to the Sailor: An Address Delivered May 28, 1862, Before the Boston Seaman's Friend Society, at the Thirty-Fourth Anniversary* (Boston: T. R. Marvin and Son, 1862), 7; Mervin M. Deems, *A Home Away from Home: The Boston Seaman's Friend Society, Inc., 1827–1975* (Bangor, Me.: Furbush-Roberts, 1975), 20, 24.

3. Deems, *Home Away from Home,* 2–5, 36–40, 60–76; *Fifth Annual Report of the Board of Directors of the Boston Seaman's Friend Society* (Boston: Perkins and Marvin, 1833), 14.

4. Deems, *Home Away from Home,* 16; Huntington, *Our Duty,* 7, 8–10.

5. Deems, *Home Away from Home,* 19.

6. Ibid., 18–19.

7. *Eleventh Annual Report of the Boston Seaman's Friend Society* (1839), 12, [27]; *Twelfth Annual Report of the Board of Directors of the Boston Seaman's Friend Society* (Boston: Perkins and Marvin, 1840), 12; *Nineteenth Annual Report of the Boston Seaman's Friend Society* (Boston: T. R. Marvin, 1847), 10; Deems, *Home Away from Home,* 19; *Tenth Annual Report of*

the *Board of Directors of the Boston Seaman's Friend Society* (Boston: Perkins and Marvin, 1838), 11.

8. *Ninth Annual Report of the Board of Directors of the Boston Seaman's Friend Society,* quoted in Deems, *Home Away from Home,* 19; *Tenth Annual Report of the Board of Directors of the Boston Seaman's Friend Society,* 10; Deems, *Home Away from Home,* 30.

9. Deems, *Home Away from Home,* 18–19, 30–31, 40–41, 51–53; *Twentieth Annual Report of the Board of Directors of the Boston Seaman's Friend Society,* quoted in Deems, *Home Away from Home,* 40; *Seventeenth Annual Report of the Board of Directors of the Boston Seaman's Friend Society* (Boston: T. R. Marvin, 1845), 20; *Forty-Seventh Annual Report of the Board of Managers of the Boston Seaman's Friend Society* (Boston: J. Howard Barnard, 1875), 8–10.

10. *Twenty-Fifth Annual Report of the Boston Seaman's Friend Society* (Boston: T. R. Marvin, 1853), 7; *Fifth Annual Report;* Deems, *Home Away from Home,* 29, 33.

11. *Nineteenth Annual Report,* 12; *Sixteenth Annual Report of the Boston Seaman's Friend Society* (1844), 13.

12. *Twenty-Fourth Annual Report of the Boston Seaman's Friend Society* (Boston: T. R. Marvin, 1852), 8, 10; *Twenty-Third Annual Report of the Boston Seaman's Friend Society* (Boston: T. R. Marvin, 1851), 7; *Twenty-Eighth Annual Report of the Boston Seaman's Friend Society* (Boston: T. R. Marvin, 1856), 10; *Boston Courier,* November 14, 1849; December 9, 1849; Deems, *Home Away from Home,* 33–34, 46.

13. Association for the Relief of Aged Indigent Females, *Ninth Annual Report* (Boston: John Wilson and Son, 1859), 9; Henry B. Rogers, *Remarks Before the Association for Aged Indigent Females, at the Opening of Their Home* (Boston: C. C. P. Moody, 1850), 9–10, ser. 1, box 1, HAW; Carol Lasser, "'The World's Dread Laugh': Singlehood and Service in Nineteenth-Century Boston," in *The New England Working Class and the New Labor History,* ed. Herbert G. Gutman and Donald H. Bell (Urbana: University of Illinois Press, 1987), 72–88.

14. Receipt for Premium for Admission to the Home, in Association of Aged Indigent Females, *Act of Incorporation, By-Laws, Rules of the Board of Managers, and Regulations for the Government of the Home* (Boston: Damrell and Moore, 1849), 11, ser. 1, box 1, HAW.

15. Association for the Relief of Aged Indigent Females, *Third Annual Report* (Boston: John Wilson and Son, 1853), 20, ser. 1, box 1, HAW.

16. *Thirty-Seventh Annual Report for the Home for Aged Women* (Boston: John Wilson and Son, 1886), 9, ser. 1, box 1, HAW.

17. Carole Haber, "The Old Folks at Home: The Development of Institutionalized Care for the Aged in Nineteenth-Century Philadelphia," *Pennsylvania Magazine of History and Biography* 1010 (1977): 240–57; Rogers, *Remarks,* 11–12; Association for the Relief of Aged Indigent Females, *Second Annual Report* (Boston: John Wilson and Son, 1852), 10, ser. 1, box 1, HAW.

18. Rogers, *Remarks,* 7–9, 10–11, 14; *Memorial to the City Government: To the Honorable the Mayor and Aldermen and the Common Council of Boston* (March 26, 1849), reprinted in Henry B. Rogers, *Address Delivered at the Opening of the New Home for Aged Indigent Females, Revere Street, Boston, Thursday, June 25, 1863* (Boston: John Wilson and Son, 1863), 33, ser. 1, box 1, HAW.

19. *Act of Incorporation and By-Laws of the Home for Aged Colored Women* (Boston: Deland and Barta, 1884), 4; Rogers, *Address,* 6; Association of Aged Indigent Females, *Act of Incorporation,* 15.

20. Association for the Relief of Aged Indigent Females, *First Annual Report* (Boston: John Wilson and Son, 1851), 35, ser. 1, box 1, HAW; *Third Annual Report,* 12.

21. Rogers, *Address,* 11–12, 16–18; Nathaniel Bradlee, "Appendix," Rogers, *Address,* 31; *Sixteenth Annual Report of the Home for Aged Women* (Boston: John Wilson and Son, 1866), 7;

Twenty-Fifth Annual Report of the Home for Aged Women (Boston: John Wilson and Son, 1875), 10, ser. 1, box 1, HAW.

22. David J. Rothman, *The Discovery of the Asylum: Social Order and Disorder in the New Republic* (Boston: Little, Brown and Co., 1971); Rogers, *Address*, 5; Rogers, *Remarks*, 11.

23. Association for the Relief of Aged Indigent Females, *Third Annual Report*, 19; *Twenty-Fourth Annual Report of the Home for Aged Women* (Boston: John Wilson and Son, 1874), 10, ser. 1, box 1, HAW; Association for the Relief of Aged Indigent Females, *Act of Incorporation*, 16–17.

24. Association for the Relief of Aged Indigent Females, *Thirteenth Annual Report* (Boston: John Wilson and Son, 1863), 5; *Fifth Annual Report* (Boston: John Wilson and Son, 1855), 8; *Seventh Annual Report* (Boston: John Wilson and Son, 1857), 12; *Fifteenth Annual Report* (Boston: John Wilson and Son, 1865), 11, ser. 1, box 1, HAW; *Act of Incorporation*, 16; *Third Annual Report*, 13; Bradlee, "Appendix," 30.

25. Michael B. Katz, *In the Shadow of the Poorhouse: A Social History of Welfare in America* (New York: Basic Books, 1986), 28; Rothman, *Discovery of the Asylum*, 145–46.

26. *Twentieth Annual Report of the Association for the Relief of Aged Indigent Females* (Boston: John Wilson and Son, 1870), 7; *Twenty-First Annual Report of the Association for the Relief of Aged Indigent Females* (Boston: John Wilson and Son, 1871), 7, ser. 1, box 1, HAW.

27. Association for the Relief of Aged and Indigent Females, *Ninth Annual Report*, 14; Home for Aged Women, Executive Committee Records, March 2, 1870; February 1, 1865; October 10, 1866; May 3, 1871; July 25, 1863; January 27 and December 7, 1864, ser. 3B, box 1, HAW; *Twentieth Annual Report*, 10.

28. *Eighteenth Annual Report of the Association for the Relief of Aged Indigent Females* (Boston: John Wilson and Son, 1868), 5, ser. 1, box 1, HAW; *Twentieth Annual Report*, 8–9; *Ninth Annual Report*, 14.

29. Executive Committee Records, November 11, 1863; April 5, 1865; May 3, 1871.

30. *Ninth Annual Report*, 14; Executive Committee Records, July 25 and November 11, 1863; January 27, 1864; May 2, 1866.

31. Executive Committee Records, May 7, 1871.

32. [Mrs. Lamson], "Account of the Origin of the Boston Young Women's Christian Association" (read by her daughter at the Pioneers Vesper Service in Lamson Hall, February 6, 1916), unpaginated typescript, folder 2, carton 1, BYWCA.

33. Mary S. Fergusson, "Boarding Homes and Clubs for Working Women," *Bulletin of the Department of Labor*, No. 15 (Washington, DC: U.S. Government Printing Office, 1898), 149, 142; *Third Annual Report of the Boston Young Women's Christian Association, Presented March 1, 1869* (Boston: J. M. Hewes, Printer, 1869), 10; *Twenty-Third Annual Report of the Boston Young Women's Christian Association, Presented March 4, 1889* (Boston: Frank Wood, 1889), 9; and *Second Annual Report of the Boston Young Women's Christian Association* (Boston: J. M. Hewes, 1868), 14–15, folder 21, carton 1, BYWCA.

34. *Seventeenth Annual Report of the Boston Young Women's Christian Association* (Boston: Frank Wood, 1883), 19, carton 1, 15v.; *Travelers' Aid Department. Young Women's Christian Association Boston, Mass.* (n.p,: n.p., [1894]), 1–3, 6, folio box 3, 53v.; *Twenty-Third Annual Report*, 9; *Second Annual Report*, 14; *Thirteenth Annual Report of the Boston Young Women's Christian Association* (Boston: Frank Wood, 1879), 11, carton 1, 15v.; *Thirty-Second Annual Report of the Boston Young Women's Christian Association* (Boston: Frank Wood, 1898), 10, folder 23, carton 1, BYWCA; Fergusson, "Boarding Homes," 143.

35. *Fifth Annual Report of the Boston Young Women's Christian Association* (Boston: J. W. Hewes, 1871), 9, carton 1, 15v; *Twenty-Fourth Annual Report of the Boston Young Women's*

Christian Association (Boston: Frank Wood, 1890), 11, folder 22, carton 1; *Twenty-First Annual Report of the Boston Young Women's Christian Association* (Boston: Frank Wood, 1887), 10, carton 1, 16v.; *Thirtieth Annual Report of the Boston Young Women's Christian Association* (Boston: Frank Wood, 1896), 12, folder 22, carton 1; *Twenty-Third Annual Report*, 9; *Eighth Annual Report of the Boston Young Women's Christian Association* (Boston: J. M Hewes, 1874), 13, folder 21, carton 1, BYWCA.

36. *Fifth Annual Report*, 10; *Twenty-Third Annual Report*, 9; *Third Annual Report*, 15.

37. *Third Annual Report*, 10; *Thirtieth Annual Report*, 12; *Thirty-Second Annual Report*, 10.

38. A flier advertising the Margaret Louisa Home of the Young Women's Christian Association of the City of New York described it as "A Temporary Home for Protestant Self-Supporting Women," box 3, v. 57, BYWCA. Its location (14 East Sixteenth Street) matches Richardson's description. Dorothy Richardson, *The Long Day: The Story of a New York Working Girl*, ed. Cindy Sondik Aron (1905; reprint, Charlottesville: University Press of Virginia, 1990), 157.

39. Richardson, *The Long Day*, 157–58, 160, 168.

40. Ibid., 159, 165–68, 171, 174–75.

41. Fergusson, "Boarding Homes," 149.

42. Evelyn Malcolm, "In a Working-Girl's Home: Board and Lodging for Poor Women at Three Dollars a Week," undated, unidentified newspaper clipping, folio box 3, v. 57, BYWCA.

43. *Ninth Annual Report of the Boston Young Women's Christian Association* (Boston: J. M. Hewes, 1875), 14–15, carton 1, 15v., BYWCA; Joanne J. Meyerowitz, *Women Adrift: Independent Wage Earners in Chicago, 1880–1930* (Chicago: University of Chicago Press, 1988), 73–91.

44. *Ninth Annual Report*, 14–15; Fergusson, "Boarding Homes," 146.

45. Junius Henri Browne, *The Great Metropolis: A Mirror of New York* (1869; reprint, New York: Arno Press, 1975), 485.

46. Stephen O'Connor, *Orphan Trains: The Story of Charles Loring Brace and the Children He Saved and Failed* (New York: Houghton Mifflin, 2001), 39, 72–76; Children's Aid Society, *The Crusade for Children: A Review of Child Life in New York During 75 Years, 1853–1928* (New York: The Children's Aid Society of the City of New York, [1928]), 7–8; Thomas Bender, *Toward an Urban Vision: Ideas and Institutions in Nineteenth-Century America* (Baltimore: Johns Hopkins University Press, 1982), 138–41; Emma Brace, *The Life of Charles Loring Brace Chiefly Told in His Own Letters* (1894; reprint, New York: Arno Press, 1976), 75–88, 153–54.

47. Brace, *Life of Charles Loring Brace*, 172–73.

48. Ibid., 171; Brace, *Dangerous Classes*, 76–77.

49. Brace, *Dangerous Classes*, 97–99.

50. O'Connor, *Orphan Trains*, 79–80, 90; Brace, *Dangerous Classes*, 44–46.

51. Brace, *Dangerous Classes*, 98, 100.

52. Ibid., 100; Children's Aid Society, *Crusade for Children*, 18.

53. Speech before the First Convention of Managers and Superintendents of Houses of Refuge and Schools of Reform, 1857, quoted in O'Connor, *Orphan Trains*, 157–58; *Fifth Annual Report of the Children's Aid Society* (New York: Wynkoop, Hallenbeck, and Thomas, 1858), 24; *Second Annual Report of the Children's Aid Society* (New York: M. B. Wynkoop, 1855), 27; *Seventh Annual Report of the Children's Aid Society* (New York: Wynkoop, Hallenbeck, and Thomas, 1858), 14.

54. [John Morrow], *A Voice from the Newsboys* (published for the benefit of the author, 1860), 63.

55. Brace, *Dangerous Classes*, 102; Children's Aid Society, *Crusade for Children*, 19.

56. Brace, *Dangerous Classes*, 100, 102–5.

57. *Eighth Annual Report of the Children's Aid Society* (New York: Wynkoop, Hallenbeck, and Thomas, 1861), 75.

58. *Seventh Annual Report of the Children's Aid Society*, 13; *Second Annual Report of the Children's Aid Society*, 27; Brace, *Dangerous Classes*, 105–6.

59. Brace, *Dangerous Classes*, 106.

60. Ibid., 106, 77.

61. Ibid., 106, 242.

62. Linda Gordon, *The Great Arizona Orphan Abduction* (Cambridge, MA: Harvard University Press, 1999), 9–10; Katz, *In the Shadow of the Poorhouse*, 106–7; O'Connor, *Orphan Trains*, esp. 148–62, 202; *Second Annual Report of the Children's Aid Society*, 26.

63. Association for the Relief of Aged Indigent Females, *Third Annual Report*, 18.

Epilogue. "Decay of the Boarding-House"

1. "Decay of the Boarding-House," *New York Times*, March 28, 1878.

2. Ibid.; Elizabeth Collins Cromley, *Alone Together: A History of New York's Early Apartments* (Ithaca, NY: Cornell University Press, 1990); Gwendolyn Wright, *Building the Dream: A Social History of Housing in America* (Cambridge, MA: MIT Press, 1981), 135–51.

3. Albert Benedict Wolfe, *The Lodging House Problem in Boston* (Boston: Houghton Mifflin, 1906), 1, 5, 42–44; Mark Peel, "On the Margins: Lodgers and Boarders in Boston, 1860–1900," *Journal of American History* 72 (March 1986): 816–34; Joanne J. Meyerowitz, *Women Adrift: Independent Wage Earners in Chicago, 1880–1930* (Chicago: University of Chicago Press, 1988), 73–78.

4. Wolfe, *Lodging House Problem in Boston*, 4–5, 27–33, 19; Paul Groth, *Living Downtown: The History of Residential Hotels in the United States* (Berkeley and Los Angeles: University of California Press, 1994), 23, 92–101, 109–15.

5. Groth, *Living Downtown*, 101, 115–19; Peel, "On the Margins."

6. Peel, "On the Margins," esp. 816, 820–23, 833–34.

7. See, e.g., "Boarders Wanted" and "Board Wanted," *New York Times*, January 3, 1920; "Board—Manhattan—Bronx," and "Board Wanted," January 2, 1935; "Board," *New York Times*, February 1, 1940; "Rooms-Board-Housekeeping," *Chicago Tribune*, November 3, 1954; "To Rent—Rms,—Room and Board," *Chicago Tribune*, December 25, 1949.

8. "Unite! Prepare! T.R. to Nation: He's for America First and Last," *Chicago Tribune*, April 30, 1916; "Colonel's Gospel for the Nation," *Chicago Tribune*, April 30, 1916; "Great Throng Gives Honor to Birth of State," August 27, 1918; "Boarding House Tales," *Chicago Tribune*, January 18 and 25, February 1, 8, and 15, March 28, April 4, May 2 and 9, 1920; *It's a Wonderful Life* (dir. Frank Capra, 1946); "Let's Talk it Over," *Calling All Boys* 4 (May 1946): 28, quoted in Susan Ferentinos, "An Unpredictable Age: Sex, Consumption, and the Emergence of the American Teenager" (Ph.D. diss., Indiana University, 2005), 150.

9. Maynard Frank Wolfe, *Rube Goldberg Inventions* (New York: Simon and Schuster, 2000), 71; Donald Payton, *The Boarding House Reach: A Comedy in Three Acts* (Cedar Rapids, IA: Heuer Pub. Co., 1948), esp. 3–4, 92–102.

10. See, e.g., *Our Boarding House*, February 4 and June 6, 1928; January 8, 1934; February 2 and 6, 1928; February 12, 1926; February 19, 1938; and January 8, 1934, Special Collections Division, Michigan State University Library; Donald Phelps, "Boarding House Days and Arabian Nights: The Life and Imaginary Times of Major Hoople," *Reading the Funnies: Essays on Comic Strips* (Seattle: Fantagraphics Books, 2001), 243–49.

11. Frederick Lewis Allen, *Only Yesterday: An Informal History of the 1920's* (1931; reprint, New York: Harper and Row, 1964), 73–101.

12. Albert Benedict Wolfe, *The Lodging House Problem in Boston* (Boston: Houghton Mifflin, 1906), 46–47, 152; Peel, "On the Margins," 813–15.

Like a house, this book rests on a foundation. And if the edifice remains shaky, the foundation—secondary literature representing a wide variety of topics and subfields—is sturdy indeed. What follows is necessarily a partial and idiosyncratic sampling that emphasizes the studies I found most helpful; by no means should it be considered an exhaustive compilation of relevant scholarship.

There is a vast literature on the nineteenth-century home, both as a material artifact and a cultural ideal. Key works include Nancy F. Cott, *The Bonds of Womanhood: "Woman's Sphere" in New England, 1780–1835* (Yale University Press, 1977); Mary P. Ryan, *Cradle of the Middle Class: The Family in Oneida County, New York, 1790–1865* (Cambridge University Press, 1981); Gwendolyn Wright, *Moralism and the Modern Home: Domestic Architecture and Cultural Conflict in Chicago, 1873–1913* (University of Chicago Press, 1980) and *Building the Dream: A Social History of Housing in America* (Pantheon, 1981); Clifford Edward Clark Jr., *The American Family Home, 1800–1960* (University of North Carolina Press, 1986); Glenna Mathews, *"Just a Housewife": The Rise and Fall of Domesticity in America* (Oxford University Press, 1987); Richard Bushman, *The Refinement of America: Persons, Houses, Cities* (Knopf, 1992); Kenneth L. Ames, *Death in the Dining Room and Other Tales of Victorian Culture* (Temple University Press, 1992); Jane C. Nylander, *Our Own Snug Fireside: Images of the New England Home, 1760–1860* (Knopf, 1993); Kathryn Grier, *Culture and Comfort: Parlor Making and Middle-Class Identity, 1850–1930* (Smithsonian, 1997); and Bernard L. Herman, *Town House: Architecture and Material Life in the Early American City, 1780–1830* (University of North Carolina Press, 2005). See Kristin Hoganson, "Cosmopolitan Domesticity: Importing the American Dream, 1865–1920," *American Historical Review* 107 (February 2002): 55–83, for a fascinating discussion of the global implications of domestic consumption.

Elizabeth Blackmar's *Manhattan for Rent, 1785–1850* (Cornell University Press, 1989) and Jeanne Boydston's *Home and Work: Housework, Wages, and the Ideology of Labor in the Early Republic* (Oxford University Press, 1990) are especially important for unmasking the fiction of domestic isolation. Both show that—the rhetoric of separate spheres notwithstanding—homes were indeed workplaces that were always connected to the marketplace, and that the apparently sturdy boundaries between private and public were always illusory. I am particularly indebted to Boydston's notion of the pastoralization of housework. For further explorations of these themes, see Joan Jensen, "Cloth, Butter, and Boarders: Women's Household Production for the Market," *Review of Radical Political Economics* 12 (Summer 1980): 14–24; Jeanne Boydston, "The Woman Who Wasn't There: Women's Market Labor and the Transition to Capitalism in the United States," *Journal of the Early Republic* 16 (Summer 1996): 183–206; Amy Dru Stanley, "Home Life and the Morality of the Market," in *The Market Revolution in America: Social, Political, and Religious Expressions, 1800–1880,* ed. Melwyn Stokes and Stephen Conway (University of Virginia Press, 1996), 74–96; Catherine E. Kelly, *In the New England Fashion: Reshaping Women's Lives in the Nineteenth Century* (Cornell University Press, 1999); Angel Kwolek-Folland, "Cows in Their Yards: Women, the Economy, and Urban Space, 1870–1885," unpublished paper, 2001; Elizabeth White Nelson, *Market Sentiments: Middle-Class Market Culture in Nineteenth-Century America* (Smithsonian, 2004); Ellen Hartigan-O'Connor, "Abigail's Accounts: Economy and Affection in the Early Republic," *Journal of Women's History* 17, no. 3 (2005): 35–58, and Robin Veder's manuscript in progress, "Shrine of Flora / Temple of Mammon: The Pastoralization of Flower Gardening in Nineteenth-Century Transatlantic Culture."

The Boardinghouse in Nineteenth-Century America joins Jeronima Echeverria, *Home Away from Home: A History of Basque Boardinghouses* (University of Nevada Press, 1999), and Stephen A. Mrozowski, Grace H. Ziesing, and Mary C. Beaudry, *Living on the Boott: Historical Archaeology at the Boott Mills Boardinghouses, Lowell, Massachusetts* (University of Massachusetts Press, 1996) as one of three books that focus exclusively on boardinghouses. Nevertheless, I rely heavily on the insights and findings of numerous works that examine boarding—albeit sometimes only briefly—in the course of discussions of class, ethnicity, race, gender, sexuality, business, employment, housing, politics, and urban life, as well as articles that focus more specifically on the subject. These include James Sterling Young, *The Washington Community, 1800–1828* (Columbia University Press, 1966); Michael B. Katz, *The People of*

Hamilton, Canada West: Family and Class in a Mid-Nineteenth-Century City (Harvard University Press, 1975); Wright, *Building the Dream;* Susan Strasser, *Never Done: A History of American Housework* (Pantheon, 1982); Ruth Schwartz Cowan, *More Work for Mother: The Ironies of Household Technology from the Open Hearth to the Microwave* (Basic Books, 1983); Christine Stansell, *City of Women: Sex and Class in New York, 1789–1860* (Knopf, 1986); Joanne J. Meyerowitz, *Women Adrift: Independent Wage Earners in Chicago, 1880–1930* (University of Chicago Press, 1988); Richard B. Stott, *Workers in the Metropolis: Class, Ethnicity, and Youth in Antebellum New York City* (Cornell University Press, 1990); Elizabeth Collins Cromley, *Alone Together: A History of New York's Early Apartments* (Cornell University Press, 1990); Anne C. Rose, *Victorian America and the Civil War* (Cambridge University Press, 1992); Hasia R. Diner, *A Time for Gathering: The Second Migration, 1820–1880* (Johns Hopkins University Press, 1992); Timothy J. Gilfoyle, *City of Eros: New York City, Prostitution, and the Commercialization of Sex, 1790–1920* (W. W. Norton, 1992); Kenneth A. Scherzer, *The Unbounded Community: Neighborhood Life and Social Structure in New York City, 1830–1875* (Duke University Press, 1992); George Chauncey, *Gay New York: Gender, Urban Culture, and the Makings of the Gay Male World, 1890–1940* (Basic Books, 1994); Juliet E. K. Walker, *The History of Black Business in America: Capitalism, Race, Entrepreneurship* (Twayne, 1998); James Oliver Horton, *Black Bostonians: Family Life and Community Struggle in the Antebellum North,* rev. ed. (Holmes & Meier, 1999); Sharon Marcus, *Apartment Stories: City and Home in Nineteenth-Century Paris and London* (University of California Press, 1999); Howard P. Chudacoff, *The Age of the Bachelor: Creating an American Subculture* (Princeton University Press, 1999); Peter Laipson, " 'I Have No Genius for Marriage': Bachelorhood in Urban America, 1870–1930" (Ph.D. diss., University of Michigan, 2000); and Jean Fagan Yellin, *Harriet Jacobs: A Life* (Basic, 2004). I regret that I learned of Betsy Klimasmith's fine study *At Home in the City: Urban Domesticity in American Literature and Culture* (University Press of New England, 2005) just after I had completed the final revisions on this book.

The most sustained treatments of the history of boarding and boardinghouses are John Modell and Tamara K. Hareven, "Urbanization and the Malleable Household: An Examination of Boarding and Lodging in American Families," *Journal of Marriage and the Family* 35 (1973): 467–79; Robert F. Harney, "Boarding and Belonging," *Urban History Review* 2 (1978): 8–37; Leonore Davidoff, "The Separation of Home and Work? Landladies and Lodgers in Nineteenth- and Twentieth-Century England," in *Fit Work for*

Women, ed. Sandra Burman (London: Croom Helm, 1979), 64–97; Rachel Amelia Bernstein, "Boarding-House Keepers and Brothel Keepers in New York City, 1880–1910," (Ph.D. diss., Rutgers University, 1984); Mark Peel, "On the Margins: Lodgers and Boarders in Boston, 1860–1900," *Journal of American History* 72 (March 1986): 813–34; Blackmar, *Manhattan for Rent;* Elizabeth S. Peña and Jacqueline Denmon, "The Social Organization of a Boardinghouse: Archaeological Evidence from the Buffalo Waterfront," *Historical Archaeology* 34 (2000): 79–96; Peter Baskerville, "Familiar Strangers: Urban Families with Boarders, Canada, 1901," *Social Science History* 25 (Fall 2001): 321–46; Susan L. Porter and Laura B. Driemeyer, "Like a Large Family: Genteel Boarding Houses in Nineteenth Century Boston," unpublished paper, 2002; Susan L. Porter, "Making 'A Home for Some of the Finest People': The Politics of the Genteel Boarding House in Nineteenth-Century Boston," paper presented at the annual meeting of the Organization of American Historians, Boston, March 2004; David Faflik, "Community, Civility, Compromise: Dr. Holmes's Boston Boardinghouse," *New England Quarterly* 78 (December 2005): 547–69; and Jared N. Day and Timothy J. Haggerty, "The Bachelor and the Landlady: A Tale of Gotham," *Seaport* 40 (Winter 2005): 14–21. Paul Groth's marvelous *Living Downtown: The History of Residential Hotels in the United States* (University of California Press, 1994) merits special mention, for it shows how the cultural hegemony of the single-family home shaped social policies that ultimately rendered large numbers of people homeless. Interested readers will also want to consult David Faflik's "Boarding Out: Inhabiting the American Urban Literary Imagination, 1840–1860" (Ph.D. diss., University of North Carolina, Chapel Hill, 2005).

There is also a growing literature on nineteenth-century hotels. In addition to Groth's *Living Downtown,* see Molly Winger Berger, "The Modern Hotel in America, 1829–1929" (Ph.D. diss., Case Western Reserve University, 1997); Catherine Cocks, *Doing the Town: The Rise of Urban Tourism in the United States, 1850–1915* (University of California Press, 2001); and Andrew K. Sandoval-Strausz, *Hotel: An American History* (Yale University Press, 2007).

Studies of social class have tended to emphasize working-class experience until relatively recently. Among the most important are E. P. Thompson's classic *The Making of the English Working Class* (Vintage, 1963); Sean Wilentz, *Chants Democratic: New York City and the Rise of the American Working Class, 1788–1850* (Oxford University Press, 1984); Stansell, *City of Women;* Mary H. Blewett, *Men, Women, and Work: Class, Gender, and Protest in the New England Shoe Industry, 1780–1910* (University of Illinois Press, 1988); Bruce Laurie, *Artisans into Workers: Labor in Nineteenth-Century America* (Hill and Wang, 1989); Charles Sellers, *The Market Revolution: Jacksonian America, 1815–1846* (Oxford University Press, 1991); and Mary H. Blewett, *Constant Turmoil: The Politics of Industrial Life in Nineteenth-Century New England* (University of Massachusetts Press, 2000). Much recent work on the middle class takes as its starting point Stuart Blumin's magisterial *The Emergence of the Middle Class: Social Experience in the American City, 1760–1900* (Cambridge University Press, 1989). Increasingly, however, scholars argue that class, like gender and race, is at least partly socially constructed. See, especially, the essays in *The Middling Sorts: Explorations in the History of the American Middle Class,* ed. Burton J. Bledstein and Robert D. Johnston (Routledge, 2001); Daniel J. Walkowitz, *Working with Class: Social Workers and the Politics of Middle-Class Identity* (University of North Carolina Press, 1999); Jocelyn Wills, "Respectable Mediocrity: The Everyday Life of an Ordinary American Striver, 1876–1890," *Journal of Social History* 37 (2003): 323–49; Robert D. Johnston, *The Radical Middle Class: Populist Democracy and the Question of Capitalism in Progressive Era Portland, Oregon* (Princeton University Press, 2003); "The Middle Class in the City," *Journal of Urban History* 31, special issue (March 2005); and "Symposium on Class in the Early Republic," *Journal of the Early Republic* 25 (Winter 2005): 523–64.

Boardinghouses were small businesses. The best overview of the subject is Mansel G. Blackford, *A History of Small Business in America,* 2d ed. (University of North Carolina Press, 2003). Boardinghouses were not only small businesses; most often, they were businesses run by women. Accordingly, this study situates itself in a growing body of scholarship on the history of women in business. Angel Kwolek-Folland's *Incorporating Women: A History of Women and Business in the United States* (Twayne, 1998) is a superb synthetic treatment; see also Virginia Drachman, *Enterprising Women: 250 Years of American Business* (University of North Carolina Press, 2002), and *Women in Business,* ed. Mary Yeager (Edward Elgar, 1999). For more focused accounts, see Wendy Gamber, *The Female Economy: The Millinery and Dressmaking Trades, 1860–1930* (University of Illinois Press, 1997) and three outstanding studies: Edith Sparks, *Capital Intentions, Female Proprietors in San Francisco, 1850–1920* (University of North Carolina Press, 2006); Susan Ingalls Lewis, *Unexceptionable Women: Female Proprietors in Mid-Nineteenth Century Albany, 1830–1885* (Ohio State University Press, forthcoming); and Tiffany Melissa Gill, "Civic Beauty: Beauty Culturists and the Politics of African-American Female Entrepreneurship, 1900–1965" (Ph.D. diss., Rutgers University, 2003). See

Andrea Tone's wonderful *Devices and Desires: A History of Contraceptives in America* (Hill and Wang, 2001) for discussions of women in the contraceptive business.

In order to write about the labor of nineteenth-century boardinghouse keeping, I needed to learn what housework entailed. Two now-classic accounts—Strasser's *Never Done* and Cowan's *More Work for Mother*—proved indispensable, as did Boydston's *Home and Work* and Nylander's *Our Own Snug Fireside*. Jack Larkin, *The Reshaping of Everyday Life, 1790–1840* (Harper and Row, 1988); Daniel E. Sutherland, *The Expansion of Everyday Life, 1860–1876* (Harper and Row, 1989); Thomas J. Schlereth, *Victorian America: Transformations in Everyday Life, 1876–1915* (HarperCollins, 1991); and Suellen M. Hoy, *Chasing Dirt: The American Pursuit of Cleanliness* (Oxford University Press, 1995) helped me understand living conditions in nineteenth-century America. Karen V. Hansen's *A Very Social Time: Crafting Community in Antebellum New England* (University of California Press, 1994) includes a brilliant discussion of visiting as labor. The most important studies of domestic service include David Katzman, *Seven Days a Week: Women and Domestic Service in Industrializing America* (Oxford University Press, 1978); Faye E. Dudden, *Serving Women: Household Service in Nineteenth-Century America* (Wesleyan University Press, 1983); and Thomas Dublin, *Transforming Women's Work: New England Lives in the Industrial Revolution* (Cornell University Press, 1994). I am also indebted to scholarship on the history of food, dining, and manners. See, especially, *Dining in America, 1850–1900,* ed. Kathryn Grover (University of Massachusetts Press, 1987); Harvey Levenstein, *Revolution at the Table: The Transformation of the American Diet* (Oxford University Press, 1988); John F. Kasson, *Rudeness and Civility: Manners in Nineteenth-Century Urban America* (Hill and Wang, 1990); Donna R. Gabaccia, *We Are What We Eat: Ethnic Food and the Making of Americans* (Harvard University Press, 1998); C. Dallett Hemphill, *Bowing to Necessities: A History of Manners in America, 1620–1860* (Oxford University Press, 1999); and Hasia R. Diner, *Hungering for America: Italian, Irish, and Jewish Foodways in the Age of Migration* (Harvard University Press, 2001). Although it concerns a very different context and a much later period, Amy Bentley's *Eating for Victory: Food Rationing and the Politics of Domesticity* (University of Illinois Press, 1998) taught me a great deal about interpreting the meanings of food.

Influential studies that examine the relationships—real and perceived—between crime, vice, and urban life include Paul S. Boyer, *Urban Masses and Moral Order in America, 1820–1920* (Harvard University Press, 1978); Karen

Halttunen's seminal *Confidence Men and Painted Women: A Study of Middle-Class Culture in America, 1830–1870* (Yale University Press, 1982); Bernstein, "Boardinghouse Keepers and Brothel Keepers"; Stansell, *City of Women*; Mary P. Ryan, *Women in Public: Between Banners and Ballots, 1825–1880* (Johns Hopkins University Press, 1990); Ann Vincent Fabian, *Card Sharps, Dream Books, and Bucket Shops: Gambling in Nineteenth-Century America* (Cornell University Press, 1990); Daniel A. Cohen, *Pillars of Salt, Monuments of Grace: New England Crime Literature and the Origins of American Popular Culture, 1674–1860* (Oxford University Press, 1993); Carl S. Smith, *Urban Disorder and the Shape of Belief: The Great Chicago Fire, the Haymarket Bomb, and the Model Town of Pullman* (University of Chicago Press, 1995); Amy Gilman Srebnick, *The Mysterious Death of Mary Rogers: Sex and Culture in Nineteenth-Century New York* (Oxford University Press, 1995); Patricia Cline Cohen, *The Murder of Helen Jewett: The Life and Death of a Prostitute in Nineteenth-Century New York* (Knopf, 1998); Karen Halttunen, *Murder Most Foul: The Killer and the American Gothic Imagination* (Harvard University Press, 1998); and Sharon E. Wood, *The Freedom of the Streets: Work, Citizenship, and Sexuality in a Gilded Age City* (University of North Carolina Press, 2005).

A lively body of literature on law, marriage, and the family helped me to better understand the social underpinnings of concerns about the relationship between boarding and marriage. For important interpretations, see Michael Grossberg, *Governing the Hearth: Law and the Family in Nineteenth-Century America* (University of North Carolina Press, 1985) and *A Judgment for Solomon: The d'Hauteville Case and Legal Experience in Antebellum America* (Cambridge University Press, 1996); Sara L. Zeigler, "Wifely Duties: Marriage, Labor, and the Common Law in Nineteenth-Century America," *Social Science History* 20 (Spring 1996): 63–96; Amy Dru Stanley, *From Bondage to Contract: Wage Labor, Marriage, and the Market in the Age of Slave Emancipation* (Cambridge University Press, 1998); Norma Basch, *Framing American Divorce: From the Revolutionary Generation to the Victorians* (University of California Press, 1999); Richard Wightman Fox, *Trials of Intimacy: Love and Loss in the Beecher-Tilton Scandal* (University of Chicago Press, 1999); Hendrik Hartog, *Man and Wife in America: A History* (Harvard University Press, 2000); and Nancy Cott, *Public Vows: A History of Marriage and the Nation* (Harvard University Press, 2000). On the history of home economics, see Kathryn Kish Sklar's *Catharine Beecher: A Study in American Domesticity* (Norton, 1973), Laura Shapiro's irreverent *Perfection Salad: Women and Cooking at the Turn of the Century* (Farrar, Straus, and Giroux, 1986), and the essays in *Rethinking Home Economics: Women and the History of a Profession,* ed. Sarah Stage and Virginia B. Vincenti (Cornell University Press, 1997). On cooperative housing, see Dolores Hayden, *The Grand Domestic Revolution: A History of Feminist Designs for American Homes, Neighborhoods, and Cities* (MIT Press, 1981).

David J. Rothman's *The Discovery of the Asylum: Social Order and Disorder in the New Republic* (Little, Brown, 1971) remains an extraordinarily useful resource for the history of institutions. For perceptive studies that analyze institutions' and reformers' reliance on familial and domestic rhetoric, see Ellen Dwyer, *Homes for the Mad: Life Inside Two Nineteenth-Century Asylums* (Rutgers University Press, 1987); Lori D. Ginzberg, *Women and the Work of Benevolence: Morality, Politics, and Class in the Nineteenth-Century United States* (Yale University Press, 1990); Peggy Pascoe, *Relations of Rescue: The Search for Female Moral Authority in the American West, 1874–1939* (Oxford University Press, 1990); Regina G. Kunzel, *Fallen Women, Problem Girls: Unmarried Mothers and the Professionalization of Social Work, 1890–1945* (Yale University Press, 1993); and Anne M. Boylan, *The Origins of Women's Activism: New York and Boston, 1797–1840* (University of North Carolina Press, 2002). Carole Haber, "The Old Folks at Home: The Development of Institutionalized Care for the Aged in Nineteenth-Century Philadelphia," *Pennsylvania Magazine of History and Biography* 1010 (1977): 240–57; and Carol Lasser, " 'The World's Dread Laugh': Singlehood and Service in Nineteenth-Century Boston," in *The New England Working Class and the New Labor History,* ed. Herbert G. Gutman and Donald H. Bell (University of Illinois Press, 1987), 72–88, are excellent accounts of the genesis and operations of homes for elderly women and men. Meyerowitz's *Women Adrift* provides an excellent account of homes for working women in Chicago; Sarah Deutsch's monumental *Women and the City: Gender, Space, and Power in Boston, 1870–1940* (Oxford University Press, 2000) delineates late-nineteenth-century reformers' reliance on the middle-class home as a model for civic life. My analysis of the Children's Aid Society would have been far poorer without the useful insights of Thomas Bender's *Toward an Urban Vision: Ideas and Institutions in Nineteenth-Century America* (Johns Hopkins University Press, 1975) and Stephen O'Connor's, *Orphan Trains: The Story of Charles Loring Brace and the Children He Saved and Failed* (Houghton Mifflin, 2001).